Great American
HOT RODS

Great American HOT RODS

KEITH HARMAN

kp books

An Imprint of F+W Publication

700 East State Street • Iola, WI 54990-0
715-445-2214 • 888-457-2873

kp books
An Imprint of F+W Publications

700 East State Street • Iola, WI 54990-0001
715-445-2214 • 888-457-2873

Colin Gower Enterprises Ltd.,
Cordwainers, Caring Lane,
Leeds, Maidstone, Kent ME17 1TJ
United Kingdom.
©2005 Colin Gower Enterprises Ltd.

ISBN: 0-89689-226-3
Library of Congress   2005924824
Designed by Casebourne Rose Design Associates
Color reproduction: Berkley Square Partnership
Printed and bound in China

Contents

Introduction

America today is full of great hot rods. In fact the scene is probably bigger and more diverse than it has ever been in its short history. So just how do you do justice to the many great cars out there cruising the highways of this country, and choose what rods to include in a book called *Great American Hot Rods*?

For a start, and as part of the overall answer, maybe it's advisable to set out what this book *isn't*. Certainly, it isn't an attempt to document, in some sort of running order, all the cars which we consider to be *the* greatest hot rods. That would indeed be an impossible task, as the matter is totally subjective. Everyone has his/her own favorite cars from hot rodding history. So, while some hot rods have undoubtedly had more long-lasting influence over the hobby than others, and are rightly considered milestone cars, they are already so well known, they do not require yet another book to underline the point.

So, instead, while we have attempted to include some of those cars, we also present you with a much wider picture of hot rodding – old and new, in many different styles – high-buck, low-buck and all points in between. They all make up the huge hobby we enjoy today. Therefore, by definition, they really are all "great" hot rods. Consequently, don't be surprised to find an "America's Most Beautiful Roadster" winner from days gone by on one page, and on the next a hardcore jalopy that's all raw welds, attitude and grinding flash. We hope that you'll appreciate the differences of build style, while still recognizing the vision and dedication required to bring both types of hot rod from dream to reality.

As well as these two contrasting styles, we have an exciting and fascinating mix of cool machinery and have tried to touch base with as many different makes, models and build styles as possible. For example, from the early days of hot rodding we have the modified Model Ts from the rural dirt tracks with their tuned 4-bangers. From the early West Coast scene are their salt flat racer cousins, whose pioneers did much to further the tuning capabilities of the Flathead Ford V8. The names of many of these builders and drivers live in the forms of well-known brand names of speed equipment.

Moving along the time line to the late 1940s, the '32 Ford, or "Deuce," introduced Henry Ford's affordable V8. It was a cheap and widely-available used car, easily worked on and easily hopped up for more power. All over the country, roadster clubs and timing associations were

formed. Speed test events and reliability runs became fun ways to enjoy the stripped-down, open-wheeled hot roadsters, or "hot rods," as they soon became known. Unfortunately, as is often the case with any new craze that the "establishment" doesn't seem to understand, some rather bad press followed – fueled by lurid tales of speed-crazy teenagers and highway wrecks, etc.

In order to counter this, the National Hot Rod Association was formed. It provided a governing body for hot rodding and promoted responsible and safe driving practices. A result of this was to take racing off the streets and provide purpose-built facilities for weekend racers. In this way, organized drag racing was born.

However, at about this point, the hot rodding story met a fork in the road, as it were. Drag racing became a whole new sport of its own, growing through the 1950s and 1960s to the major, corporate-sponsored, TV and spectator-oriented spectacle that it is today. Since rodding and drag racing share a common ancestry, we've included a few racecars in the book, but only the ones where the links between street and strip remain recognizable. In other words, still being hot rods and not purpose-built competition cars such as rail dragsters, etc.

Hot rodding grew rapidly with the onset of the 1950's boom years. With the combined influences of a growing speed equipment industry and the nationwide availability of monthly hot rod-orientated publications, it was easier than ever to put together a hot rod or cool custom car. By this time, there was also a much wider variety of rodded body styles to be seen on the streets. Roadsters were (and still are) the favorite cars to build, but hopped, chopped and dropped coupes and pickups too became drive-in favorites. Sedan body styles were still rare, though; they remained rather too "Mom and Pop" for most young rodders.

In most ways, the 1950s remain the most influential decade of all in hot rodding. Even today, by far the majority of so-called "traditional" and indeed "hardcore" rods reflect the styles of this period – as will be evident as you look through this book. After all, it was in this decade that rodding experienced the rise of the popular indoor car shows. These were where regular guys building cars at home often saw the trends first-hand – trends such as pinstriping, custom bodywork, metallic paint finishes, rolled and pleated interiors and an extensive use of chrome. All these features were soon seen regularly on

◄ A real survivor from the fifties, this '32 roadster has seen and done it all and still wears its hand rubbed black lacquer from 1959.

▶ Hardcore hot rods typically use whatever old parts look right rather than stick to a rigid formula, a '39 truck grille, REO headlamps and a Buick Nailhead V8 all come together in this cool Chevy Coupe.

street-driven cars, and a combination of these tricks usually still denotes a 1950s-style hot rod.

As the 1950s became the 1960s, fads and trends seemed to come and go much faster, probably due to parallel, rapid social changes. However, the small-block Chevrolet V8, first introduced in 1955, soon became the engine of choice for hot rodders. It quickly eclipsed the previous popularity of the venerable Flathead. Surf music came and went, but for a while, Woodie wagons were the car to have, especially if you lived on the West Coast

However, the most far-reaching trend of the 1960s was the introduction of the factory muscle car. Up to this point, most hot rods had been able easily to outperform anything that Detroit built, simply by virtue of a powerful motor in a lightweight body. But the introduction of the commercial "pony-cars" meant that horsepower was available to anyone with enough money or access to a credit

▲ For some hot rodders, you can never have enough chrome, as the fully detailed engine of this '32 Coupe proves.

line, regardless of whether or not they could wield a welding torch.

This was easily-obtained, instant street cool and had the effect of drastically reducing the number of hot rods on the streets. Many of those who stayed with rodding took their cars almost exclusively to the drag strips – getting their kicks on the quarter-mile and taking advantage of the still-growing performance parts industry. A few moved into the ever wilder show car world; that scene itself then branched off into the construction of some wild, cartoon-inspired creations that rarely saw street use – that is, if they actually ran at all!

Probably the biggest and most lasting innovation of the

▲ A mouth watering prospect for any hot rodder, an array of old Fords sits in this barn awaiting the welding torch and spray gun.

1960s still with us was the introduction of fiberglass repro-duction bodies; in particular, the Fad "T" or T-bucket. The simple design of the T roadster's frame, plus the minimal bodywork involved, made them easy to produce in simple kit form. So, the open-engined, mag-wheeled, high-topped T became *the* hot rod icon of the 1960s.

With the 1970s came a renewed interest in street driven hot rods. In addition, the formation of the National Street Rod Association did much to bring the building of pre-'49 body-styled cars back from the negative associations of the bad old "hot rod" days, re-christening them "Street Rods." The NSRA continued to promote "street rodding" as a safe family hobby through their larger and larger nationwide events, regularly attracting thousands of participants and visitors. Hot rodding was now socially acceptable.

Hollywood also played its part in renewing interest in the older cars through the release of *American Graffiti*, a movie that, for the first time, presented hot rods and the California cruising scene to a new generation of hot rodders the world over. In turn, this helped fuel the first real nostalgia boom for all things 1950's. A few rodders even started building real "hot rods" again, since the majority of the scene had become top heavy with "Resto-rods" – being mostly cars built with stock bodywork and all the original chromed barbs, their modern running gear hidden from view beneath two-tone metallic brown paintjobs and accessory luggage racks. There are even a few examples of this style in these pages, though it has yet to make a real comeback, and is treated with less affec-

tion than other styles by most 21st century rodders.

Which bring us to the 1980s and the first real new look to emerge that wasn't nostalgia-based. Somewhere between the milling machine of L'il John Buttera, the sketchpad of Thom Taylor and the workshop of Boyd Coddington, came the smooth, clean "Billet" style that would dominate the street rod look for the next couple of decades. It was the complete antithesis of the 1970s Resto-rods, with a new emphasis on clean, uncluttered lines, machined aluminum instead of chrome and body-color-painted detailing. Handcrafted independent suspension also became popular, again with components milled from billet alloy. The aftermarket wasn't slow to catch on to this new trend either. Soon, machine-finished components, including many new styles of alloy wheels. were on sale everywhere

The 1980s was also the decade of "Fat Attack" and rodders wanting to build steel cars. Finding 1930's cars in short supply, they started to turn to the bigger heavier models of the immediate post-World War II period for inspiration. These cars could be built with all the luxury features of new and late model cars, but without compromising their style. What is more, these rods made comfortable and practical long-distance cruisers. Later in the decade, a complete monochromatic look became popular. Virtually all chassis, engine and bodywork were devoid of brightwork, and instead synchronized into one color – usually a pastel shade. In order to break up this often boring overdose of color, multi-color graphics were added to the bodywork. However, they were frequently on the garish side and did little to complement the lines of the car concerned.

By the time the 1990s rolled around, rodding had a full half-century of history to draw upon, and this was evident in the many makes and styles of rods out there. In short, it was a time of anything goes. There were more fiber-glass bodies available than ever before, many of which were so-called "phantoms," or body styles that had never actually been commercially available. Of course, this all

◄ This Model A Sedan is undergoing the treatment to turn it into a killer hot rod. Its Halibrand wheels and Buick Nailhead help a lot.

▲ Alas, some old cars are just too far gone for even the most dedicated rodder, as typified by this late 1930's scrap yard coupe. Rust in peace!

added extra novelty value to the finished rod. Another feature was that wheel diameters kept getting bigger, with 17-, 18- and 20-inch rims becoming common – often combined with air-bagged suspension for radical looks and a ground-scraping stance.

Interestingly, while all this had been going on, a grass roots ground swell of interest had been gathering momentum as a direct reaction to the ever more spiraling costs of building a finished, painted and trimmed street rod. The result was the "primer is finer" school of thought. As a result, and with an eye on the past, a whole new generation of rodders started building, back-to-basics, nostalgia cars. These were rods that without the constraints of high-end paint and trim jobs, could be

▲ Many hours of metal fabrication, welding and grinding take place before any hot rod project even begins to take shape.

▲ Notice something different? Some radical engineering solutions were created in order to fit a Chevy ZZ4 motor behind the cockpit in this innovative Deuce Roadster project.

driven hard and fast, with road rash being worn as a badge of honor. These "unfinished" cars were at first dismissed as "rat rods" by the main stream rod establishment, though the guys and gals involved often didn't seem to care that much. As far as they were concerned, they were "hardcore" and you either got it, or you didn't. Besides, they organized their own events anyway.

So where are we today, you might well ask? Well, with nearly all of the above, reality. Hardcore rodding continues to go from strength to strength. Then, at the other end of the scale, well-heeled rodders are busy discovering landmark hot rods and racecars from days gone by and carrying out nut-and-bolt restorations on them. To put some perspective on this breadth of rod activity, who, a few short years ago, would have thought that there would ever have been a hot rod class at the prestigious and exclusive Pebble Beach Concours d'Elegance? Meanwhile, for the select few, bespoken completely hand-built concept rods vie for the top honors at the national indoor shows. It's quite a contrast, but speaks wonders for the enthusiasm.

To summarize, we've attempted to bring all those many styles and trends together into this one book so as to provide a one-stop window into the world of hot rodding today. At the same time, this is also acknowledging everything that has gone before. This book is above all a celebration of every rodder out there who has ever swapped a motor, chopped a top, turned a wrench or busted a knuckle. We salute you all, for the automotive world would be a very barren and dull place without you – the dreamers, racers, builders, drivers and owners of the "great American hot rods."

Keith Harman

1941 Willys Coupe

The wild and colorful custom paint job on this Willys Coupe is very reminiscent of the late 1960's style, with different effects set in panels of color, laid over a white base coat. The alloy, 10-spoke wheels are also typical 1960's gasser equipment, but rather than the old raised front look from that period, it looks like the chassis has been re-worked to bring it back up to date with a purposeful nose-down stance. Many old race cars have since been resurrected and re-built for the street with modern updates, after lying unloved and unpopular for many years.

This one certainly has all the hallmarks of an ex-drag strip hero, with its full roll cage and purposeful chrome scoop poking through the hood. An aluminum rear wing has been added to increase the competition look, but extra holes have also been cut into the front of the hood and the grille panel, probably to increase airflow to the radiator, as a concession to street driving. The sizeable exhaust pipe under the rocker panel hints at a no-nonsense engine lurking under the hood, the big rear slicks on a narrowed rear axle almost confirm the fact. Wanna race?

MAKE:	Willys
BODY STYLE:	Coupe
YEAR :	1941
ENGINE:	454 Chevrolet V8
BUILD STYLE:	Nostalgia Race Car
OWNER:	Dennis Johnston

◀ Most hot rodders agree there's only one way to build a Willys Coupe – race style!

'33 Ford Coupe

Here's how the story went back in the 1950s. Not many kids had the dough for a fancy custom, a late model or even a fully-chopped and channeled hot rod, despite what some of the old guys tell you. This '33 is probably a lot nearer the mark, so imagine if you will, a prewar Ford Coupe traded in at the local Ford dealer against a new Fairlane, then left sitting at the back of the used car lot with two flat, bald tires and a broken headlight. But, there's a local kid washing the cars on Saturday for a few dollars pocket money, who just got his license. He gets his dad to talk to the manager; a few greenbacks change hands, and our hero gets the car of his dreams.

A set of steel rims are scavenged from the local wrecking yard, painted red in the family garage and dad springs for the new whitewall tires, partly in return for chores carried out – but more for his own peace of mind. One year on, and the shop classes at school came in handy fixing up the bodywork, what's more, the same wrecking yard has given up a '40 back axle and a '39 trans which have been installed behind the V8, which now sports some serious mail order parts: Offy Heads, 97s and an intake; that's quite a few Saturday's of car washing down at the lot right there. Sound familiar? Ok, well, maybe the story is made up, but this '33 is the real thing.

▲ There's nothing too fancy here. Nothing unless whitewalls and black suede paint put a gleam in your eye!

MAKE:	Ford
BODY STYLE:	3-window Coupe
YEAR:	1933
ENGINE:	Flathead V8
BUILD STYLE:	Traditional Hot Rod
OWNER:	Dave Gazaway

'31 Model A Coupe

Let's get one thing straight; this cool Model A coupe is not a careful exercise in re-creating a period nostalgia rod. No sir, this is the real thing! This particular car was originally built in the early 1960s and was found sitting in a California garage, where it had lain hidden since 1966. Passed on from the original owner to his son, it was snapped up on an internet auction site as piece of period hot rod history – and the buyer has now shipped it over to her home in England!

By modern standards, the engineering on the car is a trifle crude, its powerful 327 with triple Strombergs, 4-speed T10 "box and drum" brakes all residing in a 75-year-old unboxed frame. But therein lies its charm; it is the real thing, from its cracked green metallic paint to its chrome Mor-Drop I-beam axle. It just oozes nostalgia and plenty of character, and that's a quality you just can't buy for your new hot rod, no matter what the price.

MAKE:	Ford
BODY STYLE:	Coupe
YEAR:	1931
ENGINE:	327 Chevrolet V8
BUILD STYLE:	Period Hot Rod
OWNER:	Melissa Gee

▸ It may have lain unused for nearly twenty years, but owner Melissa Gee is more than making up for it now! She's driving the wheels off it!

'32 Ford 3-window Coupe

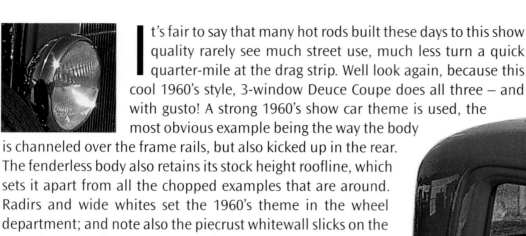

It's fair to say that many hot rods built these days to this show quality rarely see much street use, much less turn a quick quarter-mile at the drag strip. Well look again, because this cool 1960's style, 3-window Deuce Coupe does all three – and with gusto! A strong 1960's show car theme is used, the most obvious example being the way the body is channeled over the frame rails, but also kicked up in the rear. The fenderless body also retains its stock height roofline, which sets it apart from all the chopped examples that are around. Radirs and wide whites set the 1960's theme in the wheel department; and note also the piecrust whitewall slicks on the rear, the owner has another set of legal tires to swap for road use.

There's attention to detail and lots of hand-crafted touches all over this rod and we could probably spend a whole chapter on it. Chrome and stainless steel, owner-built details abound everywhere – and that's not the whole story either. The 350 Chevy engine has been bored and stroked and now displaces 383 ci. With Airflow heads and all the goodies, the engine is now putting out about 430 bhp at 5700 rpm. This means the car is easily good enough for 12-second quarters – no problem! Is that enough "show and go" for you?

▼ John Lye's outstanding '32 Ford 3-window coupe is built for show, but also comes with a good helping of go!

MAKE:	Ford
BODY STYLE:	3-window Coupe
YEAR:	1932
ENGINE:	383 Chevrolet
BUILD STYLE:	1960's Show Car
BUILDER:	John Lye

'36 Ford Convertible

Just about the earliest Ford model to lend itself well to the 1950's trend of building "customs," with the emphasis on custom body modifications, rather than on outright performance, is the art-deco styled '36 Ford – like this customized 2-door touring model. The body modifications crafted in lead on these early cars were often so extensive so as to mask completely the make of the original car. The name of the game was "low and slow" and cruising slowly was a "must" – so that as many onlookers as possible at the drive-in got a chance to check out the cool custom work.

This satin black '36 Convertible has probably had the rear frame "z"-ed to get the body as close to the pavement as possible and the rear fender skirts over the wheel openings compound the early "taildragger" look. The windshield has also been chopped, again to accentuate the low-slung look. This car runs without a hood to show off the detailed and chromed engine. At the front, the car's identity has been hidden with the fitting of a custom grille from a different upmarket 1930's car – á La Salle, possibly? Answers on a post card, please!

MAKE:	Ford
BODY STYLE:	2-door Tourer
YEAR:	1936
ENGINE:	"Y" Block Ford V8
BUILD STYLE:	Traditional 1950's Custom

▶ These early custom styles have seen a big resurgence in recent years, with the emphasis on an original "old school" look. This cool '36 was spotted on the street at Paso Robles, California.

'32 Ford Roadster

When the owner of this cool Candy Blue '32 Highboy first embarked on this project, he had several goals in mind. One was to create his dream roadster using all the parts on his wish list. Secondly, he wanted to emulate his favorite period of hot rodding, the early 1960s. He's certainly achieved both of those ambitions with this flawless example. Although everything on the car is fully polished – including the axle, suspension, engine and the Halibrand quick-change center section under the rear – the car is regularly driven to shows all around the country. No trailer queen, this one!

Typical 1960s touches on the '32 include the use of the big stock style '32 headlights, the polished and race-inspired Moon tank mounted in front of the grille and the Radir Tri-Rib wheels fitted with period whitewall tires. Not so obvious in the picture is the white pearl effect vinyl upholstery with matching '40 Ford steering wheel, or the split hood side panels built specially to accommodate the "Limefire" headers (which are usually seen on cars that run without hood or side panels). With fine details like this all round, little wonder that it picks up "Best in Show" trophies wherever it goes!

MAKE:	Ford
BODY STYLE:	Highboy Roadster
YEAR:	1932
ENGINE:	350 Chevrolet
BUILD STYLE:	1960's style show car
OWNER:	Dan Boone

◀ What hot rodder wouldn't want to make space in the garage for this candy blue beauty!

'34 Ford Coupe

If, in search of speed, you had been rebuilding a '34 Ford back in the 1950s, chances are that one of the first things you would have done was to remove the fenders to save weight and increase performance. If you had, you would have ended up with a highboy coupe like this Peppermint Green example. This one wears small rear "bobbed" fenders as a concession to legality, but still gives the car a completely different look from a stock-bodied car. In keeping with the 1950's theme, this rod features a chopped top – and instead of alloy wheels, it has color-matched steel rims, along with chrome hubcaps and beauty rings. Another nice touch is the small chrome nerf bar, protecting the lower front grille.

The stock, 3-piece hood features all the original cooling louvers – necessary since this particular coupe is running a Chrysler 392 Hemi for motive power! You can see where the hood side panel has been cut away to clear the chrome valve cover on the big V8. The owner of this coupe has really gone the extra mile to build in some unique nostalgic features – such as cutting down and fitting the steel dash panel and gauges from a 1961 Ford Galaxie. This is no mean feat in the close confines of the '34's body – but definitely worth it as a trick custom feature.

MAKE:	Ford
BODY STYLE:	Coupe
YEAR:	1934
ENGINE:	392 Chrysler V8
BUILD STYLE:	Traditional 1950's Hot Rod
BUILDER:	Johny Best

▶ The theme of this car is traditional throughout, including the big Buick finned brake drums on early Ford spindles and mounted on the dropped I-beam front axle.

'39 and '34 Woodies

There are some pretty slick hot rod Woodsters in this book, and while Woodies are always evocative of the 1960's Californian surfer lifestyle, it's unlikely that many surfers drove real peaches even back then. So, for the sake of unabashed nostalgia – and even dare we say "authenticity" – we thought we'd show these two hardcore crates in almost "as found" condition. You have to admit they're both pretty "gnarly!" Both cars were found and purchased by Rich Conklin of Radir Wheels, and (naturally) those are brand new Radir Tri-Ribs on both cars, complete with Radir Dragster whitewalls.

The '34 was bought from the Hershey swap meet by Rich. Also, as far as is known, it was a one-owner car from Illinois. The Flathead motor was replaced with another from a '36, equipped with a set of Edelbrock finned heads and a pair of 97's on a dual intake, the trans was replaced with a '39 unit. This car has now been sold and has headed west to California for a full restoration. Meanwhile, the '39 is definitely a one-family owned car from New Jersey. Apart from the rolling stock and some mechanical work to get it running, it remains stock and serves as a vintage transport for Rich when he wants to hit the beach – hardcore style!

▲ This pair of old Woodies were just too cool to leave out, apart from the new wheels and tires they are pretty much stock, with original Flathead motors. Cowabunga!

MAKE:	Ford
BODY STYLE:	4-door Woodies
YEAR:	1939 and 1934
ENGINE:	Flathead V8
BUILD STYLE:	Traditional
OWNER:	Rich Conklin

'32 Ford 5-window Coupe

The Ford 5-window Coupe has long been a favorite with hot rodders everywhere, and this one displays some very cool racecar inspired touches that just scream "hot rod" to anyone who sees it. I mean, look at it – what else could it be! The 10-spoke front wheels and big slot mags out back are typical of a strip-inspired car shod as they are with blackwall tires. In any form of racing, weight saving is paramount and if a racer can drill a hole in something to lose weight, then he will. To this end, the builder has used the same technique to convey the race inspiration by drilling the front frame horns and the chrome front wishbones as well.

The short chrome headers exiting from the hood sides, can easily be "uncorked" by removing a plate at the end of the pipe for race duty. Otherwise, when the plate is in place, the exhaust gases will continue down the pipe, under the car, and exit to the rear as normal. This hot rod employs the "Ford in a Ford" ethos, meaning that although updated, the car still runs an ohv Ford V8 in place of the old Flathead that came standard in the '32. In this case, a tuned 351 Cleveland sits under the hood, backed up with an FMX gearbox.

MAKE:	Ford
BODY STYLE:	5-window Coupe
YEAR:	1932
ENGINE:	351 Cleveland Ford V8
BUILD STYLE:	Nostalgia Hot Rod
OWNER:	Chris Juan

◀ The copper metallic paint on this 5-window is simple but distinctive, letting the clean lines of the deuce coupe speak for themselves.

'34 Ford Coupe

The first thing that hits you on this '34 Ford Coupe, apart from the stunning red paint, is the massive, polished GMC 6-71 supercharger fed by twin 600 Holley carbs on top of the engine. That engine really is the centerpiece of this fine '34, although the rest of the car is perfect too. Surprising to find that underneath all that chrome, stainless steel and braided hose, that the engine is a stock 283 Chevy, the smallest displacement V8 in the Chevy family (apart from the original 265). The stainless theme is carried out right through this car, with many custom parts hand-fabricated at home by the owner, over the course of the nine-year build.

The bodywork has been given special attention, with particular care given to fit and finish, with smooth painted running boards replacing the stock rubber items and the chopped top adding to the sleek look. As well as the bright-

work and the extreme detailing work that's gone into the engineering and building of this cool coupe, it features a full tan leather tuck'n'roll interior with matching carpets inside, as well as a fully trimmed rumble seat for extra passengers.

▼ The distinctive Budnik Famosa alloy wheels are highly polished and contrast well with the VW red paint on this fine '34 street rod.

MAKE:	Ford
BODY STYLE:	Coupe
YEAR:	1934
ENGINE:	283 Chevrolet
BUILD STYLE:	Contemporary Show Car
BUILDER:	Bill Gibb

'34 Ford Coupe

When some builders undertake the building of a classic Ford hot rod, some prefer to keep it simple and let the beauty of the original design shine through without distracting loud paint or radical modifications. This '34 Coupe is a classic case in point. Black paint has been chosen because nothing shines like a freshly-polished black car; plus it was always one of ol' Henry's favorite colors! Similarly, this car keeps many of the original body details, such as chrome grille, screen surround and chrome door handles. It even retains the black rubber running board covers for practicality. In fact, it's only the low stance of the car, the chopped top and the highly polished American Racing 5-spoke wheels with low profile radial tires that give it away as a hot rod.

Underneath the skin, however, it's a different story. A traditional aluminum dropped I-beam front axle supports the front end, while between the frame rails lurks a Chevrolet ZZ4 V8 engine displacing 350 ci. This puts the power through a B&M Transmission and down to the rodders' favorite, a Halibrand quick-change rear axle. All of which makes for a decidedly hot rod update on the car's original running gear.

MAKE:	Ford
BODY STYLE:	Coupe
YEAR:	1934
ENGINE:	350 ZZ4 V8 Chevrolet
BUILD STYLE:	Performance
OWNER:	John Emery

▸ A common term for the style of street rod that retains many of its original bodywork and trim features is "resto rod" – though this style hasn't been as popular in recent years.

'34 Hudson 4-door Sedan

Some call 'em Rat Rods, but the guys that drive them call them "Hardcore" and so that term will do for us. So, if ever a big old 1930's sedan was "hardcore," it's this one. Probably a case of "if you can't get what you want, then use what you got." On that basis, Jay Taylor went at it with this 4-door sedan, starting by chopping 4 inches out of the top (that's a lot of pillars to cut!) and then channeling the body down 8 inches over the chassis. Combine this with a massive 14-inch kick up in the rear frame, and you end up with one low sedan. A shot of black suede suffices for a paint job. And who needs a roof insert if it's not raining?

A straight tube front axle, mounted suicide style and a set of hairpins, keeps

the front frame rails off the floor and a Moon tank and corroded Model A grille add panache! A 350 ci Chevy small block provides the power and three 2s give an ol' timey look to the V8 motor. Add a set of swept back headers and lakes pipes, and you're ready to terrorize the show'n'shine crowd. Yee-hah!

▼ Jay has dubbed his Hudson "Aces and Eights" and had the name sign written across the steel sun visor of the big Hudson taxi.

MAKE:	Hudson
BODY STYLE:	4-door Sedan
YEAR:	1934
ENGINE:	Chevy 350 V8
BUILD STYLE:	Hardcore
OWNER:	Jay Taylor

'41 Willys Coupe

Old race cars never die, they just get turned into immaculate show-winning hot rods. Such is the case for this former quarter-mile hero. This classic example of one of the perennial favorite gas coupe's of the early 1960s has been re-born with a complete ground-up rebuild, culminating in an eye-poppin' Candy Apple Red paint job. In the picture, you can clearly see the straight axle mounted on parallel leaf springs used on these cars to achieve the high-stepping stance and to aid weight transfer under hard acceleration. Rarely did the owners go to the extra expense of finishing off the cars to this standard, with every component under there polished or chromed. Rather, they preferred to spend their money on the latest speed equipment.

Interestingly, this car seems to be running a narrowed rear axle, to ensure those wide rear tires remain tucked well inside the stock width wheel arches. Back in the old days, the axle would have probably remained stock width from the donor car, maybe an Olds or a Ford 9-inch from a station wagon. This would have seen those racing slicks protruding out at least 6 inches each side of the car. Sadly, this car's racing days are over; but at least it's been given a new lease on life on the show circuit.

MAKE:	Willys
BODY STYLE:	Coupe
YEAR:	1941
ENGINE:	392 Blown Chrysler Hemi
BUILD STYLE:	Ex-competition Show Car
OWNER:	Paul Bath

◀ With the popularity in recent years of nostalgia race events, more and more of these cars can be seen at events such as the California Hot Rod Reunion series.

'26 Ford T Modified

Long before the T-bucket craze of the 1960s, the typical rodded Model T would have appeared much like this green and white cutie. Known as a "Modified," it would have been equally at home racing on the dry lakes or getting a bit sideways on a local cinder track. The narrow T chassis rails usually meant that 4-cylinder engines were the norm in these little cars, and this one right here is no exception. The Lakes Modified style has seen somewhat of a revival in recent years due to the relatively low outlay required to build them. Not sure what motor this one is running, but you can see the twin K&N air cleaners poking thru the hood on the left, while the side-mounted exhaust exits parallel with them on the right-hand side.

Front end on the '26 is a drilled I-beam mounted on quarter elliptic leaves, with hairpin radius rods and Houdaille shocks. The drilled bracket theme is evident throughout the car, adding to its overall appeal and build quality. The Sprint Car style cowl steering is fitted by way of a very short column and a steering box mounted under the dash. A Deuce grille shell and early wires are good choices to complete the "look" on this cool Modified.

MAKE:	Ford
BODY STYLE:	Modified Roadster
YEAR:	1926
ENGINE:	4-cylinder in-line
BUILD STYLE:	Traditional Lakes Modified

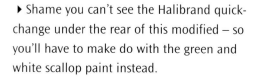

▸ Shame you can't see the Halibrand quick-change under the rear of this modified – so you'll have to make do with the green and white scallop paint instead.

'32 Ford Tudor Sedan

One way to get your ride noticed at events is to wow the troops with a real radical ride – and it doesn't need to be a coupe or roadster either. This sedan subscribes to the "how low can you go" school of thought. The 2-door sedan body has been severely channeled down over the frame, achieved by cutting out the floor, positioning the body at the desired height and then re-forming a new floor that is mounted higher up inside the body. The builder of this car has gone the whole hog and severely chopped the top (a hot rod term for lowering the roof) for a super low profile. The resulting driving position is now probably more akin to driving a low-slung formula racing car than a 1930's sedan.

Obviously, the fenders and running boards have been junked and you can see that the grille shell has also been cut down to match the profile of the cowl. If this wasn't statement enough, the choice of power plant is a story of its own, the builder deciding to install a Chrysler Hemi unit up front for maximum bhp fun. The exhaust is just eight short pipes ensuring that you'll hear this hot rod well before you see it! The choice of unpolished 5-spoke wheels with piecrust whitewalls just serves to complete the picture – cool!

MAKE:	Ford
BODY STYLE:	Sedan
YEAR:	1932
ENGINE:	Chrysler Hemi V8
BUILD STYLE:	Radical Nostalgia Hot Rod

▶ With no fenders to mount the rear lights, the 1950 Pontiac units have been frenched into the lower rear body panel, a popular trick on fenderless cars.

'36 Chevrolet 5-window Coupe

No one said all hot rods have to be Fords, although there are plenty who do indeed subscribe to that theory. The guy in the process of building this wild gasser coupe is certainly "daring to be different" by basing his project on a different make and model.

Hot rods are a labor of love and so we make no apologies for showing you this "in progress" car. You can tell already that it'll be a "killer" coupe once it's finished, even though at present we are looking at bare sheet metal. It looks like all the hard work is done, the engine is installed and you can just see the front shackle mounts for the front leaf springs, where the wing meets the grille panel. It just needs glass, paint (or maybe just primer) and whatever minimal creature comforts are required for the interior.

Where once sat a sturdy old flathead 6-cylinder engine, now resides a firebreathing monster Chrysler Hemi V8. Not only that, but it is supercharged and looks like it is running an early injector setup instead of carburetors. This kind of arrangement is somewhat of a rarity for a street-driven car, for sure – so maybe the car is destined to be a strip-only machine. Either way, it's going to be out there on the wild side of hot rodding, if it's not there already! Note those racing slicks on the rear sticking way past the rear fender sheet metal.

MAKE:	Chevrolet
BODY STYLE:	5-window Coupe
YEAR:	1936
ENGINE:	Blown and Injected Chrysler Hemi V8
BUILD STYLE:	Nostalgia Race Car

◀ The shortage of good, original metal-bodied cars these days is making rodders look to models like this that a few years ago would have been passed over. This '36 Chevrolet is a good example.

'30 Ford Model A Coupe

Here's a mean-looking Ford Model "A" Coupe that's built for the street, but with plenty of "attitude." The top has been chopped about as much as is practical and the top has been filled with a steel panel. A common update on Model A's for years has been to fit a '32 Ford or "Deuce" grille shell like the one shown here. To achieve the correct profile hood to fit both the cowl and the grille shell, a special hood has to be made with the right front and rear radius at each end. It is now possible to buy reproduction steel hoods, though before this facility, guys would have to make them themselves. The car is cruising on a hot day and you can see the vintage air-conditioning in action – or, rather, the opening windshield is wound out.

The car has been built to be deliberately business-like with a minimum of exterior brightwork. The fenders have been removed as has the bar onto which the headlamps are usually mounted. Tiny front turn signals have been mounted on the splash apron that covers the front frame horns to comply with local traffic laws. The wide tires extending from the arches were a common site on 1970s-built hot rods, but certainly don't look out of place on this one.

MAKE:	Ford Model A
BODY STYLE:	Coupe
YEAR:	1930
ENGINE:	Big-block Chevrolet V8
BUILD STYLE:	Street

▶ A polished set of American Racing
5-spoke wheels set just the right flavor on
this Model A with a set of big and little tires.

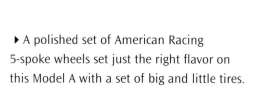

'29 Ford Model A Roadster

This car is a neat interpretation of one of the most traditional ways of updating an early Ford Model A. Right from the early days, rodders were taking the Model A roadster body and mounting it on the later Model B frame rails. The frame rails of the B are much easier on the eye when building a fenderless early rod, as the top rail is the same width as the body giving a more integrated look. Henry Ford even had the foresight to incorporate a swage line into the frame rails, running along the lower edge of the rail and curving up to the point where the four bar is now mounted.

The frame rails would also have been "pinched," which involves cutting out the chassis cross members and pulling the rails in so that they match the narrower Model A cowl.

This car probably runs a modern set of reproduction rails, which can be purchased already done. The stock height windshield and the choice of steel wheels, with chrome rings and early Ford script hubcaps, add to the nostalgic air of this neat roadster. Any old hot rodder from the early 1950s would instantly recognize the theme running through this car.

MAKE:	Ford
BODY STYLE:	Roadster
YEAR:	1929
ENGINE:	Small block Chevrolet V8
BUILD STYLE:	Traditional Street Rod

▶ Although built with an eye on early hot rod trends, notice that as a concession to modern driving, the car is installed with a modern brake setup on the front hubs.

'34 Ford Model 40

Sporting the classic highboy fenderless treatment is this '34 Ford Roadster. The 33-34 Ford, with its all-chrome grille sweeping down to a point just behind the front fender, is not such a common choice for the highboy look. A lot of rodders like the swoopy fenders on the 33-34, or Model 40 as it's known, and leave them on the car. They look just as fine without as well, as this one proves – and the deeper body panels here mean that the chassis is hidden from view beneath the car, which adds to the clean look. Classic black paintwork is all that's needed on this roadster to make the "Trad" statement. Early rodders didn't have the funds to paint their cars fancy colors, and since black was the most common color back then, that's the way most rods stayed.

Not only has this rodder kept to the early theme of steel rims and hubcaps for the roadster, he's also using the tall bias-ply tires, which is good, as lower profile radials just don't look as good on an early style car. Once again, close examination reveals that the dropped and drilled I-beam front axle has had modern disc brakes installed in the interests of modern driving safety. Many rodders will build a car this way as a compromise between the cool, early look and the best of modern running gear.

MAKE:	Ford
BODY STYLE:	Roadster
YEAR:	1934
ENGINE:	350 Chevrolet V8
BUILD STYLE:	Traditional Hot Rod

▸ There are only subtle differences between a 1933 and a 1934 Ford front grille and it takes a real expert to tell. There is a slight difference to the shape of the surround, plus the positioning of the crank handle hole. This one is a 1934 model.

'48 Ford Anglia

You could be forgiven for not instantly recognizing this neat little sedan. It's a Ford Anglia, a British import with a long model run. It was built from the late 1930s until the 1950s over in England. Quite a few made it across the Atlantic where it was sold as a true economy car, with its tiny flathead, 4-cylinder engine and rod-operated brake system. Many of these cars ended up on drag strips during the 1960s, where their short wheelbase and light body weight made them ideal for the gasser classes back then. Since then, some of these Anglias – or Populars as they're known in the UK – have made cool and interesting little street-driven hot rods.

When built for the street, rodded Anglias often still reflect their quarter-mile heritage and this yellow '48 is no exception. The top has been chopped and the decreased headroom, plus the installation of a big V8, means that the driver's seating position is often way back where the confined rear seat used to be! It's no mean feat to fit a V8 with suitable transmission and a stout back axle into these little cars, but it can be done. The rear axle would have needed a major narrowing job to fit it in and keep those big rear tires inside the narrow rear fenders.

MAKE:	Ford
BODY STYLE:	2-door Sedan
YEAR:	1948
ENGINE:	350 Chevrolet V8
BUILD STYLE:	Performance

▶ Solid, race style wheels give this little Anglia a modern high-performance feel, as does the chrome hood scoop and the wheelie bars just visible at the rear.

'32 Ford Model B Roadster

There are some who say that with the amount of reproduction fiberglass bodies produced over the last thirty years, that there are more '32 Ford Roadsters on the road now than there were back in the 1930s! These days, it's even possible to purchase a complete reproduction steel body, virtually indistinguishable from the original. From this picture, it's impossible to tell which this is, but it's a fine example of one of the most popular hot rods on the road. The stance is quite low, a stock framed highboy would sit higher than this without modifying the rear cross member.

This one is set apart by the unusual color combination of pink flames on a red background, as flames are often painted in a more striking contrasting color for maximum effect. The side-opening, one-piece hood is an aftermarket addition, the stock hood would have had a four-piece affair, with a "piano" hinge running down the center. The wheels are traditional early slot mags, maybe Halibrand's, and the center spinners are a nice finishing touch.

MAKE:	Ford
BODY STYLE:	Roadster
YEAR:	1932
ENGINE:	350 Chevrolet V8
BUILD STYLE:	Street Rod

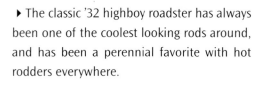

▶ The classic '32 highboy roadster has always been one of the coolest looking rods around, and has been a perennial favorite with hot rodders everywhere.

'47 Austin Devon Sedan Delivery

Back in the late 1940s, the British motor industry threw it's heart and soul into producing cars and trucks for export to recover from the financial ravages of World War II. This even included supplying down-sized economical vehicles to the USA. The Austin Devon model range – available in sedan, pick-up, and sedan delivery – was one of the most up-to-date, and prettiest post-war designs around. The sedan delivery shown here is a very rare piece indeed, on either side of the Atlantic.

It must have taken many hours of hard work to get those panels in good enough shape for the superb red paint on this cute commercial. There's also a lot of work gone into the rear door and rear panel area. The rear doors have been punched with four rows of louvers apiece and the rear license plate has been neatly recessed into the rear panel, a technique known as "frenching." A pair of '42 Ford rear lights has been used in the rear panel too, and they certainly don't look out of place. The highly-polished Centerline wheels really set off the red paint.

MAKE:	Austin of England
BODY STYLE:	Sedan Delivery
YEAR:	1947
ENGINE:	Small Block Chevrolet V8
BUILD STYLE:	Street Rod

▶ With the popularity in recent years of nostalgia race events, more and more of these cars can be seen at events such as the California Hot Rod Reunion series.

'40 Ford Coupe

After the Model As and Bs of the early 1930s, the 39-40 Ford has to be right up there as one of the hot rodder's favorite models – and many hot street rods have been built using the '40 as a starting point. Not only is the '40 shown here a cool street rod, it's all hot rod as well. From it's choice of Hoosier tires on polished race-style rims, to the hot flames licking around the hood and front fenders, the builder has blended carefully these high-performance styling cues with a flawless restored body and much of the original brightwork and trim.

Any owner of the '40 knows they have something good to show under the hood. Here, it is left open to show off the highly-detailed motor within. It is difficult to tell what engine is powering the coupe, but it is a fair bet that it's a small block Chevy, the hot rodder's favorite motor of choice. But one thing is clear; there is a highly-polished and detailed supercharger sitting on top of the motor to provide some extra high horse-power fun. Of course, you can't beat the whine of a blown engine either – but you'll have to imagine that part!

MAKE:	Ford
BODY STYLE:	Coupe
YEAR:	1940
ENGINE:	Chevrolet V8
BUILD STYLE:	Street Rod

◀ This picture captures typical hot rodding in California, with a bunch of cool cars out for a daytime cruise, before stopping at the malt shop for a little light refreshment.

'27 Model T Touring

Just about everybody involved in the car hobby knows that Henry Ford's initial success was founded on the mass production of the Model T Ford, which lasted from its inception in 1908 until 1927. The T models built in the last few years of production have always been the basis of cool hot rods. Indeed, the very first hot rodders started by developing ways to get more power from the T's four-banger engine. The 4-door T Tourer shown here when participating in a little night cruisin' shows off well some of the ways in which a T can make for a cool hot rod.

There's also some interesting metal work on show here, with the frame shrouded in some louvered tinware, both underneath the body and also covering the front frame horns.

The fenders and hood have been discarded to show off the detailed engine, which appears to be a small block Ford with a single carb. There's plenty of room for the fabricated exhaust headers to exit over the frame and run alongside, before tucking back under the car. As the back seat is not in use, a tarp or a tonneau cover is fixed in place; it probably extends over the front seats too when the car is unattended. A practical and fun car, if you need more space than the average roadster provides.

MAKE:	Ford Model T
BODY STYLE:	4-door Touring
YEAR:	1927
ENGINE:	Small Block Ford V8
BUILD STYLE:	Traditional

▶ A set of early 15-inch Kelsey Hayes spoked wheels have been painted orange and provide an ol' timey look to the car, especially when mounted on spindles with early drum brakes, like this car.

'32 Ford 3-window Coupe

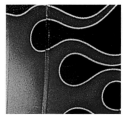

Ford made two models of 2-door coupes in 1932 and either style is often referred to as a "Deuce Coupe." But it's worth noting that the two models are further distinguished by the number of windows in the body, not counting the windshield. Hence, what we have here is a one hot-looking Deuce 3-window; that is, it has one side window each side and a rear glass. This one has all the ingredients for a timeless hot rod. The classic yellow and red flame job has been edged with a fine white pinstripe that looks fantastic over the metallic purple paint.

The roof has been expertly chopped on this '32 to give just the right proportions to the profile ; and the top has been filled. The car retains the chrome screen surround to add just enough brightwork to the upper body, while the polished American Racing mags are exactly the right choice for a car like this. Trends may come and go, but cars like this will always strike the right chord with hot rodders young and old.

MAKE:	Ford
BODY STYLE:	3-window Coupe
YEAR:	1932
ENGINE:	Small block Chevrolet V8
BUILD STYLE:	Street Rod

◄ To many rodders, the 1932 Ford was definitely Henry Ford's finest hour. Some prefer roadsters, but for those who like a roof on their ride, a Deuce Coupe like this one is right on the money!

'32 Ford 5-window Coupe

Of course, hot rodding really took off in the late 1940s, when many skilled young men got back from World War II with money in their pockets and looking for speed and thrills. This is an example of what a rodded '32 Ford would have looked like back then – before there were such things as an aftermarket wheel industry, and speed shops were few and far between. Most rodders back then had to work their craft in their own back yards.

To the uninitiated, the car looks mostly stock, and bodily it probably is. The top is unchopped and remains at stock height and the car wears a typical muted shade of green, again probably a stock Ford color. You'll notice though that the car has a pronounced slope or "rake" to the front. The owner has probably installed a "dropped" or "dago'd" front axle, so called as the modification is believed to been first carried out in the San Diego area of California. Later, smaller diameter Ford wire wheels have been installed and painted a contrasting apple green. The tires add the finishing touch to this period-perfect, early hot rod.

MAKE:	Ford
BODY STYLE:	5-window Coupe
YEAR:	1932
ENGINE:	Flathead Ford V8
BUILD STYLE:	Early Hot Rod

▲ Although mostly stock in the looks department, early rodders would have spent many hours "hopping up" the versatile Flathead V8 that came as standard in the Model B.

'32 Ford Roadster

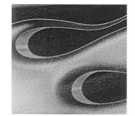

Rodders are constantly looking for new ways to interpret their own vision of the perfect '32 Ford roadster, while at the same time adding their own stamp of individuality to the car. This cool California roadster mixes some old and some new styles with flair to achieve exactly this. The body, while retaining its stock dimensions, has been smoothed out. Notice the lack of door handles and also the smooth hood sides with no cooling louvers. This has given the painter a clean and smooth canvas on which to work his art. In this case, the classic flame job has been given an extra elemnet by giving a three-dimensional effect to the licks of the flames.

Complimenting these contemporary touches are some decidedly traditional ones too. The steeply-raked windscreen is generally known as a "DuVall" screen and dates back to the 1930s. Similarly styled ones were fitted on to the upmarket luxury sports cars of the day, and rodders have been using them on roadsters ever since. The wheel and tire combo on a rod can dictate a theme or style instantly. In this case, classic early five-spoke slot mags are used with "knock off" or spinner center caps for a classic look.

MAKE:	Ford
BODY STYLE:	Highboy Roadster
YEAR:	1932
ENGINE:	Small Block Chevrolet V8
BUILD STYLE:	Street Rod

◀ There is only one front axle set up that looks right on a rod like this. The I-beam and transverse leaf has been in use on roadsters for years and is attached to the chassis either by "hairpins", or a four bar as shown here, instead of the original wishbone arrangement.

'27 Model T Roadster

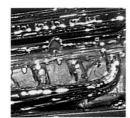

Already famous across the country for his work with customs, California's George Barris took a shot at the Oakland Roadster Show's "America's Most Beautiful Roadster" trophy back in 1962 with this wild '27 T. Needless to say, he won it with the combination of a "Metalflake" green turtledeck T roadster body mounted on a similarly painted '32 Ford frame. "Tall" was "in" in the early 1960s, and so the car has a stock height windshield and frame ahead of the white pearl naughahyde upholstery which featured matching "flake" inserts.

Other outstanding features on the T, which was dubbed the "Twister T," were the custom grille insert in the deuce grille shell, quad chrome headlights, and the Buick 15-inch wire spoke wheels. Naturally, for a show car of the period, the undercarriage was fully chromed and polished too. Although built to compete on the show circuit, it was a fully functioning hot rod, unlike some show cars of the period. To prove it, *Rod and Custom* magazine ran a full road test on the rod in 1963 – with impressive results.

MAKE:	Ford
BODY STYLE:	Turtledeck Roadster
YEAR:	1927
ENGINE:	270 ci Dodge Red Ram V8
BUILD STYLE:	Show Rod
BUILDER:	George Barris

▼ The fully chromed-out motor in the Twister T was a stock '56 Dodge V8 with four Stromberg 97 carbs.

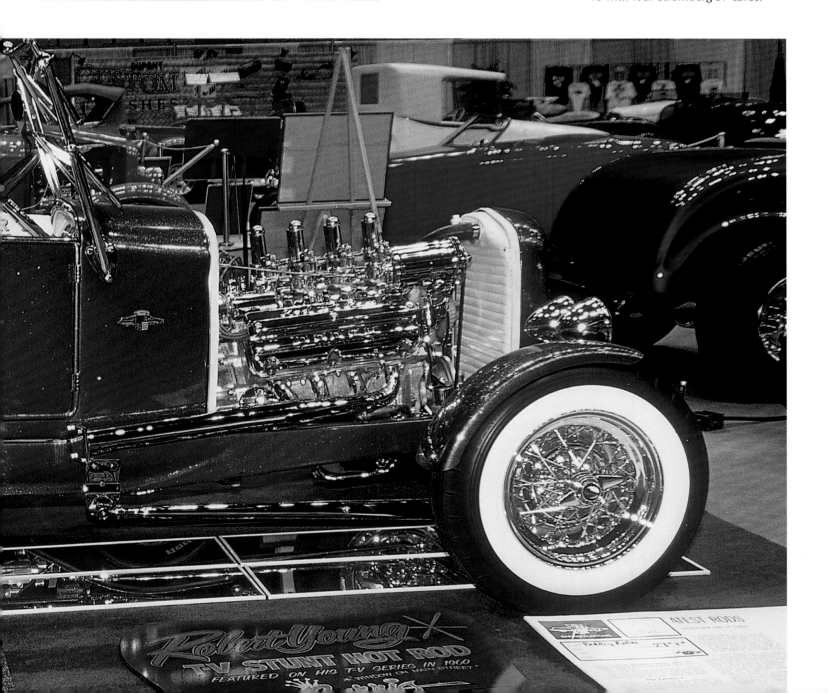

'29 Model A Roadster

The ultimate expression of the hot rodder's quest for more speed is, of course, the race car; and they don't get more "ultimate" and still look like an early Ford than this '29. Built by Don Waite, the '52 De Soto engine was set so far back in the frame that the cockpit area was paneled over and the driver relegated to where the trunk used to be. Sitting low in the car, the driver is protected by a small roll-over bar and a minimal plexiglass windshield. Being a competition car only, cooling was not a major issue and so the Deuce grille shell features a polished aluminum insert. Some neat metalwork also surrounds the front frame and suspension area.

This famous race car was featured on the cover of *Hot Rod* magazine back in 1962. The power plant was a stroked and injected 252 ci De Soto V8, although it later was fitted with a big Mercury engine, hence the lettering on the hood side panel. Its best result ever was a 10.5 second pass at 140 mph in the quarter-mile.

MAKE:	Ford
BODY STYLE:	Roadster
YEAR:	1929
ENGINE:	Mercury 255 V8
BUILD STYLE:	Restored Race Car
BUILDER:	Don Waite

▶ This old race car has now been fully restored to its former glory and is regularly seen at indoor shows and NHRA Reunion events.

'29 Model A Roadster

Originally built in the early 1950s by California hot rodder Ken Fuhrman, this '29 was unique for many innovative features over the years. Most obvious was the fact that not only was the roadster body set on '32 rails, which was a common trick at the time, but those rails were completely chromed - along with most of the running gear! Ken was also a pioneer in the use of "Lucite," a form of plexiglass, which he used to form a see-through hood for the roadster and through which you could view the fully-detailed flathead engine. This feature alone was an absolute showstopper back then.

Originally built as a fenderless roadster with steel wheels and early Ford hub caps, the fenders and the American Racing Equipment Torq-Thrust 5-spokes are later additions from the early 1960s. But the detailed engine with three carbs is true to the original build, including the twin spark plug conversion to the flattie's cylinder heads.

MAKE:	Ford
BODY STYLE:	Roadster
YEAR:	1929
ENGINE:	Ford Flathead V8
BUILD STYLE:	Show Rod
BUILDER:	Ken Fuhrman

▶ The '29 roadster was featured in a Fawcett publication from 1953 called *Best Hot Rods*, which clearly shows the car wearing a 1950 license tag. Some 55 years later, it's still being featured – in this book!

'27 Model T Roadster

In 1953, Dick Williams won the coveted "America's Most Beautiful Roadster" award at Oakland with this outstanding and very low '27 T. To get the car so close to the ground, the body has been channeled over the frame – and it certainly looks from the picture that a full belly pan has been installed underneath the car. This was an early streamlining trick derived from salt flat racing. Of course, much of the suspension has been chromed, including the neat hairpins that secure the axles to the chassis in place of the original wishbones.

A Deuce grille shell has been used in place of the original T item and it has been cut down to fit between the chassis rails, in keeping with the low theme of the car. Another popular update was to replace the front brake drums with polished alloy finned items from a Buick. The fins were designed to dissipate heat build-up; but on a show car like this one they just look plain cool. The flathead engine is, of course, fully detailed on a white-painted engine block. Better make sure there are no oil leaks on that one!

MAKE:	Ford
BODY STYLE:	T Roadster
YEAR:	1927
ENGINE:	Ford Flathead V8
BUILD STYLE:	Show Rod
BUILDER:	Dick Williams

◄ The chrome-plated steel wheels on the roadster are shod with bias-ply black wall tires and Mercury plain hubcaps. The super-wide back wheels were added later, probably when the car was restored.

'40 Ford 2-door Sedan

It wasn't just early Fords that got the show car treatment back in the 1950s: This '40 Ford two door sedan got the full treatment in 1955, courtesy of George Barris' Kustom City. Named the "L'il Beauty," the big sedan was channelled 5 1/2 inches over the frame and the running boards removed, before the fenders were extensively trimmed back to expose the wheels front and rear. The fenders have also been molded to the body for a smooth seamless finish and the edges of the fenders have been flared to provide a slight lip, which has then been accentuated with a pinstripe over the Candy Apple Red paint. Cool stuff! Not so obvious in the pic is the sectioned hood, which has also been punched with four rows of louvers for good measure.

A custom license plate holder has been molded into the trunk lid and, in place of bumpers, chrome nerf bars have been incorporated into the long custom tailpipes. A neat and original touch. At the front of the car, a custom grille was installed along with '57 Lincoln canted headlights and more chrome nerf bars. Wheels are chrome reverse steels with plain hub caps. A heck of a lot of work, resulting in a stunning custom rod.

MAKE:	Ford
BODY STYLE:	2-door Sedan
YEAR:	1940
ENGINE:	Ford Flathead V8
BUILD STYLE:	Custom Show Rod
BUILDER:	George Barris

▸ The door and trunk handles, as well as the stock trim, on this '40 have been removed for a clean look. This process is known as "shaving" the trim.

See Trophies Awarded
To Winning Cars
MONDAY NIGHT
LAST NIGHT OF SHOW

'33 Ford Pickup

This little '33 truck was originally rodded back in the 1980s before being bought by Shag, a member of the Autoholics, a Californian club. We don't know what it looked like back then, but it couldn't be any better than this cool 1950s rendition. The cab has been channeled over the frame and the pickup bed has been radically shortened, so that the tailgate is now inside the furthestmost point of the bobbed rear fenders. At the front, the fenders have been dispensed with completely, leaving only the grille shell echoing the cool red and white paint.

The use of a white tarp over the bed of the rodded truck is a typical 1950's touch and complements well the red and white theme, which is carried over to the steel rims and wide white wall tires. The small block Chevy in the Ford has been detailed with paint and chrome and boasts lakes-style headers with caps that reappear behind the cab as chrome tailpipes running along the edge of the truck bed.

MAKE:	Ford
BODY STYLE:	Pickup
YEAR:	1933
ENGINE:	Chevrolet V8
BUILD STYLE:	Traditional 1950's Rod
BUILDER:	Shag

▶ It's the details that make this truck so cool – such as the white accents on the red paint, the chrome tailgate hinges and the rear nerf bar, which house the tail lights and license plate.

'30 Ford Pickup

Well, this is a difficult hot rod truck to classify! The spindle-mounted, 12-spoke front wheels and whitewall rear slicks just shout "competition-only" machine, especially as there are no brakes fitted to the front hubs! Indeed the only visible way of slowing down the truck from speed seems to be the twin parachutes mounted on the tailgate. The channeled cab and use of a '32 Ford grille shell are very much traditional custom touches on this radical hot rod.

The dressed-out, small-block Chevy is certainly detailed enough for show, and the twin 600 carbs and performance distributor, point to a healthy power output, especially with the long swept-back headers. Then there's that olive drab military themed paint job?

Anyhow, it may not fit into any recognized rodding pigeonhole. But then, perhaps that was the builder's idea in the first place? In which case, it is mighty successful. We like it!

MAKE:	Ford
BODY STYLE:	Fenderless Pickup
YEAR:	1930
ENGINE:	Chevrolet Small Block V8
BUILD STYLE:	Traditional
BUILDER:	Beetle Bailey

▲ We're not sure that Uncle Sam ever commissioned any military trucks to this specification. A shame, as it would have worked wonders at the recruiting office!

'33 Ford SpeedStar Coupe

With not nearly enough original steel bodies to go around, for years now rodders have been relying on fiberglass aftermarket panels and complete bodies. In line with one of the modern trends towards building smooth, cutting-edge cars that constantly push the boundaries of hot rodding, many companies have gone one further and developed their own swoopy interpretations of the original Ford design that are recognizable – but share not one panel with the original car. One such company is Cruisin' Products of Detroit, Michigan, who offer several such body styles such as this Speedstar Coupe based on a '33 Ford Coupe.

Ron Cremo of Cupertino, California, is a customer of theirs, and owns this very slick, green-flamed, SpeedStar Coupe. Powered by a Chevrolet LT1 crate engine, backed up with a 4L60 heavy duty transmission and with a fully polished independent front suspension that is a world away from the old I-beam set ups, it represents just how far hot rodding has come since the early days.

MAKE:	Ford
BODY STYLE:	SpeedStar Coupe
YEAR:	1933
ENGINE:	Chevrolet LT1 V8
BUILD STYLE:	Street Rod
OWNER:	Ron Cremo

▸ Despite being a full-on 21st century hot rod, this '33 still manages to pay homage to the past with its polished 10-spoke front wheels and rear slot mags.

'41 Ford Convertible

Just say the name "Foose," to any hot rodders and they'll know immediately you are talking innovative and quality built hot rods. Depending on their generation, they'll either think of Chip Foose, a talented artist and car builder with the skill to turn his sketches into dream cars, or his father Sam, from whom Chip learned his many skills. Case in point is this subtle but extensively modified '41 Ford convertible built in the mid-1990s. With this car, it's almost what *hasn't* been done rather than list what has. Taking a cue from all the great custom body men that have gone before, Sam has used almost every trick in the book – and then some – to create this smooth custom ragtop.

Traditional "old school" custom body mods include "peaking" the hood, to create the distinctive vertical nose, frenching both the headlights at the front, and the rear license plate into the rolled rear pan. Further changes include chopping the windshield and creating the low custom convertible top, molding all the fenders to the body, removing all the trim and handles and creating the unique custom grille were also attractive modifications. Popular later additions include creating the V-butted bonded windshield without the center post that would have been standard and adding the late model passenger car door mirrors! Phew! And we haven't even touched on the interior or running gear!

MAKE:	Ford
BODY STYLE:	2-door Convertible
YEAR:	1941
ENGINE:	TPI Chevrolet V8
BUILD STYLE:	Contemporary Street Rod
BUILDER:	Sam Foose

◀ Modern directional and polished billet wheels with low profile rubber compliment the smooth lines of this typical '90's high-tech street rod.

'32 Ford Roadster

To some people, a black'n'flamed road-ster is the quintessential hot rod. After all, you could never mistake it for anything else. It doesn't matter how much time you spend hanging around or working on hot rods, when you see a cool one like this '32 cutting through traffic, you are always going to get a kick out of just seeing it move up the street; and that's just how it should be. This Deuce achieves that effect with a wicked yellow and orange flame job licking over a black basecoat in a time-honored fashion. The flames are pinstriped in blue by renowned hot rod artist Dave Bell.

The roadster features an owner-built chassis, with a 4-inch dropped axle from the Super Bell Company, who also supplied the Mustang discs. A Posies spring provides the bounce and it's secured to the frame with a stainless steel 4-bar. Even if you get passed on the freeway by this hot Deuce, you may just have time to appreciate the Winters Grand National Quickchange rear end tucked under the back – before it disappears from view. Super reliable cruising is guaranteed by the '93 Z28 350 Chevy underneath that flaming 4-piece hood. A true American classic.

MAKE:	Ford
BODY STYLE:	Highboy Roadster
YEAR:	1932
ENGINE:	Chevy 350 V8
BUILD STYLE:	Traditional Rod
OWNER:	Barry Larson

▶ This aerial shot of this classic, flamed hot rod shows off the rich oxblood rolled leather trim job.

'46 Ford 2-door Sedan

Just to prove that hot rodding is constantly evolving with every passing decade, take a look at the bang up-to-date treatment of this fat-fendered Ford. Hottest trick in the last few years has been to have your car "bagged" to get that ground scraping stance when parked up at a show. This is achieved by fitting a hydraulic suspension system based on compressed air or "Airbags." These can be easily inflated to give a superior ride quality but then deflated to achieve the "look." This system is very popular with the rodders running the larger and more practical 1940's-style cars that are ideal for carting the whole family away for a weekend rod run.

Smooth bodywork and a lack of exterior brightwork, typify the 21st century hot rod look. All exterior trim has been removed and all holes filled, the fender has been molded, painted body color and moved in close to the front lower panel, the grille also has been de-chromed and painted in the body color of tangerine pearl. The headlamps have also been frenched into the fenders, which is a traditional custom trick that will never go out of fashion. With the hood open, you can see a pair of small rams that neatly replace the old and cumbersome original hood springs. That's technology for you!

MAKE:	Ford
BODY STYLE:	2-door Sedan Roadster
YEAR:	1946
ENGINE:	TPI Chevrolet V8
BUILD STYLE:	Contemporary Street Rod

▶ It's left to the wild tribal flames and the big diameter rolling stock to break up the bright monochromatic paint on this fine Ford sedan.

'29 Model A Roadster

Wow! Are these guys having fun, or what? The car may be a competition style '29 A roadster, built to compete in the B/Gas class of Street Roadster, but it doesn't stop them enjoying a cruise around the parking lot of the local rod run. Although retaining the front fenders, the side splash aprons and the running boards have been removed and the rears shortened or "bobbed." A set of old unpolished slot mags are good enough for racing and get the job done; and the windshield has been removed, the highest point on the car being the safety rollbar behind the seat.

Since the A roadster still runs a set of headlamps and is wearing street treaded tires instead of slicks, we assume the car is just about street legal in this case. The Chevy engine in the little hot rod can be seen due to the lack of hood side panels – though you'll notice that it's not nearly as shiny and detailed as some of the street roadsters elsewhere in this book. The modified hood top hints at a large multi-carburetion system set-up for racing hidden under there.

MAKE:	Ford
BODY STYLE:	Roadster
YEAR:	1929
ENGINE:	Chevrolet V8
BUILD STYLE:	Competition Street Roadster

▶ Hot rodded model As and Bs similar to this one have formed the backbone of the street roadster classes at drag strips all over the country for years. Long may they reign!

'48 Ford Convertible

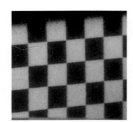

Now here's an interesting one. As a 1948 Ford, it is the last model from Henry with separately styled fenders before the "shoebox" design was introduced. As such, it will qualify as a Street Rod for most large rod events, there being a pre-1949 cut off for body styles as set out by the National Street Rod Association. Under the broader umbrella of hot rod terminology, however, it is more likely to be referred to as a "custom" or "Leadsled" – the latter term being coined due to the fact that most body repairs were carried out with lead filler in the days before modern plastic fillers were developed.

So what makes it a Leadsled? Well, the modifications have to be traditional customizing techniques from the old school, so lowering the car is a must. Fender skirts have been added at the rear to make the car appear even lower and the handles have been shaved too. Shown cruising at a rod event, the windshield on this car has been chopped and a new "Carson" convertible top has been made, eliminating the rear side windows, to give the car more of a coupe look. The satin black paint and flames add to the early look of this "kemp."

MAKE:	Ford
BODY STYLE:	Convertible
YEAR:	1948
ENGINE:	Chevrolet V8
BUILD STYLE:	Early Custom

▶ The lack of a hood on this cruiser shows off the checkerboard-painted firewall and the big Caddy-style air cleaner, again early custom additions to the Ford.

'31 Ford Tudor Sedan

At some time in the late 1950s-early 1960s, someone invented "Metalflake" paint, which as its name suggests, used real flakes of metal suspended in the color. It immediately became "the" finish to have on custom machinery, cars and motorcycles alike. It was available in many colors, and you can clearly see here, the sparkly effect obtained, on the Deuce grille shell and body of this early 1960's-style, fenderless Model A Sedan. Once applied, Metalflake paint requires many additional coats of lacquer, as it is has a very thick and rough finish straight from the spray gun, and so needs the lacquer to give it a smooth finish and high shine.

As well as the "flake finish," it was also a custom trend to paint and detail components in white or cream to further illustrate just how clean the finished car was. This chopped A sedan is mounted on a '32 chassis that has been finished this way, with the firewall behind the engine being painted white also. This theme is carried on through the white vinyl top and the wide white wall tires. That firewall has also having been recessed to make room for the big block V8 that's been fitted.

MAKE:	Ford
BODY STYLE:	Tudor Sedan
YEAR:	1931
ENGINE:	Big Block Chevrolet V8
BUILD STYLE:	Traditional 1960's Hot Rod

▶ The wild, serpentine exhaust headers on this hot rod look as if they are a set of fenderwell headers designed to clear the frame of another car – one that would have had an engine compartment with much more limited space than this Model A.

'34 Ford Tudor Sedan

We thought it was time to throw a curve ball for all you rod spotters out there. So, before you all write in and say this is a '32 sedan and not a '34, have another look. Sure, it's a Deuce sedan alright, but we can assure you it was manufactured in 1934. Just check out the fenders on the car, not a custom trick, they've always been there, as have the rear- hinged suicide doors. The rod also features a '34 style dash and hidden hinges for the opening windshield.

The reason for all this auto-confusion is not a "Bad day at Dearborn," but the fact that this car was originally built in England for the British market. Back then, it was too expensive in the UK to re-tool for new bodies every year (as, of course, happened in the USA), due to the reduced size of the British market, so the '32 body was used for a few extra years with some later updates. It still makes for a fine-looking hot rod, along with the subtle touches of steelies and white walls, plus the "Moon" fuel tank ahead of the grille to add a bit of "hot rod" to the restrained exterior.

MAKE:	Ford
BODY STYLE:	Tudor Sedan
YEAR:	1934
ENGINE:	Buick 215 ci V8
BUILD STYLE:	Street Rod
OWNER:	Gary Kybert

▸ In keeping with it's unusual origins, this cool sedan has an unusual engine too. It runs an aluminum Buick V8 with a four-speed transmission. Another American export!

'33 Ford 3-window Coupe

We don't know why, but it seems that as soon as you strip the fenders off of a Model 40, it almost just shouts "Hot Rod" right away. Of course, a few extra touches don't hurt either – such as a dropped and drilled I-beam front axle and matching hairpins, fully chromed and polished, naturally. A similarly highly polished set of big'n'little Halibrand traditional wheels with black wall tires don't hurt either. This Michigan-based '33 coupe also boasts a neat set of nerf bars, especially that subtle bar protecting the edge of the rear pan.

Featuring a cool roof chop and filled hood sides with just three rows of small louvers, the absolutely flawless copper metallic paint on this 3-window is a great choice. It's a color that has seen a comeback on hot rods in recent years, after seemingly years of nothing but red ones! No flames, graphics or other distractions are needed when a rod looks this cool. The choice to retain the large stock headlights on the rod was a good one too.

▲ Taken from this angle, the shot really accentuates the swoopy lines of a Model 40, with a slight rake created by the right choice of rolling stock.

MAKE:	Ford
BODY STYLE:	3-window Coupe
YEAR:	1933
ENGINE:	Chevrolet V8
BUILD STYLE:	Street Rod

Lakes Modified Roadster

To be perfectly honest, we don't know which make of steel body the owner of this radical little Lakes Modified roadster used to create his high horsepower wild ride. But it was such a cool hot rod we just had to include it in the book. Usually, these types of cars are based on Ford's 2-seat Model T roadster body, with the rear "turtledeck" removed. This minimal bodywork look gave rise to the term T-bucket. The body on this rod looks as though it has fixed posts for the windshield surround, which is not typical of a T, though it could easily be owner fabricated. We don't even recognize the chopped-down grille shell used here, though it does look familiar.

Judging from the lettering on the cowl, the car hails from Georgia; so if anyone down south knows what it is, we'd love to know. What we do know is that those are the unmistakeable chrome valve covers of a Chrysler Fire Power Hemi sitting between those home-brewed megaphone headers. That's an awful lot of power for such a small lightweight car, and more than enough power is available to make those rare Halibrand "kidney bean" vintage slot mags spin the tires on the asphalt. More than a handful, in fact.

MAKE:	Unknown
BODY STYLE:	Lakes Modified Roadster
YEAR:	Unknown
ENGINE:	Chrysler Fire PowerHemi V8
BUILD STYLE:	Lakes style Hot Rod

▲ The unpainted bare metal body and untrimmed interior have been left that way intentionally. This roadster wasn't built for show, just maximum fun!

'38 Lincoln Zephyr 3-window Coupe

Acquired by the Ford Motor Co. in the 1920s, the Lincoln brand soon became Ford's flagship marque, the Lincoln Zephyrs of the 1930s becoming one of their most distinctive designs. Not many survive as street rods and you are more likely to find them in a classic museum. However, as this picture shows, if any cars exemplified the "Art Deco" looks of the late 1930s, these do – and they make unusual and striking rods. The streamlined body is so distinctive that it doesn't really need much modification, other than maybe a little cleaning up of unnecessary exterior trim; even those fender skirts are stock items.

Despite its Show Car looks, this particular hot rod Lincoln does more than its fair share of highway miles to various events. This is no surprise, since its owner, Jake Moran, is an official of the National Street Rod Association and as such drives this car to events all over the USA, though you'd never know it to look at the quality of the candy blue paintwork. Where originally a big V12 engine used to be, now resides an injected small-block Ford V8.

▼ Original steel Lincoln Zephyrs like this one are rare hot rods, but it is now possible to buy or build your own fiberglass replica from a company called Deco-Rides.

MAKE:	Lincoln Zephyr
BODY STYLE:	3-window Coupe
YEAR:	1938
ENGINE:	Injected 302 Ford V8
BUILD STYLE:	Art Deco Street Rod

'47 Ford 2-door Sedan

No wild or radical custom mods on this '47 Ford Sedan. On the contrary, the body is straight and it still retains all the chrome and stainless exterior trim that it bore when it first left the showroom all those years ago. But that's the point; there are great hot rods like this one all over the USA, providing fun and reliable transport for the whole family whenever it's required. The earlier pre-World War II coupes, roadsters and sedans just don't have enough room and comfort for the family-oriented hot rodder, so the post-war cars are an ideal alternative. With many chassis and suspension components available to update them, these cars are the first choice for anyone planning any serious, long-distance driving.

With its straight red paint, this Ford represents an almost perfect restoration. Yet, underneath that vintage sheet metal, you can be sure there are plenty of modern updates for driving pleasure – such as power steering, power brakes, independent front suspension and rack-and-pinion steering. A big sedan like this provides plenty of comfort for all the family, plus enough trunk space too for those longer trips. With air-conditioning and full stereo also included, why drive a modern car?

MAKE:	Ford
BODY STYLE:	2-door Sedan Roadster
YEAR:	1947
ENGINE:	Chevrolet V8
BUILD STYLE:	Street Rod

▲ From a distance, you'd be forgiven for mistaking this as a stocker, if it wasn't for its lower stance and polished American mag wheels.

'40 Ford Coupe

Black as coal and meaner than a junkyard dog, the Helger Bros "Headhunter" is coming for you! This '40 Coupe looks about ready to wreak havoc in the staging lanes with its sky-high stance, courtesy of a stainless straight axle front end. The coupe really looks the part as a period gasser, its design coming from the same era as the classic Willys coupes.

In fact, the Willys would have had a considerable weight advantage over the Ford, hence their popularity; but that doesn't stop this Coupe from making a welcome appearance at any nostalgia race event.

It's quite possible that this one is wearing a fiberglass flip front end to save weight, judging by the blanked off headlamp buckets, albeit with some stock '40 stainless trim on the hood and a repro '40 grille. Under the hood and powering the fat fendered forty to 10-second runs is a 600 hp small block Chevy backed up with a 2-speed Powerglide and a stout '57 Oldsmobile rear axle – plus what looks like a very substantial set of ladder bars to minimize spring wind-up on those green light moments. The fender well headers can be clearly seen between the front wheel and front arch, exiting just behind the rearmost edge of the fender.

MAKE:	Ford
BODY STYLE:	2-door Coupe
YEAR:	1940
ENGINE:	Chevy 327 V8
BUILD STYLE:	Gasser
OWNER:	Ray Helger

◀ This car has all the classic gasser hallmarks, including a set of early Halibrand wheels – with vintage unpolished finish, of course.

'34 Ford Pickup

The owner of this cool, late-1950s Ford pickup patterned the truck after one that had impressed him as a child many years before. It just goes to prove that you can get bitten by the hot rod bug at a very early age. To re-create that memory, a '34 cab was channeled 6 inches over the frame, which itself has been narrowed to take the steel Model A pickup bed. Although the truck has no fenders at the back, the wild front fenders were formed in steel by modifying a set from a '34 Ford. A '32 Ford car grille has been used at the front and modified to fit between the frame rails.

Neat period features abound on this rod, but the centerpiece has to be the engine. A '57 Ford Thunderbird Y-block was fully detailed, and fitted with an Offenhauser inlet manifold with 3 Holley 2100 carbs. Those wild, stainless steel headers were crafted by the owner and are fitted with motorcycle baffles in order to subdue the big V8. The truck is also fitted with a four-speed stick shift as well for even more 1950's fun. Inside, the interior is trimmed in black and white pleated Naugahyde for more of that old timey feel.

MAKE:	Ford
BODY STYLE:	Pickup
YEAR:	1934
ENGINE:	Ford Thunderbird 292 ci V8
BUILD STYLE:	Traditional 1950's Hot Rod
BUILDER:	Paul Brewer

◄ The whitewall slicks on the back, the '50 Pontiac taillights and the cool nerf bars are the icing on the cake on this period perfect Hot Rod truck.

'31 Ford 2-door Sedan

Here's a neat Model A that will make you green with envy, thanks to the unusual color choice that manages to still look great with the trad red steelies, whitewalls and '46 Ford 'caps. What's more, the combo of this wheel treatment looks great on just about any hot rod. It's also a much cheaper option than expensive machined billet wheels as well. The car features a mild chop to the roofline and an aftermarket Rootleib hood with smooth sides and a side opening one piece top match the cowl up with the Deuce grill shell. The hood sides have slots in the side to clear the Lakes Style headers.

The whole deal sits on squarely on a color-matched '32 frame with drilled I-beam and polished stainless hairpins. Stock headlamps and a spun aluminum Moon tank complete the picture at the front end. The red-and-white theme is carried through to the interior of this A sedan, with pleated two tone seats and matching headliner. A '40 Ford dash also painted in the green body color adds extra interest inside, as does the use of a 1950's passenger car steering wheel with chrome horn ring. How cool is that?

MAKE:	Ford
BODY STYLE:	2-door Sedan
YEAR:	1931
ENGINE:	Chevrolet V8
BUILD STYLE:	Traditional Hot Rod
BUILDER:	Jeff Davis

◀ The artwork on the side of the cowl bears the nickname of the rod "L'il Stinker" with a cartoon skunk to match. There's a story in there somewhere, but we don't know it…

'32 Ford Pickup

Looking at the aged green paint and faded lettering on the doors, this truck appears to be one of those rare "barn finds" that all hot rodders dream of stumbling across. Nothing could be further from the truth, however. The ol' pickup was actually found at a swap meet and constructed as a working hot rod truck to tow the owners sprint car project. Although the running gear is all newly-installed hot rod hardware, the paint has been cleverly applied to give the truck a "faux" patina of faded green with hints of primer and even rust showing through. Even the pinstriping on the fenders looks like it was applied at some time in the truck's distant past.

A small block Chevy V8 provides the motive power and as this was built to be a tow truck, it's been built with reliability as the key factor, with tried and tested components. The body remains completely stock, apart from the hot rod louvers in the rear tailgate. Note the front spreader bar on the frame. This would normally be a straight tube affair, although there are custom variations on the market. But, in this case, it has been made from a section of drilled I-beam front axle. The truck has the complete component underneath the truck painted in red to match the other details.

MAKE:	Ford
BODY STYLE:	Closed Cab Pickup
YEAR:	1932
ENGINE:	Chevrolet 350ci V8
BUILD STYLE:	Traditional Street Rod
BUILDER:	Dan Shaw

▶ Built on a modest budget, this '32 truck draws as much attention as shiny hot rods that have cost three times as much, with clever use of detail making up for a lack of big bucks.

'40 Willys Sedan

The Willys coupe body is a firm favorite and popular with nostalgia drag racers and rodders alike, but you won't see many Willys sedan bodies with the hot rod treatment. This is mainly because the sedan was naturally a 4-door, and rodders, if building a sedan, have traditionally preferred 2-door cars. Here is the exception to the rule, as this '40 has been skilfully converted to a 2-door sedan by welding up the rear doors, though you'd never know, as the proportions are perfect. This Hot Rod Willys has been built to full race car specifications including an NHRA certified 10-point roll cage and it runs as good as it looks.

Nine years in the building was time well spent to create a rod that looks, well, as "hot" as this one does! A fully rebuilt and injected '57 Chrysler Hemi, topped with a 6-71 GMC supercharger driving through a polished Torqeflite transmission to a narrowed 9-inch Ford rear axle provides the running gear. The car is built on a custom chassis, which was narrowed at the rear to allow for the wide rear rubber. Polished Halibrand spindle mount front wheels add to the "race car with tags" ethos running throughout this car. Yes, it is street legal!

MAKE:	Willys
BODY STYLE:	2-door Sedan
YEAR:	1940
ENGINE:	Blown and injected 392 Chrysler Hemi V8
BUILD STYLE:	Race Car with Tags
BUILDER:	Shane Weckerley

◀ Look under the hood and you'll see the bug catcher injection set up on top of the polished blower. The motor deliberately looks like it has come straight out of a 1960's fuel dragster.

'32 Ford Roadster

▲ All the standard elements for a cool "highboy" are there, the stainless hairpins, the lakes pipes, even the flames but it's the way it has all been put together that makes the telling difference.

There are plenty of '32 Roadsters in this book; and no apologies for that, as most rodders (if they haven't got one) still aspire to owning one at some time. But this one is a bit special, for sure. Careful selection of modern reproduction parts, including a Brookville steel body, has resulted in a hot rod that drives so well that the owner has taken it across country on several major long-distance events; but it will still turn the quarter-mile in less than 14 seconds in full street trim. The main goal, when undertaking the build of this car, was not only that it should look 1960's cool, but also that it should be good enough to drive easily on a daily basis; and by any measure, this highboy achieves this hands down.

A lime-green color-coded, 350-crate engine equipped with a Holley 650 carb, is backed up by a Tremec 5-speed manual gearbox for maximum driving involvement in this roadster, and if you haven't driven a hot rod with a clutch pedal installed, Man, you haven't lived! Despite the lack of obvious fitting points, the '32 does have a folding top for those not so sunny days. Nostalgic appearing wheels are Budnik 15-inch Murocs.

MAKE:	Ford
BODY STYLE:	Roadster
YEAR:	1932
ENGINE	350 Chevrolet V8
BUILD STYLE	Street Rod
OWNER	George Poteet

'32 Ford Cabriolet

The '32 shown here might not be the shiniest or the fastest in these pages, but it have one of the most interesting histories. For a start, one thing that makes it unusual is that it is the rarer Cabriolet, with the fixed windshield, rather than the Roadster on which the screen unbolts from the body. Then, there is the fact that this car was originally produced for export and spent most of its life on the other side of the Atlantic. It was there that it was first hot-rodded, with a small block Chevrolet engine, making it one of the first to be built in this way in the UK. At one time, it even had full Jaguar independent suspension all round, though the owner has since changed it back to a conventional dropped beam and "live" axle.

Now back in North America, the car retains all its original steel sheet metal and many other original parts, the owner having owned it now for nearly forty years! Built to drive, the Chevy V8 is backed up with a T10 manual transmission and a Ford 9-inch rear axle and gets used regularly. Later updates for reliability include electronic ignition and a modern aftermarket Walker radiator.

MAKE:	Ford
BODY STYLE:	Cabriolet
YEAR:	1932
ENGINE:	Chevrolet 327 ci V8
BUILD STYLE:	Street Rod
OWNER:	David Waring

▲ The chassis is the original '32 frame and always has been. The steel wheels feature '50 Ford hubcaps and chrome beauty rings.

'34 Ford Phaeton

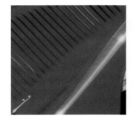

No, your eyes don't deceive you; that is a flip-bodied hot rod built for the street! This unusual 4-door convertible or "phaeton" was first built in the early 1980s by ex-drag racer Jim Green. If we tell you that Jim was famous for racing "funny" cars, you'll know why he built the fiberglass bodied rod like this. Because he could! When lowered, the '34 looks like any other resto-rod of the period with plenty of original style parts, such as full convertible top, luggage rack and chrome fenders. A favorite with resto-rodders, the car wears a set of fine-spoke chrome wire wheels, which look good, but include a high maintenance factor to keep clean.

A full custom-built chassis was created especially for the car's body, which is supported by hydraulic rams when raised. A big block SOHC Ford engine powers the phaeton. Not only that, but it's blown too. Jim may have hung up his racing boots but that doesn't mean he's lost his taste for a big engine up front. The car was featured in *Hot Rod* magazine way back in 1982; but as you can see in the pic taken 22 years later, it still looks great.

MAKE:	Ford
BODY STYLE:	4-door Phaeton
YEAR:	1934
ENGINE:	Ford 427 SOHC V8
BUILD STYLE:	Resto-rod Plus!
BUILDER:	Jim Green

▸ In case you're wondering about the vertical board mounted ahead of the front fender, the rod was conducting push car duties at the drags when we took the picture.

'41 Ford Pickup

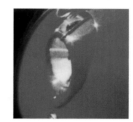

These early 1940s Ford pickups make great rods, just like their passenger car versions. However, it's a lot harder to tell the model years apart, especially when they've been rodded. Featuring the use of very similar sheet metal between the years, they often have details from the car range added for extra detail – such as chrome headlamp embellisher rims, for example. This one has the original painted rims color-matched to the orange paint and the hood has been smoothed of its original bright trim parts and some subtle pin striping added instead. To contrast the orange, the grille has been blacked out as this was often body color as standard. New turn signals have also been added to the front.

A nice low stance makes this '41 really stand out. This is achieved by using a complete independent front suspension unit from a compact Ford passenger car at the front. Simultaneously, this upgraded the truck to disc brakes and power assisted rack and pinion steering. A lowering kit has been installed at the rear to get that end down where it belongs. A black tarp over the bed area is a practical and useful addition when hauling stuff in this truck.

MAKE:	Ford
BODY STYLE:	Pickup
YEAR:	1941
ENGINE:	283 Chevrolet V8
BUILD STYLE:	Street Rod
OWNER:	Ian Smith

◄ The lack of fenders adds to the clean, uncluttered look of the truck, while the wheel treatment is kept simple with a set of baby Moon hub caps.

'46 Ford Business Coupe

The big '46 Ford coupe wouldn't normally be your first choice for a race car; but back in 1958, when Phil Pofahl first paid $75 for it, it seemed like a good idea. Four years later, it was painted the Glade Green that's still on it now and the sign in the window proudly draws attention to the fact. Built to run in the C/Gas class in the early 1960s, it has a stainless steel straight front axle with '32 Ford spindles and a '51 Mercury rear end, narrowed on one side. This isn't a traditionally-built hot rod; this is the real deal!

Along with the nicely aged, old paintwork, the '46 still runs much of its original trim including the rear fender. Originally raced with a 303 ci Oldsmobile engine, this has now been stroked out to 387 ci and runs Hilborn injection to feed the gas from the 2-gallon Moon tank. A member of the "Geezer Gassers" association, this ol' hot rod now regularly runs at nostalgia drag race events in the northern Midwest, where its best time to date is 11.77 at 111mph.

MAKE:	Ford
BODY STYLE:	2-door Coupe
YEAR:	1946
ENGINE:	Stroked 387 Oldsmobile V8
BUILD STYLE:	Show
BUILDER:	"Firesuit" Phil Pofahl

◀ This old Ford exemplifies the way race cars use to be back in their day. Check out the old front slot mags and the long fenderwell headers. Classic gasser stuff.

'27 Ford Doctor's Coupe

When you think of a Model T hot rod, the first thing that usually comes to mind is the T bucket style. But there are many other styles, such as this tall "Doctors Coupe," as they're often known. Much rarer (owing to the fact that few, if any, have ever been reproduced in fibreglass) nevertheless, they make for a cool and unusual hot rod. This one, looking fine in Henry Ford black, is understated and classy-looking. Although parked on a grassy slope, it maintains a cool rake due to the dropped stainless tube front axle and big and little tires.

A point worth mentioning is that the tire-to-fender gap on a hot rod is something that many rodders can be critical of on a hot rod, preferring to have the wheel fit in there as closely as possible with minimum gap. On a T, however, some quarter must be given as the fenders are very flat in design and have virtually no valance to curve down over the edge of the tire. The stock bodywork on this T is flawless, with its chrome grille shell and four-piece hood.

MAKE:	Ford
BODY STYLE:	Model T Coupe
YEAR:	1927
ENGINE:	Chevrolet V8
BUILD STYLE:	Street Rod

◄ Much rarer at rod shows than T roadsters, this type of closed-cab coupe has an unmistakeable tall look. The polished American mags contrast well with the straight paintwork.

'29 Ford Model A Cabriolet

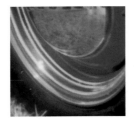

There's nothing too fancy about this sweet little '29. It just looks "right," that's all; and that's good enough for us. A nice low stance has been achieved with a dropped I-beam and the front mounted Moon tank and nerf bars are just enough to give it a late 1950's-early 1960's feel. Once again, red painted Ford steel wheels have been brought in to good effect, especially with the ribbed beauty rings and 50's F100 truck hubcaps. Just for a change, the top has been left up on this car, the fixed windshield posts denoting that this is as a Cabriolet.

The small block Chevrolet V8 is visible under the hood, but the owner has taken a different approach to detailing the engine. The valve covers visible are finned Chevy script ones that have been color-coded to match both the block and the body color. Stock Chevy Rams horn cast manifolds have been used instead of expensive headers. The hood itself is a one-piece top and the car runs without the side panels.

MAKE:	Ford
BODY STYLE:	Cabriolet
YEAR:	1929
ENGINE:	Chevrolet V8
BUILD STYLE:	Traditional Street Rod

▶ Equally at home parked at a rod run or cruising down the road, this clean and practical little A looks like a lot of fun without breaking the bank.

'34 Ford 5-window Coupe

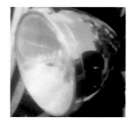

There's been a big move recently by some in the hot rod scene to shift away from the high-dollar cars and return to home-built machines – that while lower on bucks, are big on character and innovation. This '34 is certainly displaying some of those traits – and looking cool in the process. The un-chopped, 5-window body has been channeled over the frame for the low look and the rod runs without bumpers, running boards or front sheet metal. The body has been left in a flat gray primer finish also popular on these early style rods.

That's not the most unusual feature though, since the builder of the coupe has opted for an inline 6-cylinder engine instead of either a flathead or even a later ohv V8. To accommodate the six-pot, the radiator had to be moved forward. Consequently, so had the grille shell, giving the car a longer stretched appearance. It looks like the engine has received a little tuning equipment by way of a twin carb set-up and split exhaust manifold. There is also a polished valve cover on there for added dress up.

MAKE:	Ford
BODY STYLE:	5-window Coupe
YEAR:	1934
ENGINE:	GMC Straight Six
BUILD STYLE:	Traditional Retro Rod

◀ Early steel wheels are fitted on the rear, but even earlier Kelsey wires are good enough for the front, all shod with bias-ply blackwall tires.

'40 Willys Coupe

We make no apologies for including some classic gassers in this book. If they're not true hot rods, then nothing is! A case in point is this restored '40 Willys Coupe that raced under the team name of Stoltz and Velasquez. Even back then, the car was famed for its gorgeous Candy Apple Red paint, campaigning as it did in the BB/Gas Supercharged class. Photos taken at the time often show the car running with chrome Cragar S/S 5-spokes, but this latest incarnation has the period slot mags fitted as shown the pic.

Now that the car is enjoying its well-deserved retirement, its standard of restoration probably exceeds the standard of finish it enjoyed while racing back in the mid-1960s. The GM blower is fully polished, as is the Hilborn injection set-up on top. No doubt the rest of the engine is the same. Underneath, you can see the stainless front axle with the parallel leaves that have been chromed. The fender well headers are just visible behind the front wheel and these have also been chromed.

MAKE:	Willys
BODY STYLE:	Coupe
YEAR:	1940
ENGINE:	392 Chrysler Hemi V8
BUILD STYLE:	Restored race car
OWNER:	Nelson Stolz

◄ If anyone ever asks you what makes a hot rod a gasser, just reach for this book and show them this picture.

'32 Ford Roadster

Probably the most well-known paint scheme in hot rodding is the scalloped, two-tone paint design as evident on this So-Cal Speed Shop-built '32. It dates back to the original racing team campaigned by So-Cal founder Alex Xydias. The company was founded in 1946; and cars built by the Southern California shop went on to make their mark in history at both the Bonneville Salt Flats and the Pomona Drags. The company takes its history very seriously and has built a reputation as the leading supplier and builder of traditional style cars and parts on the West Coast – and further.

Needless to say, along with another couple of '32 hot rods just like these serve as rolling showcases for the company's products. With many vintage parts getting harder and harder to find, the company is always looking to improve it's product line by taking original concepts (such as the traditional I-beam suspension and hairpin set-ups) and improving on them. If we started to list the components on this archetypal California roadster, we'd begin to sound like their shop catalog. But you have to admit it's a great looking car. So, we'll leave it to them. After all, they do it so much better!

MAKE:	Ford
BODY STYLE:	Roadster
YEAR:	1932
ENGINE:	Chevy 355 V8
BUILD STYLE:	Traditional Street Rod
BUILDER:	So Cal Speed Shop

▸ The simple red and white scalloped paint on the So-Cal '32 dates back to the 1940s and the shop's original racing team. It still looks fresh today.

'23 T Roadster

Hot rodding had always been the symbol of four-wheeled teenage rebellion, from its early days right through to the early 1960s; but then something happened. After the surfing craze on the West Coast, Detroit suddenly discovered young people and introduced the Ford Mustang. As sales of the fast "pony" and then muscle cars grew, so hot rodding, in its true sense, began to lose ground to these instant thrill machines – cars that didn't require long nights of wrenching to acheive attention on the streets. Throughout this period, it was the Fad T phenomenon that kept rodding alive with cars very much like the superb wine red T-bucket shown here.

This car has all the hallmarks of a classic T-Bucket roadster from that era – the full-height windshield with long windshield braces, the chrome drop tube axle mounted "Suicide" style and the chrome sprint car headers. With such exposed "hardware" and absolutely minimal bodywork, the finish and workmanship needed to be top notch. There was nowhere to hide botches! Hence, most T- bucket rodders spent many dollars at the chrome platers – and this one is no exception. The focus of attention has to be the 6-71 Dyers blower on top of the 350 ci Chevy V8 that is fed by a variable venture Predator carb with more (even more!) chrome provided by the classic Cragar S/S 5-spokes. This T runs without fenders, of course!

MAKE:	Ford
BODY STYLE:	T-Bucket Roadster
YEAR:	1923
ENGINE:	Chevy 350 V8
BUILD STYLE:	Traditional Fad T
OWNERS:	Randy and Tanya Green

◄ The blown T-bucket is a classic hot rodding icon, and is still the epitome of a hot rod to the guy in the street!

'32 Packard Cabriolet

It's true to say that the majority of hot rods are based on the mass-produced makes and models of domestic cars. After all, these models have always been plentiful and – at one time anyway – relatively inexpensive. It's always interesting then, to see a quality street rod made from one of the rarer luxury pre-war makes like this 1932 Packard Model 900 Rumble seat Cabriolet. The majority of this project was treated primarily as a restoration, with the rare and classy body being massaged back to 1930s factory condition before receiving an all-over coat of Mercedes Benz red. Only the lowered stance and the new chrome fine-wire spoke wheels with radial tires give away the car's Resto Rod identity.

The Packard retains its original strong frame, but is updated with a dropped tube front axle secured on coil overs shocks, and a 4-bar at the front. At the back, and maintaining its luxury car status, is a Jaguar fully-independent rear end, again with coil overs (although all Jaguars have them as standard anyway). Under the long hood that was built for a flathead straight eight, there now resides a Chevy V8. A big-block 454 engine now powers the Cabriolet and the big-inch Chevy is kitted out with polished aluminum heads and four 48-mm Weber carbs on a custom manifold for added class.

MAKE:	Packard
BODY STYLE:	Rumble-seat Cabriolet
YEAR:	1932
ENGINE:	Chevy 454 V8
BUILD STYLE:	Resto Rod
OWNER:	Eric Ball

◄ Resto-rod or Luxo-rod? Whichever way you cut it, a '32 Packard street rod is one unique and very classy way to go cruising.

'29 Sedan Delivery

This neat black Model A has risen like a phoenix from the ashes of a very sad looking '29 Tudor body that it once was. Found with no upper panels, a Gibbon conversion kit was installed to transform it into the cool sedan delivery in the picture which doubles as a rolling billboard for the owner's street rod building business. While the conversion was taking place, the top was chopped at the same time and a set of Polyform glass fenders installed, along with a Rootlieb hood with solid sides. Once the bodywork was complete, several coats of black urethane enamel gave the Model A a truly deep shine.

The original frame was beyond help – so a T.C.I. reproduction chassis was tweaked and slipped underneath the body, ready for the 4-inch Magnum dropped I beam on stainless 4-link at the front and the narrowed Ford nine-inch rear axle. Power for the little truck comes from an '84 Chevy 305 ci, which remains basically stock – with the exception of a 600 Holley on an Edelbrock Performer manifold. A Turbo 400 transmission shifts the gears helped along by a Trans-go shift kit. A set of Weld Superlite 15-inch rims with B.F. Goodrich keep the delivery rolling down the highway.

MAKE:	Ford
BODY STYLE:	Sedan Delivery
YEAR:	1929
ENGINE:	Chevy 305 V8
BUILD STYLE:	Street Rod
OWNER:	Willie Hartshorn

▶ "Willie's Street Rod Service" is the cool logo on the side of this neat Model A Delivery shop truck.

'32 Ford Coupe

Packing big tires, a big engine and an even bigger attitude, this Pro-Street Coupe is one muscle-bound Deuce for sure. A Pro-Street chassis was custom built for this Coupe, ensuring that not only would the narrow frame accommodate the big rubber planned, but include the correct profile '32 front frame horns as well. A narrowed Ford 9-inch, with Richmond 4.11.1, gears is fitted at the back, with Aldan coil covers and a 4-link securing it in the frame. Meanwhile, at the front is a Speedway Motors 4-inch dropped axle installed with early Ford spindles. The wheel combination is a set of Cragar Street Stars, 15-inch diameter with 6s on the front and big 12-inch wide rims on the back.

The 3-window Deuce body is by Fiberglass Unlimited, and features a 3-inch chop – as if this Coupe wasn't tough enough already. The body, frame and grille shell are all finished in a Swiss Aqua acrylic lacquer with a few coats of clear added for good measure. Keeping this bad boy Deuce all Ford is a 460 ci big block blue oval engine, equipped with a BDS 6-71 blower and twin 750 Holley carbs. To handle the high-horsepower engine, a Ford C-6 transmission is used with a shift kit and heavy-duty internals. Is that "tuff enuff" for you?

MAKE:	Ford
BODY STYLE:	3-window Coupe
YEAR:	1932
ENGINE:	Ford 460 V8
BUILD STYLE:	Pro Street Rod
OWNER:	Don Martin

◀ A big-inch Ford V8 keeps this Deuce a blue oval product all the way, apart from some serious hot rod hardware, of course.

'27 Ford Model T Roadster

No matter how far up the ladder of fame you rise, everyone has to start somewhere. This even includes successful drag racers, and they don't come much more famous than Don Garlits. With a racing career spanning some fifty years and countless wins and championships, they just don't get much larger than "Big Daddy" himself. But this is where it all began – well, almost. Don had been racing ever since the bug hit him at sixteen, but at that time they were all hopped-up regular daily driven cars. But when he was unable to beat the local hot shot, he decided to build this little '27 T Roadster to turn around that very situation.

Using a bored and stroked Flathead that he had already owned and used in two previous cars, he installed it in the T frame, also moving the body rearwards in order to increase weight transfer and improve traction. Even with a set of Offy heads, an Isky cam and three Strombergs on a Sharp manifold, it wasn't quick enough. So Don went back to the workshop. Next time he came out to race, the T sported a front axle that had been moved forward by 13 inches; and he had welded the rear axle (from a '48 Ford) directly onto the T's frame. This had the desired effect and – suddenly – Don Garlits had his first "Top Eliminator" title. The rest, as they say, is history.

MAKE:	Ford
BODY STYLE:	T Roadster
YEAR:	1927
ENGINE:	Flathead V8
BUILD STYLE:	Drag Race Roadster
OWNER:	Don Garlits

◄ From this little yellow T Roadster, with its innovative safety roll-bar, grew the career of the undisputed King of Drag Racing, "Big Daddy" Don Garlits.

'34 Chevy Pickup

The great thing about hot rodding is that nowhere else in the automotive hobby spectrum can you find such a combination of individual imagination and skill at work. This is ably demonstrated in the construction of this one-of-a-kind hot rod truck that also comprises some way-out custom tricks. Originally a Chevy 1-ton truck, the rear frame was shortened by four feet, with new kick-ups formed to clear the Ford 9-inch on Chassis Engineering replacement rear leaves. At the front, for a softer ride, the stock leaf springs were disassembled, re-arched and then put back using only half the leaves. An MAS dropped axle was then mounted on top, with '54 Chevy spindles and GM brakes.

However, the coolest feature on the truck has to be the custom bed, made from the rear bodywork of a '60 Buick Sedan by narrowing it some 26 inches and using parts of the Buick's roof to construct the lower rear quarters. Unfortunately, we can't see the rolled rear pan made from a '53 Buick grille and turned upside down. That's the custom part. The hot rod bit is the 350 Chevy crate engine wearing three 2s on an Edelbrock manifold, backed up by a beefed-up 700R transmission, good enough to consistently chirp the tires in second gear! By the way, those cool wheels are Radir Tri-Ribs, shod with Coker bias-ply whiteband tires.

MAKE:	Chevrolet 1-ton truck
BODY STYLE:	Pickup
YEAR:	1934
ENGINE:	Chevy 350 V8
BUILD STYLE:	Hot Rod truck
OWNER:	Aaron Grote

▶ This Custom Truck substitutes the usual high-end custom parts for imagination and old-school know-how, to create a wild and nostalgic hot rod hauler.

'34 Ford Tudor Sedan

If any one model year and body style of the pre World War II Ford lends itself to the Resto-rod style, it could well be the '34 Ford Tudor Sedan – just like the Ford Dark Jade green example shown here. Not only has its steel body been restored with all its factory original features and chromed trim, but some period accessories have also been added. These include the fold-down rear luggage rack, the spare wheel carried on the rear panel, and the front fender-mounted accessory chrome grille guard. The classy '34 sits on its original chassis, which has been boxed for strength and now features Chevy Corvair front suspension and Mustang II steering. The stock Ford transverse spring has been retained and now suspends a Ford 9-inch from a '57 Station Wagon.

The Ford-in-a-Ford theme continues under the Rootleib 4-piece hood, with a 302 small block engine dressed up with much chrome and breathing through a Carter 650 carb on an Edelbrock aluminum intake. A GM HEI distributor lights the fire and a C4 transmission with a shift kit completes the running gear. As with many Resto-rods, a set of chromed fine wires are the wheels of choice, and complete the vintage look of this fine street rod.

MAKE:	Ford
BODY STYLE:	Tudor Sedan
YEAR:	1934
ENGINE:	Ford 302 V8
BUILD STYLE:	Street Rod
OWNER:	Frank Ficaro

▶ While it may not have the down and dirty look of some hot rods, a good Resto job has a charm all of its own.

'41 Chevy Coupe

There's no doubt about it, these fat forties coupes by Chevrolet are good looking cars, especially when they feature the combination of an immaculately restored body with all the factory brightwork, and a high-horsepower blown bowtie engine. A '69 Camaro front clip grafted to the stock Chevy chassis forms the basis for this tough street contender, which also features a Ford 9-inch rear end filled with 4.56:1 gears to handle the power from the awesome engine. Weld wheels add the racer's edge to the aggressive stance courtesy of the big and little tires. Those are fat Mickey Thompsons filling the rear fenders, by the way.

Replacing the old GM 6-pot is a hulking great 468 cube Chevy big-block which is loaded and then some, featuring as it does, '70 HP square-port heads, MSD distributor, Competition Cams bump-stick and lifters, TRW valves and Dove Engineering rocker arms. The crowning glory on all this race-proven hardware is a pair of Holley 650's on a Cragar intake feeding an Imbrogno Supercharger. Now you know why it needs a stout 9-inch! A KB Automatics uprated TH350 handles the shifting duties. A big Hilborn scoop on the hood merely hints at the awesome power waiting to be unleashed beneath.

MAKE:	Chevrolet
BODY STYLE:	2-door Coupe
YEAR:	1941
ENGINE:	Chevy 468 V8
BUILD STYLE:	Street Rod
OWNER:	"Big" Wilson

▶ The color of the paint and the restored chrome trim might say "mild," but the stance and the big-inch engine definitely shout "wild" on this '41 Chevy Coupe.

'46 Studebaker Pickup

Studebaker is a name that doesn't feature too much in the hot rod world. When it does, it's usually accompanied by the term "Pickup." Even if the Studie cars have never caught on, the trucks from South Bend, Indiana, have a quirky but interesting look for anyone wanting a change from Ford or Chevy. First job on any rodded truck is to reduce the altitude and increase the attitude, by bringing it way down to a weed-eating stance.

This pastel pick up does it with the help of a Chevy Nova sub-frame grafted on to the chassis, thus bestowing the truck with other automotive creature comforts such as power-assisted steering and power disc brakes.

A monochromatic theme was set for the truck which also features a custom made truck bed with Ford style flares to the top of the bed, and a custom rear pan housing the flush tail lights. The door handles have been shaved and the running boards smoothed out prior to painting. This truck was never built to fry the tires, so we find a mild 350 Chevy under the hood equipped with a four barrel with a Turbo-Hydramatic transmission for some easy weekend rod run cruising. Air conditioning, cruise control and a late model steering column all add further driving pleasure to the already comfortable bucket seat interior.

MAKE:	Studebaker
BODY STYLE:	Pickup
YEAR:	1946
ENGINE:	Chevy 350 V8
BUILD STYLE:	Street Rod
OWNER;	David and Joy Clark

◀ A monochromatic pastel theme in Turquoise Aqua highlights the curves of the Studebaker's lines, with contrast provided by the highly polished billet wheels.

'46 Ford Convertible

Looking for all the world like a complete stocker, this fine example of a post World War II Ford can justifiably claim to be a true wolf in sheep's clothing. With a complete and perfect body restoration, right down to the last piece of exterior trim, only the slightly wider steel wheels color matched to the blue lacquer paint with stock hubcaps hint at the late model running gear. In fact, the aim was to retain as much of the original '46 Super Deluxe as possible, while improving the power and drivability of the classy antique auto. To this, power steering has been added to the original front suspension along with gas shocks, and a 9-inch Ford has been hung on the 2-leaf rear springs, again with gas shocks for an improved ride.

Replacing the venerable Flathead supplied in the car as standard, a decidedly punchy alternative was sought in the form of a FoMoCo 351 Windsor, complete with ported and polished heads, a High-Energy camshaft and hydraulic lifters. The lower end of the engine remains stock, but extra sauce is added up top with a Holley carb on an Edelbrock manifold.

A C4 transmission provides drive through a now-open drive shaft to the upgraded rear end. The car is definitely a ride encompassing the best of both worlds.

MAKE:	Ford
BODY STYLE:	Super Deluxe Conv.
YEAR:	1946
ENGINE:	Ford 351 V8 Windsor
BUILD STYLE:	Resto Rod
OWNER:	William Jacobsen

◄ This otherwise "Antique" '46 Ford is actually a much modified street rod, with all the modern comforts; including power steering, cruise, A/C and a power folding top.

'47 Ford Phantom Pickup

Since Ford never did make a '47 Ford Roadster Pickup, nor even a '38 model, the only way to ever own one is to custom build one. If you did, it might end up as trick as this phantom Ford that never was. Starting with a boxed '35 Ford Roadster frame, a combination of Mustang II front suspension and a Ford 8-inch rear axle was installed in the frame – the latter being fitted with the help of some aftermarket components from the Chassis Engineering catalog. With the addition of a set of Cragar Drag Star wheels, a basis was formed for the hybrid hauler to come to life.

The '47 Ford cab section was both channeled 6 inches and sectioned 2 inches before having the top lopped off to form a chopped convertible roadster pickup. In fact, a new top was constructed from steel tubing and mesh, before being trimmed in blue Hartz cloth. Next, a '38 Ford passenger car front sheet metal assembly was installed, the hood having to be pie-cut to match up to the '47 cowl section. Much more went into this pickup than we have room to detail, but the regularly driven truck is powered by a fuel-injected Ford 5.0-liter Mustang engine, with goodies from Street and Performance.

MAKE:	Ford
BODY STYLE:	Roadster Pickup
YEAR:	1947
ENGINE:	Ford 5.0 L V8
BUILD STYLE:	Street Rod
OWNER:	Jim Richards

▾ It doesn't take long to see that this truck isn't at all that it seems – though it takes a little longer to figure out what really went into creating this Phantom Ford.

'39 Ford Convertible

It doesn't take a genius to work out why convertible cars exposed to the weather don't last long in junkyards. As a consequence, ragtop vehicles, which generally have the lowest production run of any model year, also suffer the highest attrition rate of decay. This makes them the rarest; and if you do find one, they are the toughest cars to bring back to life. This '39 Convertible is one of those that made it back. Having said that, this one worked out. A complete new frame had to be sourced, boxed and strengthened, before the Mustang II front suspension, power steering and Chevy Nova rear end could be installed. Although a new floor pan also went into the mix, many hours still had to be spent on bodywork before the flame red paint could be applied.

In the interests of economy over any performance agenda, a 229 ci Chevy V6 from an '81 Monte Carlo was used for motive power. This was dressed with Moroso valve covers and other goodies, featuring a Rochester Quadrajet carb on a Holley Street Dominator intake. Instead of only 2-pedals, this little red roadster has three, the third helping the '74 Borg Warner Vega manual transmission shift smoothly. Three years from the project's inception, the De Luxe Convertible looks nothing like junkyard dog it once was.

MAKE:	Ford
BODY STYLE:	De Luxe Convertible
YEAR:	1939
ENGINE:	Chevy 229 V6
BUILD STYLE:	Street Rod
OWNER:	Karol Gaines

◄ This '39 Convertible was completed back in the late 1980s as a car to be regularly driven on a daily basis, which probably explains it's slightly high stance.

'30 Ford Woodie

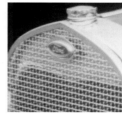

For those who like their Model As still in the packing crate, may we present this fine Woodie. All auto manufacturers have a history of using wood-bodied vehicles, going way back to the horse and carriage days. Sometimes it was used as internal structure, but hidden from view. For commercial use, it was often exposed to form both the structure and exterior finish of the vehicle. Even with bodies made from a hard wood like ash, Woodies were not equipped to stand the ravages of the years without being intentionally preserved under cover. Popular with the surfers on the west coast in the 1960s (just listen to the classic "Surf City" by Jan and Dean), few original examples survive.

Many seen at contemporary hot rod shows now sport re-manufactured or owner-built bodies and this is not a problem for an accomplished carpenter. This one uses a clean and neat 2-door station wagon body built on a '30 Model A floor pan, fenders and cowl section. A Flathead V8 is used, with aftermarket heads for a truly vintage feel. It almost looks like an original Ford model – except, of course, Henry never offered the A with the V8. It was left to hot rodders to do that! Cream painted steels with hubcaps and white walls complete the period look.

MAKE:	Ford Model A
BODY STYLE:	2-door Woodie
YEAR:	1930
ENGINE:	Flathead V8
BUILD STYLE:	Street Rod

◄ Only the wide steel wheels and radial white walls give this away as a hot rod Woodie, the grille guard is a period accessory.

'32 Ford 5-window Coupe

Make just a few changes, mainly the color, to this early 1960's style Deuce and you could easily pass it off as a clone of Milner's Coupe in the movie "American Graffiti" – and it wouldn't be a surprise to find that's how it was first built before being re-painted. The top is chopped just about the right amount, but – more significantly – so is the filled grille shell up front. The bobbed fenders are there, and so is the open engine compartment and the four-carbs on a small block Chevy, with sprint style headers. Many of these features are the period-correct items for a Deuce Coupe street racer circa 1962 from Northern California, where that movie was set.

While the style emulates the movie car, in actual fact, the fit and finish of this clean and green machine is far superior to its famous yellow cousin. That car only featured enough flash for the movie cameras and remains authentically the same to this day. Notable modern additions to this 5-window are the front spreader bar between the front frame rails. This is an aftermarket part and houses the front turn signals and the wide front radial tires. This one is also wearing chrome hubcaps on the reverse chrome wheels, something the movie car didn't have.

MAKE:	Ford
BODY STYLE:	5-window Coupe
YEAR:	1932
ENGINE:	Chevy 350 V8
BUILD STYLE:	1960's Street Rod

◀ A cool white interior upholstery job compliments the Deep Pearl Green finish on this obviously movie-inspired Deuce 5-window.

'28 Chevy Roadster

Starting out with a junkyard-found Chevy roadster body, Hugh Tucker rose through the ranks from being a 19-year-old kid racing his everyday car to becoming a National Champion and winning the AA/SR street roadster class five years straight. Since Hugh already had a '34 chassis, he mounted the Chevy body on top, installed a cheap and plentiful Oldsmobile V8 with a few goodies in it, and went racing. Although it was initially classed with the Altereds rather than the Street Roadsters, he won — and won regularly. Throughout the1960s, the car evolved through several running gear combinations, but always managing to stay on top.

The steel Chevy body was retained, albeit with the '32 Grille shell, until 1964. Then, a rule change allowed lightweight fiberglass bodies to be substituted. Tucker took advantage of the fact that no one knew the correct dimensions of a '28 Chevy and so gained a significant advantage by effectively shortening the wheelbase of the roadster. The silver roadster's racing spec culminated in a 430 ci blown Hemi and a Chrysler Torqueflite trans that helped the car run its best ever time of 9.25 in 1966.

MAKE:	Chevrolet
BODY STYLE:	Roadster
YEAR:	1928
ENGINE:	Chrysler 430 ci Hemi V8
BUILD STYLE:	AA/SR Roadster
BUILDER:	Hugh Tucker

▸ Hugh Tucker's winning Chevy Roadster has been restored and is now part of the NHRA Motorsport Museum, although it regularly is taken out to nostalgia race meets.

'40 Chevy Coupe

Hot rodding can frequently be a family thing too, you know. Sometimes, it's just in the genes and is passed on from father to son. That's certainly the case here with this '40 Chevy Coupe Gasser. Purchased back in 1958 for the awesome sum of $7.50 as a somewhat bent stocker, it first saw the strip in 1961, running a 261 ci straight six Chevy engine. This engine stood the old 40 in good stead for some 10 years, by which time it was running 13.90 in the quarter-mile. Although a V8 was finally installed in the early 1970s, it didn't see much action and was put into storage for the next 27 years.

The G.B. Automotive logo on the door refers to its owner, Gary Blasey. However, since 2001, when it was brought back to life, Gary's son Bryan now takes the wheel at nostalgia drag racing meets all over the Mid-West. These days, it runs Chevy small block power in the form of a built 360 ci, which is easily good for 11-second runs. As well as the classic gasser stance, this cool Coupe runs neat blue Plexiglas windows and Perspex hood side panels. A fiberglass flip front is now fitted to the car, which means that the streamlined '40 headlamp pods normally seen on these models are no longer in place.

MAKE:	Chevrolet
BODY STYLE:	2-door Coupe
YEAR:	1940
ENGINE:	Chevy 360 V8
BUILD STYLE:	Gasser
OWNER:	Gary Blasey

◀ "Like father, like son!" The driving duties of this family heirloom Chevy have been passed on from Gary Blasey to son Bryan.

'37 Willys Coupe

The Olympic rings on the door of this Willys Gasser are usually associated first with the successful cars run by Californian racer, K. S. Pittman. In fact, they appeared on all the cars but one, campaigned by the incredibly successful S&S Racing Team, out of Falls Church, Virginia. From 1961 until 1970, the team was one of the winningest non-pro teams of all time. During the years they raced, the members between them set no less than 21 National Records in the various gas classes. Several Willys Coupes were built over the years by the guys and this one is a restoration of Dave Hales C/Gas '37 Coupe that was first built in 1962.

The steel car was found in rough shape on a farm in southern Maryland, and quickly had its rusty front sheet metal replaced with a Hill & Zartman (other S&S members) fiberglass front end. It first hit the strip in June 1963, competing in D/Gas, with an over-bored '56 Chevy engine displacing 268 ci, a T10 4-speed and an Olds back axle. The car was constantly improved over the years, until in 1965 it moved up to compete in C/Gas, which is the guise that you see it in here and where it briefly held the class record. The engine size was increased to 301 ci in 1966. By 1967, with a new set of Crane heads and a new cam, it went back and set a new National Record in D/Gas.

MAKE:	Willys
BODY STYLE:	2-door Coupe
YEAR:	1937
ENGINE:	Chevy 301 ci V8
BUILD STYLE:	Gasser
OWNER:	Dave Hales

◄ Resplendent in Chevy Matador red, which became the team colors for the S&S team, this re-creation of the old '37 Coupe of Dave Hales is right on the money.

'15 Ford Roadster

The track-nosed T Roadster is firmly up there as one of the classic styles of early hot rodding. There is early Sprint Car-derived styling, the fully enclosed noses (usually stuffed with as much high horse-power 4-banger power as was available, sometimes even Flathead V8s), but usually very traditional in build style. Well, what if someone built one with more modern racecar styling, building on the circuit heritage that the car already has? The result would probably look something like this model. Using a fiberglass 1915 T body, with its distinctive high back to the body, this unique one-off features an owner-built tube chassis, plus plenty of custom aluminum parts.

This low-slung turtledeck Roadster, with its huge aluminum racecar-style rear wing, gets its "go" from a (mostly) stock 2.8 liter Ford V6 engine. However, there's a 350 Holley on top to get the fuel in – and those cool owner-built Lakes pipes get the burnt gases out. Running gear consists of a C4 transmission and a 4-bar suspended '57 Chevy back axle that is hung on Jaguar coil overs. The 4-bar mounted front suspension is also all owner-built, featuring hidden inboard front shocks inside the track nose – plus '40 Ford spindles and Corvair steering. Not obvious in the photo are the unusual, rectangular headlights by KD. Adding to the racecar influence is the choice of 15-inch Centerline wheels, 3-inch on the front and 12-inch on the back.

MAKE:	Ford
BODY STYLE:	Roadster
YEAR:	1915
ENGINE:	Ford 2.8 V6
BUILD STYLE:	Track T
OWNER:	Bill Deese

▸ This T roadster with its noticeably high backed body and racecar styling is an interesting variation on the traditional track-nose styling.

'23 T Roadster

Almost epitomizing the fad T cult of the late 1960s and early 1970s that helped kick start the dormant street rod hobby, this T-bucket has attitude and plenty of it. Considered one of the top contemporary T-buckets in the country, this hot rod nicknamed the "Moonkist T" has picked up many awards at National events. Deep black gloss paint on the body and frame is detailed with fine orange pinstriping, picking out the panels and chassis details. This is complemented by a matching orange upholstery job inside the bucket. Many Ts of this style feature a massively shortened pickup bed on the back of the tub; but on this one, the top is also padded with orange upholstery fabric.

The chopped-height windshield with custom flip-back fabric top adds an air of menace to the look of the T, but it's the killer engine, plus the huge rear slicks, that really sets this hot rod apart. A big block Chevy with trick heads, crowned by a polished blower and triple-threat four-barrels, dominate the appearance, with the long zoomie headers underlining the fact in nicely "blued" chrome. A chrome dropped tube axle on stainless hairpins is mounted suicide style with a transverse chrome leaf — but then again, every T should have one.

MAKE:	Ford
BODY STYLE:	T Roadster
YEAR:	1923
ENGINE:	Chevy Big Block
BUILD STYLE:	Show Rod
OWNERS:	Rich and Sharon Hoefling

▸ Being mounted without front brakes on the tube axle, spindle-mounted and polished 10-spokes add to the "Street Altered" look of this T.

'39 Ford Convertible

While the hot rodders were dicing it out on the salt (or on the street, for that matter), in their never-ending quest for more speed, over in the custom camp, the emphasis was on re-styling and customizing. Their philosophy was to produce the coolest-looking rides around and the style was everything. Demonstrating this early 1950's approach to this branch of the rodding world is this subtle, but very cool, '39 Ford. Yes, it's a Ford – although it's likely that the '40 Buick grille fooled you. This car was originally built in 1951 and was featured in a 1954 issue of *Hot Rod Magazine*. It was re-discovered in 1982 and a full restoration and update were carried out in order to bring it up to the condition shown here.

To get the right "custom" stance, the frame was boxed and the rear was C'd way back when. Then, during the latter update, the rear end was swapped for a Ford 8-inch and the front suspension updated to a Mustang II set-up, with rack and pinion steering for improved driveability. Although we said speed wasn't a priority for the customizers, the builder of this car thought otherwise. He opted for a 331 ci Cadillac engine with dual quad Carters and a Vertex Magneto that sure makes it pickup its fender skirts and run. The sneaky, custom, low profile is due to the chopped 4-inch top and removable Carson top.

MAKE:	Ford
BODY STYLE:	2-door Convertible
YEAR:	1939
ENGINE:	331 ci Cadillac V8
BUILD STYLE:	1950's Custom
OWNER:	Donn Lowe

▶ A classic "custom" in every sense of the word, this '39 Ford combines many of the customizers' tricks of the early 1950's along with modern Street Rod technology.

'32 Club Sport Coupe

Of course, Ford never did build a '32 Club Sport Coupe in 1932. But if they had, it probably would have looked like this phantom rendition right here. Built from a '32 3-window Coupe by Ken "Posie" Fenical, who has a history of debuting cool and innovative rods on the unsuspecting rodding public, usually causing quite a stir in the process. The '32 featured an interesting treatment of the top and rear roofline. In fact, what appears to be a soft top isn't, with the coupe now being converted to a 4-seater. The screen area has been squared off and the "B" pillars canted forward to complete the illusion of a Sport Coupe.

The smooth styling of the phantom Deuce clearly defines it as a 1980's-built car, with its smooth hood sides and shaved handles. The fender-mounted lights and lack of headlamp bar also point to this fact, as does the graphics on monochrome paint. The car retained the "wow" factor inside too, with a classy and luxurious burr walnut effect, wood-grained dash panel not seen in a car quite like this one before. In the "nuts and bolts" department, the rod as constructed on a set of Just-a-Hobby rails and used a Ford 351 ci V8 for motivation that is linked to a C4 auto. Classic slot mags are by Real Wheels of California.

MAKE:	Ford
BODY STYLE:	Phantom Club Sport Coupe
YEAR:	1932
ENGINE:	Ford 351 V8
BUILD STYLE:	Street Rod
BUILDER:	Ken "Posie" Fenical

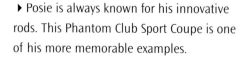

▶ Posie is always known for his innovative rods. This Phantom Club Sport Coupe is one of his more memorable examples.

'41 Ford Pickup

H ere's a completely different approach to "traditional," especially on a truck. The owner of the pre-World War II pickup has taken the 1950s "custom" look and applied it to this '41 Ford.

As is the way with the custom trend, it's the body modifications that set the mood on this particular rod. First, it's obviously been lowered several inches from the original truck ride height; and skirts have been added to the rear fenders to emphasize this. The Bubblegum Pink paint is pure 1950's kitsch and so is the mint green used on the wheels, the detail work on the door and on the fender irons. The biggest single job has been to chop the cab roof to lower the profile. This also has the added effect of making the truck look longer.

There are more subtle body mods in the shape of the custom grille, which has been lengthened to extend further down the front panel than stock. Shaved door handles, ribbed fenders and custom mirrors are all further additions to the custom hauler. A custom wouldn't be complete without a set of whitewalls, beauty rims and passenger car hub caps completing the picture of a truck fully dandied up for the high school hop.

MAKE:	Ford
BODY STYLE:	Pickup
YEAR:	1941
ENGINE:	Chevy 305 ci V8
BUILD STYLE:	Trad 1950's
BUILDER:	Gilles Bouchard

◀ The pickup bed features a custom cover with a rack for the "his and hers" 1950's pushbikes, color co-ordinated, naturally!

'37 Ford Club Cabriolet

The '37 Ford was the first pre-World War II Ford to feature the headlamps built integrally into the front fenders; that is, instead of on separate units bolted on. This added a new, smooth look to this model year. Although not a favorite of early hot rodders, it suddenly became the rod to have in the 1980s. The design lent itself perfectly to the de-chromed, color-coded look that was so big in that decade. Typical of the breed is this "cool as ice" cream and understated '37 Club Cabriolet. The chopped top and low stance are very reminiscent of the early customs. In fact, this particular car was originally a Club Coupe, and was skillfully converted to its new convertible identity.

Upgrades to the stock boxed frame include the ever-popular Mustang II independent front end, complete with power steering; and a Ford 8-inch rear axle hung on a TCI parallel leaf kit. This combination is almost a blueprint for many a similar late-1930's car, with parts available from an ever-growing number of rod part manufacturers. Built for reliability over performance, the power comes from a stock Chevy 305 and Turbo 350 transmission. The Frost Beige exterior is set off with a set of chromed Cragar Drag Stars with Goodyear rubber.

MAKE:	Ford
BODY STYLE:	Club Cabriolet
YEAR:	1937
ENGINE:	Chevy 305 V8
BUILD STYLE:	Street Rod
OWNER:	Bill Quimby

▸ Clean and understated, the '37 Ford had a big resurgence of popularity as Street Rod material during the 1980's – and this one is typical of the breed.

'34 Ford Cabriolet

Ford Roadsters of all years have always been plentiful on the rod scene, being probably the most popular body style from which to build. Yet, there is another variation of Ford's soft-top car that is less common. We are talking about the Cabriolet models of the early 1930s. These differ from true roadsters by way of having a fixed windshield frame that is integral to the body, unlike a roadster frame that can be unbolted. That was all much easier if you were running your early car at the lakes. Having a painted windshield frame the same color as the rest of the sheet metal adds a very different look, as we see here on this Hot Pink '34.

The all-steel Cabrio features the 1980's uncluttered and color-matched look on the exterior, with sophisticated Street Rod technology in the form of a Kugel suspension set-up. This was developed especially for early 1930's models and incorporating JFZ brakes and Carrera coil over shocks. There's plenty of power on tap too, with an '89 Corvette 350, complete with TPI (Tuned Port Injection) and a set of Kerker headers leading to a Borla 2-inch stainless exhaust system. Wheels of choice on this Peach smoothie are Budniks all round.

MAKE:	Ford
BODY STYLE:	Cabriolet
YEAR:	1934
ENGINE:	Chevy 350 V8
BUILD STYLE:	Street Rod
OWNER:	Karl and Jeanie Roberts

◄ The effect of a color-matched screen
frame is obvious on this peachy '34.
Don't call it a roadster; it's a Cabriolet.

'40 Chevy Sedan

The Chevy sedans of the 1940s are big cars and right for big, comfortable highway cruisers – as long as they have a engine installed that's suitable for the job. The '40 Master 85, 2-door sedan – to give it its correct title – has received a hefty 4-inch chop. While reducing its profile, this makes the body seem lower and wider at the same time, essential qualities for the blue bowtie bomber. Louvers are a big feature on this sedan too, with 92 stamps in the hood and a whole bunch in the trunk lid too. The Midnight Blue lacquer is set off with some subtle graphic paintwork just for good measure. The exterior trim is tasteful on this model, so it's good to see most of it is still in place.

The license plate on this '40 gives a clue as to the power plant under the hood of this Fat '40 – "Rat On" of course referring to a big 454 Chevy engine. The already big-cube engine has been further beefed up with a pair of Carter AFBs on an Edelbrock Performer intake, providing even more horses to eat up those highway miles. The transmission and running gear consist of a B&M modified transmission and a Ford 8-inch rear, hung on the stock '40 rear springs. The front end is Mustang II hardware throughout.

MAKE:	Chevrolet
BODY STYLE:	2-door Master Sedan
YEAR:	1940
ENGINE:	Chevy 454 V8
BUILD STYLE:	Street Rod
OWNER:	Ed Belkengren

▶ With a healthy chop, and plenty of louvers, there is no mistaking the hot rod pedigree of this big-inch Chevrolet Sedan.

'31 Town Car Delivery

When you look back in detail at the history of early Ford cars, it's amazing just how many variations of body style were available at the time. Some remain very familiar and have always made great hot rods; others are not so popular. This is also true of the commercial ranges and so what we have here is probably one of the rarest. Only 190 were ever made of this Town Car Delivery, which is something of an enigma anyway. The intention was that a Town Car was an early limo, with the idea that the privileged owners would ride in the back under cover, while the open driver's seat was occupied by a chauffeur (who, presumably, didn't mind getting wet in the rain!) But where's the logic in a Town Car Delivery?

Its puzzling history aside, it certainly makes for an interesting Street Rod, with its all-Jaguar suspension and brakes – fully chromed of course – and it's deep Candy Apple Red paint. Should this rare commercial Model A ever need to do more deliveries, the 427 Chevy engine up front will guarantee it gets there on time, especially with a GMC 6-71 blower and a Muncie 4-speed transmission installed. Inside the little truck, the load area is finished in solid walnut wood and plenty of sumptuous red leather.

MAKE:	Ford
BODY STYLE:	Town Car Delivery
YEAR:	1931
ENGINE:	Chevy 427 V8
BUILD STYLE:	Street Rod
OWNER:	Mike Winfrey

▸ Originally constructed from a 4-door sedan, the Town Car Delivery is one of the rarest early Ford truck body styles. This must be the only rodded example anywhere.

'29 Tudor Sedan

The traditional flame paint job can be found on just about every type of hot rod – and in every color combination too. So, it can be difficult to come up with a new variation when it comes to breaking out the spray gun and masking tape. This Model A Tudor achieves it by using the traditional black with red/yellow hot licks, but using them to give the car a striking fifty-fifty paint scheme that really works. However, before the paint was applied, the sedan received a 4-inch chop, a filled roof and a steel sliding sunroof.

The car is just as hot under the skin too, with a Chassis Engineering frame hung with a Super Bell axle on a 4-bar at the front and a full Corvette independent rear axle at the back. A 350 Chevy V8 lives under the steel hood, complete with a Competition Cams bumpstick; and a Holley/Edelbrock intake combo is used. The transmission is a TH 400 unit. The fiery rod was almost entirely built by the owner, with only the pleated upholstery being farmed out to a specialist auto upholsterer. Chrome Tru-Spoke wire wheels add the final touch.

MAKE:	Ford
BODY STYLE:	Tudor Sedan
YEAR:	1929
ENGINE:	Chevy 350 V8
BUILD STYLE:	Street Rod
OWNER:	Mike Essy

▶ This '29 Sedan comes up with an interesting twist by simply re-positioning the point where the flames separate the contrasting colors on the rod.

'32 Ford Roadster

If you took the average sports car fan's favorite car of the Ferrari, and combined it with the hot rodder's favorite, the '32, you would end up with a pretty unique roadster – right? Well not only did California rod builder Roy Brizio build this one for customer Jim Ells in 1986, but it was actually the second Italian-American Deuce to win the prestigious Oakland Roadster Show. The first was named "The Deucari" and was built by Dick "Magoo" Megugorac for Brian Burnett and it won in 1979; but this one was longer, leaner and lower and after being narrowly beaten in 1986, came back for the AMBR trophy in 1987.

Both cars featured a stretched frame to accommodate the long, "Italian stallion" V12, Brian's being fed by 3-carbs whereas the Brizio car featured six sidedraft twin-choke Weber carbs on its fully-detailed engine, the quad-overhead cam engine normally being found under the hood of Ferrari's 365 GTB. In line with its thoroughbred image, the Deuce was kept clean and minimal in all areas of construction, and the front chassis was shorn of its traditional '32 front frame horns. State of the art for the time, billet alloys were used and those exhaust headers are a work of art.

MAKE:	Ford
BODY STYLE:	Highboy Roadster
YEAR:	1932
ENGINE:	Ferrari V12
BUILD STYLE:	Show Rod
OWNER:	Cliff Hansen

▶ This Ferrari-powered rod was only ever going to be red, just like its predecessor. Both of them won the AMBR award.

'29 Ford Pickup

Apart from his cars constructed for movie and TV work, George Barris' most recognizable show car was probably the "Ala Kart" '29 Pickup. Many rodders probably started out building the popular AMT Model kit, but for one such guy, this just wasn't enough. So, Howdy Ledbetter built this full-size clone of the original. Virtually all the metal work on both cars was hand-built, the original featuring a back cab section from a '27 T roadster. Here, a '29 Touring rear section is used to similar effect. The fenders were all bobbed and pointed and a special feature was that the candy and pearl scallops were mirrored exactly on both the top and the underside of them, the truck's top is a one-piece removable item.

The "Kart," which is actually a roadster pickup, was loaded with wild and innovative features – such as coil springs all round and incorporating adjustable air bags, plus an electrically-operated emergency brake. All of this, together with the incredible metal work and pearl paint finish, was good enough to take the truck to two consecutive AMBR awards in 1958 and 1959. The truck also features a custom grille with quad headlamps, the lights' assemblies coming from a '57 Lincoln. The original truck is still in existence and awaiting a full restoration.

MAKE:	Ford
BODY STYLE:	Roadster Pickup
YEAR:	1929
ENGINE:	Chevy 350 V8
BUILD STYLE:	Show Car Clone
OWNER:	Howdy Ledbetter

◀ The original "Ala Kart" featured a built and injected Dodge Red Ram with a Lincoln Zephyr transmission, though this one replaced that with a small block Chevy engine.

'37 Ford Pickup

I t takes a lot of restraint when building a project not to get carried away with wild body modifications and over-the-top fancy paint in order to get your ride to stand out in the crowd at rod runs, shows and events. A strong sense of self-discipline is required when, all around, advertising campaigns are bombarding you with messages of how cool your car (or truck) would look with their latest products. This little '37 manages to look great without any of that superfluous stuff. Everything about it is understated, but superbly executed. In short, its quality shines through regardless.

Originally found abandoned in the Mojave Desert, the truck went through a couple of owners before being built to this standard. One change had been to cut off the front frame rails at the firewall. Fortunately, they were able to be restored and modified to take the Mustang II front end the truck now wears. At the back, the 9-inch rear axle is attached by a TCI leaf kit and Pete'n'Jake shocks. A '71 Chevelle gave up its 307 ci small block to the '37, and this has been neatly detailed in the same cream color as the steel rims – which, in case you were wondering, are early 70's Dodge police car items, modified for extra offset.

MAKE:	Ford
BODY STYLE:	Closed-cab Pickup
YEAR:	1937
ENGINE:	Chevy 307 ci V8
BUILD STYLE:	Street Rod
OWNER:	Paul Burnham

◄ From a desert wreck to a truck that rocks, this '37 looks almost factory fresh.

'33 Ford Roadster

At some point, probably in the late 1990s, it seems that the era of the concept rod was born. Rather than take an old body and then spend many hours cutting, grinding and welding it into the shape you wanted, hot rods were initially sketched out on paper. They were then refined, just like in a new car styling studio. Finally they were hand-crafted in metal by a few top names in the industry. Initially sketched as a Coupe by talented California designer Chip Foose while still at college, the "Shockwave" became a reality, when Chip built the car using some of the best talent available for customer Fred Warren. The final, stunning execution of the project took Fred to the AMBR winners rostrum for the second time at the 50th Anniversary of the famous roadster show.

The body of "Shockwave" was completely hand-fabricated by Marcel's Auto Metal and mounted on a custom chassis by Larry Sergejeff, starting with a pair of SAC frame rails. The engine underneath that custom "alligator" hood is a fully rebuilt Corvette LT4 V8 color coded to the exterior, with custom-built covers for the fuel injection and matching valve covers. No wires or hoses seem to be visible and the engine seems to sit alone in the compartment. All suspension components for the car were crafted especially in billet aluminum.

MAKE:	Ford
BODY STYLE:	Concept Roadster
YEAR:	1933
ENGINE:	Chevy LT4 V8
BUILD STYLE:	Show Rod
OWNER:	Fred Warren

◀ The 17- and 20-inch polished rims were designed by Chip Foose and manufactured for "Shockwave" by Budnik Wheels.

'29 Ford Roadster

Although probably not the first roadster built in the early fifties to sport an aerodynamic thirties race-car inspired nose, the "Dick Flint Roadster" is probably the most instantly recognisable of the breed. The Model A-V8 was built in 1951 and within a year made the cover of both *Hop-Up* and *Hot Rod Magazine*, the latter being the more memorable as it featured the car and its occupants pausing as an attractive young lady crosses the road. Its first year after completion also saw it win awards at many indoor shows on the West coast too. But the red track roadster wasn't just a show queen, Dick took it to the lakes at El Mirage where it topped out at 143.54 mph!

Most of the chassis and body was built by Dick himself using parts from three different Model A roadsters, but his good friend Dean Batchelor was responsible for fabricating, in aluminum, the distinctive front end treatment and the full belly pan underneath. While this undoubtedly helped the car achieve its lakes timing slip, it couldn't have done it without the engine up front, a 284 ci Merc Flathead, with Edelbrock heads and a Winfield cam. The car was restored a few years ago and was re-introduced to the public at the 50th Grand National Roadster show at Oakland. Since then, the car was car showed and won at the Pebble Beach Concours d'Elegance – in the hot rod class, of course.

MAKE:	Ford
BODY STYLE:	Roadster
YEAR:	1929
ENGINE:	284 ci Flathead V8
BUILD STYLE:	Track Roadster
OWNER:	Don Orosco

▶ Displayed in front of its memorable *Hot Rod Magazine* cover, the Dick Flint Roadster was restored in time for the Oakland Roadster show in 2000.

'32 Ford Roadster

When you've built a whole bunch of hot rods over a period of years, there often still remains a personal "holy grail" car; one that you've always wanted but never quite been able to get to. For many rodders, this car is a steel '32 roadster. However, with the price of the early real steel cars increasing each year and with no sign of stopping, this can be a problem. Fortunately, there is a solution. New steel '32 Ford roadsters have been reproduced for a few years now by the Ohio-based Brookville Company; and this Highboy is one of those "born again" roadsters. The car was assembled very much with an eye on traditional hot rod style and parts, but with a contemporary interpretation of the classic flame job. The final result is the House of Kolors Purple Candy over silver tribal graphics.

From the very outset, there were many cool parts on the "wish list" that just had to be included on this roadster. These included the 4-inch dropped axle with Buick drums, the Duval windshield, and the Halibrand quick-change rear axle – all traditional and desirable stuff for sure. Also high on the list of priorities was the Goodwrench small block Chevy engine and, with a semi-traditional theme still running through the car, a Hot Rod Carburetion tri-carb setup was installed on the detailed engine. That was also painted Candy Purple to match the flames and the whole package finished off with highly polished Halibrand Kidney bean wheels as another nod to traditional hot rodding.

MAKE:	Ford
BODY STYLE:	Highboy Roadster
YEAR:	1932
ENGINE:	Chevy 350 V8
BUILD STYLE:	Street Rod
OWNER:	Mike Key

▼ A combination of a killer stance, a Duval raked windshield and classic Deuce Highboy lines make this a dream rod that was worth waiting for.

'25 T Ford Roadster

Soon after seeing Norm Grabowski's T (featured on pages 724-725), TV and movie actor "TV" Tommy Ivo decided to build his own version of a Fad T-bucket roadster. Like Norm, he used a cut-down touring car body, a '25 Phaeton found in the desert, and a similar radically-shortened Model A Pickup bed. Tommy was heavily into racing, however, and once the car was finished, he would compete the roadster regularly at the drags. The T was virtually unbeatable in its class, and even took the California Street Roadster Championship by regularly posting 11-second quarters. When Tommy finally sold it, the car competed on the show circuit before being stored by owner Bill Rowland. Years later, it was restored and is now on display at the NHRA Motorsports Museum in California.

Tommy's T has a much lower stance than Grabowski's by virtue of its z'ed frame; an innovative feature was the 4-link front suspension that Tommy copied from the sprint car world. As with all racers, Tommy experimented with many different induction systems on the big Buick Nailhead engine, the restored hot rod displaying the cool Hilborn injected setup. Whitewall tires always featured on the car and these matched the white interior trim and of course the white pinstriping deftly applied by Von Dutch himself. "TV Tommy" went on from this T to build more many race cars and eventually turn professional on the 1960's Top Fuel circuit.

MAKE:	Ford
BODY STYLE:	T Roadster
YEAR:	1925
ENGINE:	Buick 401 Nailhead V8
BUILD STYLE:	Traditional
BUILDER:	Tommy Ivo

▸ Both this car and the Kookie T have been credited with influencing the building of many similar T-bucket roadsters over the years.

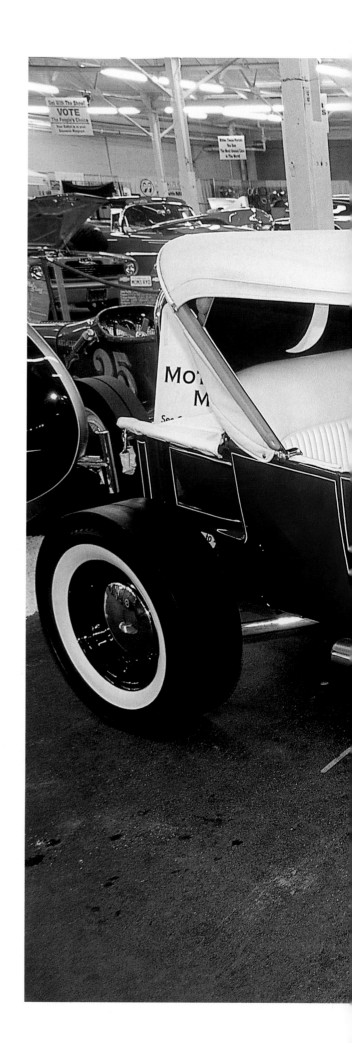

DON'T MISS IT!
See Trophies Awarded
To Winning Cars
MONDAY NIGHT
LAST NIGHT OF SHOW

SEE
SOUVENIR
PROGRAMS
For Details On
CUSTOM CARS ON
EXHIBIT

VOTE

www.HOTWHEELS.com

Chevrolet Camaro
OFFICIAL PACE CAR
2nd ANNUAL INDIANAPOLIS 500 MILE RACE
MAY 30, 1966

1924 Ford Model T
(CIRCA 1948)
STREET ROADSTER

1923 FORD MODEL T
(CIRCA 1957)
STREET ROADSTER

The Cover Car for the August 1957
Issues of Hot Rod and Car Craft
Magazines.

The car also appeared in several
Movies and TV shows.

Builder/Driver:
"TV Tommy" Ivo

Engine:
364 Cu.In. Fuel Injected Buick

Best Performance:
12.00 E.T. - 117 MPH

Restored By:
Ron Jones

Owned By:
Jack Rosen
Riverside, CA

'32 Ford Victoria

During the 1980s, the smooth, seamless finish – not to mention the bright red color – became almost synonymous with Boyd Coddington's "Hot Rods by Boyd" rod shop. Many body styles and makes have been given the Boyd treatment over the years, and this '32 Vicky built for one of his customers bears all the hallmarks and attention to detail of a Boyd-built car. With all the chassis and bodywork being handled in-house, the standard of workmanship and ultimate finish could be guaranteed for his customers. This also led to an associate company designing and manufacturing billet alloy wheels as well.

Boyd's minimalist approach was all about perfecting and enhancing the lines that already existed within the design. It also involved removing features that drew the eye away from these lines. To this end, this Vicky has had a very subtle 1-inch chop plus also a 2-inch section taken out of the grille shell with a matching tapered hood and smooth side panels. The rest of the car is totally free of any other distracting features, such as door handles etc. with the only bolt-on part remaining being the headlamp bar and lights themselves. Although not to everyone's taste, the look is nevertheless dramatic and has won many fans over the years.

MAKE:	Ford
BODY STYLE:	2-door Victoria Sedan
YEAR:	1932
ENGINE:	Chevy 350 V8
BUILD STYLE:	Street Rod
OWNER:	Carl Katerjian

◀ A hi-tech anodized finish was applied to the specially-built running gear of the 350 Chevy-powered Vicky.

'34 Ford Coupe

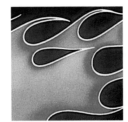

Unlike many cars made famous by the movies or on the small screen, Pete Chapouris' '34 Coupe was already a "known" hot rod, when it was cast in the made-for-TV movie *The California Kid.* By the time the film aired, the car had already been featured in the November 1973 issue of *Rod and Custom Magazine*, along with another chopped '34 belonging to Pete's business partner, Jim Jacobs. Both cars made quite a stir, suddenly thrusting the "Hot Rod" ethos back into the staid early-1970's Resto-Rod world. The "Kid" didn't capture the wider public's imagination in the way other on-screen hot rods did due to its limited exposure on the show, but among hot rodders, it was right up there at the top.

The traditionally-built Coupe already featured a filled roof and hard roof chop when Pete Chapouris acquired it. He then installed a '68 302 ci small block Ford, which he had been running in his previous car. The engine was tuned to go, with high compression cylinder heads, TRW forged pistons and an Edelbrock/Holley intake and carb combo. The transmission is a Ford C8 unit and the rear axle is 9-inch Ford. Pin striping, Nerf Bars and lots of louvers also featured heavily on the "Kid," which still retains the same engine and running gear that it's always had.

MAKE:	Ford
BODY STYLE:	3-window Coupe
YEAR:	1934
ENGINE:	Ford 302 V8
BUILD STYLE:	Hot Rod
BUILDER:	Pete Chapouris

◄ In the movie "The California Kid," instead of its usual polished Halibrands the '34 wears a set of red steel wheels with caps and rings for more of a 1950's feel.

'32 Ford Roadster

With a hot rodding history as long as your arm, the Doane Spencer Deuce set the standard for street-driven '32 roadsters way back in the late 1940s with its above average (for the time) engineering and finish. It saw a lot of action at the salt flats in those early days, with its 258 ci '46 Mercury V8 with Navarro intake and 2 Strombergs working to great effect. But its state of tune never affected reliability and the car regularly crossed the country on long road trips. As an endorsement of this, Doane has stated that he had toured 42 out of the (then) 48 States in the car. Always looking for fresh challenges, Doane took the roadster off the road in the early 1950s with the intention of entering the Carrera Panamericana Mexican road race. Many chassis modification were made towards this end. However, for safety reasons, the race was cancelled before he could compete.

The car changed hands several times over the years, always with owners sympathetic to the car's history, which is probably why it survived so well. Eventually, it was acquired by Californian collector Bruce Meyer, who immediately had it completely restored to its early Flathead specification. Since then, it has been regularly displayed at shows and at the Petersen Museum, among other events and locations. In 1997, it took top honors at the Pebble Beach Concours d'Elegance in the Historic Hot Rod class, a worthy tribute to the late Doane Spencer and the car's history as a quintessential example of the classic American Hot Rod.

MAKE:	Ford
BODY STYLE:	Roadster
YEAR:	1932
ENGINE:	Mercury Flathead V8
BUILD STYLE:	Traditional Hot Rod
OWNER:	Bruce Meyer

▲ With a low, purposeful stance and many neat and innovative features, the Doane Spencer Deuce set the standard for all '32 roadsters that were to follow.

'29 Ford Roadster

▲ As the first AMBR winner, many still consider Bill Niekamp's '29 gem to be the nicest street roadster ever built.

There are many hot rods included in these pages that have won the title of AMBR at the Oakland Roadster Show. But, in 1950, this was the first. Demonstrating the typical late-1940s features of a streamlined track nose and a full aluminum belly pan, this was then truly state-of-the-art stuff, hence the trophy. In those days, rods often did double duty, and if they weren't waxed up and on display at indoor shows, they were tearing up the salt flats at El Mirage, etc. Indeed, in 1952, this slippery roadster itself achieved 142 mph from its flathead Ford engine. A few years later, it was raffled by its owner in order to help a fellow injured Lakes racer. The raffle winner and new owner replaced the Flathead with a new Chevy small block. He also painted the car Tahitian Red. Over the years, several other engines and paintjobs followed over the years.

The all-enclosing body on Niekamp's roadster was built over a set of '27 Essex frame rails and finished in Plymouth Medium blue. This might have had something to do with the fact that Bill worked as a painter at the Plymouth car plant at the time. The front suspension was a chromed tube axle, with early hydraulic shocks and '40 Ford brakes. A '42 Mercury Flathead with Evans cylinder heads powered the car via a '39 Lincoln Zephyr transmission. In 1969, the car was totally restored by Jim Jacobs. (He went on to be the "Jake" in the well-known Pete and Jakes outfit.) This was probably the first of the old Lakes roadster to receive a proper and full restoration to its original specification.

MAKE:	Ford
BODY STYLE:	Roadster
YEAR:	1929
ENGINE:	Mercury Flathead V8
BUILD STYLE:	Period Restoration
BUILDER:	Bill Niekamp

'32 Ford Coupe

It's doubtful that when George Lucas started filming "American Grafitti," his low-budget movie based on his own teenage years growing up in Modesto, Northern California, that he would realize the effect it would have on a whole new generation. Not only did its cast of young unknown actors become some of Hollywood's greatest talents, but its cast of cool hot rods and customs would introduce cruising to a worldwide audience too. Actors aside, the real star of the show was this chopped '32 5-window, otherwise known as "Milner's Coupe" after the character in the movie that drives it. Set in 1962, the '32 was the bad boy in town, "the fastest car in the valley" that once more gets challenged to a dawn drag race on the outskirts of town. (*See also page 162*).

Bought as a chopped, primered, fully-fendered, but partly disassembled hot rod, the bobbed rear fenders were cut from the originals, with the fronts being made from a van spare wheel cover. The grille shell and radiator were cut down and the aluminum headlamp stands were installed. The entire front end was sent out for chroming and the sprint style headers were made for the car. The Chevy engine is a '66 327, with a rear Man-a-Fire intake and four Rochester 2G carbs. The gearbox is a manual Super T-10, and this drives a buggy-sprung '57 Chevy rear end. To this day, the car remains much as it did in the movie.

MAKE:	Ford
BODY STYLE:	5-window Coupe
YEAR:	1932
ENGINE:	Chevy 327 V8
BUILD STYLE:	60's Hot Rod
OWNER:	Rick Figari

▶ The "Graffiti Coupe" was never intended to be a Show Car and it was painted yellow and finished to a good enough standard for the movie camera.

'33 Ford 3-window Coupe

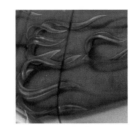

The ultimate hot rod engine – or overkill? Either way, you can't ignore Kevin Care's wild '33 with a engine as tall as an apartment building! The engine (are you ready for this?) is a '58 Chrysler 392 ci Hemi with a BDS 8-71 blower mounted on a hi-rise intake. On top of that is an Inglese manifold with four Weber 48 IDA carbs. Not stopping there, the carbs are equipped with velocity stacks for added altitude. Imagine needing a ladder to adjust your carb mixture! The engine also features a 100 bhp nitrous-oxide system, a 4-inch intercooler and custom headers with Borla mufflers.

If you're going to build the engine up, you better chop the top down, and as a result the coupe has received a 9¹⁄₂-inch chop, plus a raked-back windshield to enhance the profile. The body has also been formed over the frame before receiving its Sunflower Yellow paint and cool but, hot chilli pepper graphics. The car rolls on ET wheels, the wide rears being mounted on a narrowed Ford rear axle and the 10-spoke fronts on a drilled I-beam.

MAKE:	Ford
BODY STYLE:	Coupe
YEAR:	1933
ENGINE:	392 Chrysler Hemi V8
BUILD STYLE:	Show Rod
OWNER:	Kevin Care

◄ There's attracting attention – and there's attracting attention! Do you think anyone would notice this '33 Coupe sneakin' into the parking lot?

'23 Ford T-bucket

The T–bucket style was one of the first of the early Ford body styles to be reproduced as a fiberglass replica back in the 1960s, their simplicity making them easy and quick to assemble. For the home builder wanting to get on with the job and not wanting to get involved in reconstructing a rusty old metal body, they were an ideal first step. You would think that being open to the elements they would have appealed only to the warmer states, but they proved popular all over – and still are.

This cute red T displays many elements of the classic T, with its brass rad shell, skinny wire front wheels and super wide American Racing rears shod with Mickey Thompson tires. The front suspension is so exposed on these cars that it has to look good, and so is a combination of chrome and polished stainless steel, just as any self-respecting T should have. Note the very subtle and unobtrusive front fenders, and complete absence of rears.

MAKE:	Ford T
BODY STYLE:	Roadster
YEAR:	1923
ENGINE:	Chevy Small block V8
BUILD STYLE:	Street Rod
BUILDER:	Bill La Chance

▶ Not the most comfortable hot rods in which to ride long distances, but there's not much to beat a T-bucket for just plain fun!

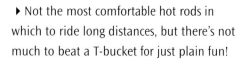

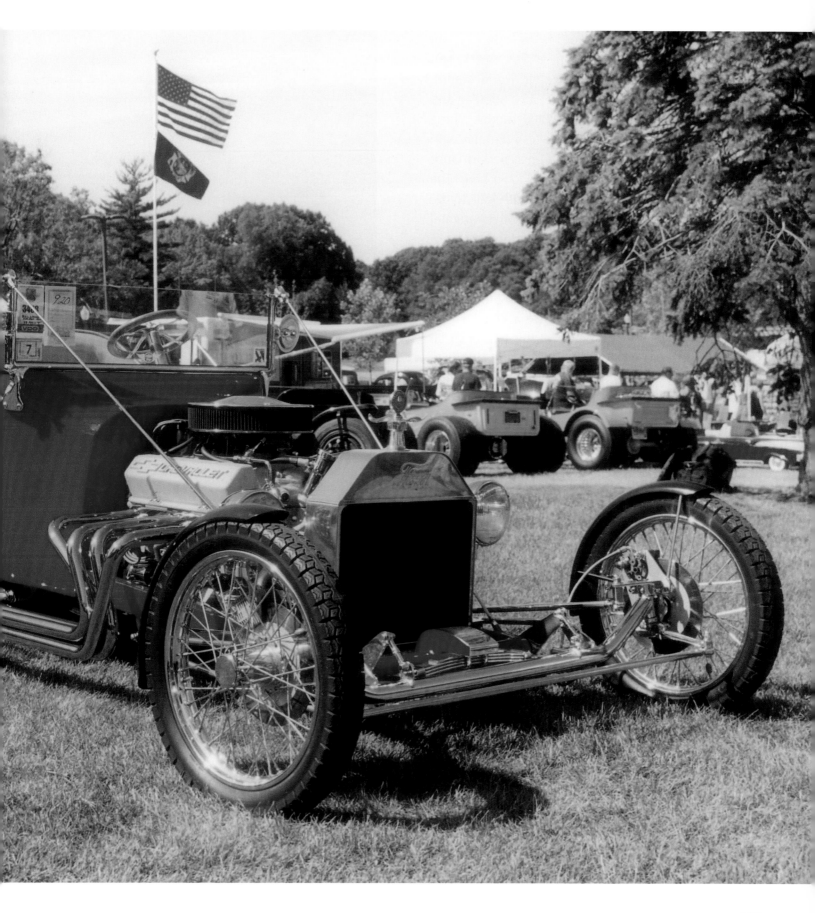

'48 Ford Pickup

The Ford F-1 was the half-ton pickup series marketed directly after World War II, and before the very popular and long-running F100 model. These early trucks are also popular with rodders, but not many of them end up as performance oriented as Jim Green's red example shown here. The flawless Mars red color gives a very smooth look to the truck despite the truck retaining most of its original brightwork. Unusually, the front fender has been removed but the apertures for the fender irons are still evident. Perhaps Jim removes it to race! Did we say race? Well if your truck turned 11.2 at 112 mph in the quarter-mile, wouldn't you want to race it? We would.

Providing the key to the power of this particular l'il red wagon is a stroked 355 ci Chevy with a 6-71 Littlefield blower with twin Edelbrock 750 carbs. This puts the power down through a Richmond 5-speed transmission and a 9-inch Ford rear axle with Moser shafts. Keeping your truck in a straight line at those top end speeds is essential, so Jim has installed a fully independent front end under the truck. Wheels are chrome 5-spokes with Hoosier rear tires.

MAKE:	Ford F-1
BODY STYLE:	Pickup
YEAR:	1948
ENGINE:	355 ci Chevy V8
BUILD STYLE:	Performance Rod
BUILDER:	Jim Green

▶ I bet you didn't expect to find an old pickup truck under the performance category in the book. This '48 is a cool exception to the rule.

'40 Ford Deluxe Coupe

There are some car designs that are hard to improve upon, and when you see a '40 Ford like Bob and Anita Damstrom's Deluxe Coupe, you just know that sometimes it's best to leave well enough alone. All this car needs to give it flair and set it apart from the resto-crowd is that gorgeous coat of Dupont Deep Cranberry pearl gloss paint. Complement that with a set of crème steel wheels and whitewalls and you have a very cool '40 indeed. All the stock trim has been retained on this car, including the fenders, guards and rubber running board covers.

Things are not so stock under the skin, though. So, while it's true that the car still runs a flattie, in this case it's a stroked 276-cube unit with Offenhauser heads, Jahns pistons and Mallory ignition. The V8 is fully dressed and also sports some period tuning equipment – in the form of an Offy twin-carb manifold, with two Stromberg 94 carbs. Long gone is the old "three-on-the-tree" transmission. Instead, a new T-5 transmission now does the job and, similarly, the old banjo rear axle has been replaced with a stout Ford 9-inch.

MAKE:	Ford
BODY STYLE:	DeLuxe Coupe
YEAR:	1940
ENGINE:	276 ci Flathead V8
BUILD STYLE:	Traditional
OWNERS :	Bob and Anita Damstrom

◄ We reckon there's more than a few that have been surprised by the sprightly performance of this otherwise stock-looking '40.

'33 Ford 3-window Coupe

▲ Is it a custom? Is it a rod? Well hey, it fits right into both camps and it's just plain cool!

O ne school of thought in hot rodding that is often overlooked, is the custom rod. It was popular in the early 1960s for a spell, particularly with the show car crowd, but it's not often seen these days. Basically, it was the custom of using wild body mods as more commonly used on customs and then applying the technique to earlier hot rod body styles. A perfect example is Scottt Porges' '33. Like many of the rods in this book, it has been chopped and channeled, but the body mods didn't stop there. The rear end has been completely re-styled, with the rear pan extending right up to meet the belt line of the '33, thus rendering the rear deck almost flat, but with raised moldings down the center. The raised moldings then continue across the roof and are echoed by another molding on the cowl. The rod wears rear fenders only, and these have been bobbed and molded to the body – but still barely cover the wide Fenton rear wheels.

Celery pearl gloss paint finishes off this cool custom rod, with red accenting on the Deuce grille insert and red engine detailing on the small block Chevy. The engine has been breathed on and features an early Fenton 3-pot inlet manifold with three carbs. We're pleased to note that the cool headers are significantly heat "blued," indicating that this car gets driven. This is no "no-go showboat!"

MAKE:	Ford
BODY STYLE:	3-window Coupe
YEAR:	1933
ENGINE:	Small Block Chevy V8
BUILD STYLE:	Custom Rod
BUILDER:	Scottt Porges

'30 Ford Roadster

We've nearly all come across the term "Rat Rod" by now. Some don't mind the phrase, whilst others hate it. Then again, some rodders don't "get" them anyway, while others love the no frills, bare-bones fun approach to them, being somewhat free from conventional rod building rules. Jim Gove is one of the latter and living on the East Coast. He put together this typically Eastern style roadster. Now, East Coast cars were traditionally low, not like the mainly West Coast/California "highboys" style. This one achieves the look with a 12-inch kick up to the rear frame, plus a 7-inch channel to the body. Also distinctive is the use of a '39 Ford truck grille up front that has been sectioned to fit.

▼ This style of "back to basics" hot rodding is not for everyone. But for those who own such rods, the fun is the building and driving, not the cleaning and polishing!

Nothing less than a '50 Cadillac gave up it's 331 ci V8 to power this roadster – fully rebuilt, of course – and with an Isky cam, an Edelbrock four-pot manifold and 2 pairs of Stromberg 97's on top doing the fuel/air mixture thing. An Offy adapter plate mates the early V8 to a '69 Ford Toploader gearbox, stirred with a Hurst shifter. A 55 Chevy axle is hung from a '48 Ford transaxle under the rear. This fun, but righteous, roadster stays truly hardcore, with a maroon suede paint job and gold-painted steel wheels.

MAKE:	Ford
BODY STYLE:	Roadster
YEAR:	1930
ENGINE:	Cadillac 331 ci V8
BUILD STYLE:	Traditional Hardcore
BUILDER:	Jim Gove

'28 Ford Model A Touring

Not as popular as coupes and roadsters, and with a lower survival rate than sedans, these 4-seat touring bodies nevertheless make great hot rods, especially when done with a late 40's "Jalopy" style. Unusually, this one features an Australian-built body and is mounted traditionally on a detailed '32 Ford chassis. To fit "right," the cowl has been tapered to match the rails and the windshield has been chopped in height and taken back some 30 degrees for a more rakish look. There were no custom wheels around back then, so a set of 16-inch wires with whitewalls set the post-war mood on this "tub," as the type is known.

Modifications to the running gear in those days consisted mainly of swapping parts from later model Fords – and so we find a 24-stud Ford Flathead with a single Stromberg 94 carb under the hood of this Model A. The rear end has been updated with a mixture of Ford and traditional, early speed parts, with a '32 Ford rear end from a 4-cylinder car and a Cyclone quick-change center section on a transverse buggy spring with Houdaille shocks. Simple engineering, but a truly hot set-up back in its day.

MAKE:	Ford
BODY STYLE:	4-seat Touring
YEAR:	1928
ENGINE:	Ford Flathead V8
BUILD STYLE:	Traditional 40's Rod
BUILDER:	Richie Willett

◄ The maroon-painted and detailed chassis contrasts nicely with the understated gray paint on this period-perfect Model A Tub.

'39 Chevrolet Business Coupe

Fords don't have it all their own way in the rodding world. These big, pre-World War II Chevy Coupes make great street rods too; and this one exemplifies the current trend for a well-executed car, sitting low over big diameter wheels. This car achieves its ground-hugging stance courtesy of an Air-Ride Technologies suspension system and a combination of Colorado Custom 15-inch and 17-inch wheels. The running boards have been smoothed and painted and the fenders dispensed with to clean up the lower body area. Another subtle modification is the removal of the bullet-shaped stock headlamps that normally sit between the top of the wing and the hood, plus the fitting of the lower, more streamlined headlamp pods from the next year, the 1940 model.

You can expect a big, comfortable rod like this Chevy to have all the luxury appointments for

long-haul runs. Power steering, power brakes (with discs all round) and air-conditioning are all pretty much guaranteed in a car like this. For motive power, this '40 uses a small block Chevy with TPI fuel injection for muscle and economy. The gearbox is the popular, 4-speed 700R4 transmission.

▾ Silver and yellow may sound an unusual choice as color combination, but as you can see, it works well with the Mystic silver metallic over the PPG Banana yellow pearl.

MAKE:	Chevrolet
BODY STYLE:	Business Coupe
YEAR:	1939
ENGINE:	Chevrolet 350 LT1 V8
BUILD STYLE:	Street Rod
OWNER:	Jack Evans

'47 International Fire Truck

There's always someone who has to go bigger and better than everyone else. In this case, who cares, when it turns out as wild as Brian Bower's Fire Truck! Where do we start with the body alterations? How about, a 32-inch stretch to the cab? Then there is a 32-inch shrink to the bed length, a 4-inch chop to the roof of the cab and a 6-inch chop to the height of the rear bed. Not only that, but the truck has had the full Pro-Street treatment with a narrowed Ford 9-inch and narrowed frame rails enabling the monster rear rubber to sit inside the stock truck wheel arches. Custom running boards have been also fabricated from sheet diamond plate steel.

A big truck like this needs a big engine to haul it and so the old International lump has been heaved, and replaced with a big 454 Chevy engine complete with an 8-71 BDS blower fed with a pair of dual quad carbs. A Hilborn intake scoop hints at the horsepower lurking beneath the hood. Reckon it'll get to the fire quick enough? A full set of genuine fire equipment accessories add authenticity to the big, red, rod.

MAKE:	International
BODY STYLE:	Fire Truck
YEAR:	1947
ENGINE:	Chevy 454 ci V8
BUILD STYLE:	Fire Rod?
OWNER:	Brian Bowers

▾ To get that front end down closer to the tarmac, a complete Chevy Nova suspension clip has been used providing easier steering suspension and engine mounting for the big rig.

'30 Ford 5-window Coupe

Now we know you're looking at this Model A coupe and maybe wondering why something just doesn't look quite right. Is it the angle of the pic, you're wondering; or what? Well, to put your mind at rest, it's not your eyes playing tricks on you. This A coupe has actually had a full 12 inches taken from the length of the body. It was a 5-window coupe originally, but now – as you can see – it is a unique, 4-inch chopped, 3-window. The fact that the car also runs a "suicide" front end also distorts the proportions and confuses the eye.

Apart from this tricky modification, the rest is all pure "old school". A 3-carb equipped Chevy engine with Moon covers and breathers, chrome reverse rims and Halibrand front wheels shod with whitewalls always look cool, especially against the polished black paint. A Deuce grille shell further disguises the li'l coupe's true identity. Those sprint style headers also help the "bad boy" image.

MAKE:	Ford
BODY STYLE:	Coupe
YEAR:	1930
ENGINE:	Chevy Small Block V8
BUILD STYLE:	Traditional Hot Rod
OWNERS:	Steve and Ryan Kopchinski

▸ There's not much room in a Model A Coupe at the best of times, let alone one that's been shortened by 12 inches! Makes for a cosy interior!

'34 Chevrolet Sedan Delivery

Back in the 1930s, one way to capitalize on auto sales was to market a commercial version based on the 2-door sedan body already in production. Known as a Sedan Delivery, it featured a 2-door commercial body on a passenger car chassis, with a single side-hinged rear door. These cars were popular with tradesmen wanting the comfort but with the additional practicality. They make great street rods, with enough space to travel long hauls in comfort and with ample baggage. They're not common, however, so it's a treat to see one as nice as Rich and Joan Molinaro's '34 Chevy. A contemporary smooth style is the chosen look for this delivery with little to interrupt the eye-popping Chrome Yellow gloss.

▼ Despite the modern monochrome color approach to this rod, the owner has chosen a set of polished A.R.E. 5-spokes, with spinners as a respectful nod to tradition.

Looking closer at the '34, you'll notice the smooth running boards, the smooth hood sides with the single sculpted vent, and the lack of exterior door handles. There are small side repeaters in the lower inner corner of the front wings and the frame and components have been color co-ordinated in yellow. Even the small door mirrors have a paint finish rather than chrome. Underneath the car, the frame features a fully independent front suspension system for modern driving and handling characteristics.

MAKE:	Chevrolet
BODY STYLE:	Sedan Delivery
YEAR:	1934
ENGINE:	Chevy Small Block V8
BUILD STYLE:	Street Rod
BUILDERS:	Rich and Joan Molinaro

'32 Ford 3-window Coupe

There's nothing too fancy or wild about this particular "Little Deuce Coupe," apart perhaps from the blown engine. Nevertheless, the black suede 3-window certainly has the look and is reminiscent of many similar '32's that would have been running around some fifty years ago. Maybe there was one like it in your home town? A healthy slice has been taken out of the top, but the rod remains un-channeled in this case. Fancy custom wheels were a bit "high-buck" for many early rodders, so many took stock steel wheels, fitted new centers to create "reverse" rims, then dipped them in the chrome vat to end up with the look we have here. A set of bias-ply wide whites finishes the rolling stock to perfection.

There's plenty of shine up front on this hot rod. The '58 Chevy 283 has been bored out 0.30 over to 288 cubes and is fitted with the rare and desirable camel-hump cylinder heads with polished Moon valve covers. We mentioned the blower earlier – a polished Dyers 6-71 unit fitted with twin Carter 500 AFB carbs – and this certainly fills the gap between the cowl and the grille shell. A set of chromed headers remove all the spent gases from the hot Chevy mill.

MAKE:	Ford
BODY STYLE:	3-window
YEAR:	1932
ENGINE:	Chevy Small block V8
BUILD STYLE:	Traditional Rod
OWNER:	Tony Muscatella

▶ The spun-alloy Moon tank, mounted here ahead of the grille, first saw duty on drag race machinery of the period and the look was soon taken up for the street.

'28 Ford Model A Roadster Pickup

There is an indefinable quality in some hot rods that you just can't put your finger on. You can't buy it, and it's more than the sum total of the parts; but most rodders know it when they see it. We believe that this A-bone roadster pickup has it in spades, and we call it "attitude." From the black suede body with contrasting white top, to the whitewall slicks on old ET slot mags, this is one mean little truck. Those are finned Buick drums mounted on early Ford spindles and back plates; and the fact that the I-beam is an un-dropped stock item also helps in giving the rod an almost nose-up stance that is reminiscent of old gas cars. The Moon tank on the front spreader bar doesn't hurt the image either.

A killer engine in a lightweight-bodied car is going to result in just one thing – awesome performance. So we've tucked it under that category, despite many traditional cues.

The engine in question is an early small block Chevy, hiding under a huge Mooneyham magnesium blower, which, in turn, is topped with six "deuces" (2-barrel carbs for the uninitiated). A set of Cal custom-finned alloy breathers help dress up the engine, which would have no trouble turning those rear slicks into rubber smoke at a moment's notice.

MAKE:	Ford
BODY STYLE:	Roadster Pick Up
YEAR:	1928
ENGINE:	Chevy Small Block
BUILD STYLE:	Pure Hot Rod
OWNER:	Jim Malaro

◄ As if the running gear wasn't "beefed" up already, check out the cow pattern seat trim in the pick up!

'39 Ford 4-door Convertible

Out there in hot rod land, there may well be some who frown and say that 4-door cars don't make for cool rods. We don't necessarily agree, especially when they turn out as nice as Mike Russo's '39 Convertible. OK, so this Ford is probably more custom in execution than out-and-out hot rod; but it's cool, nonetheless. Bodily, the big "vert" has been left as stock, save for the addition of a superb coat of Merlot pearl gloss paint and a set of fender skirts. (The skirts were possibly a factory option anyway). On cars like these, just the lowering job on the suspension would have been enough to give the car a bit of "attitude" down at the drive-in. This one goes one better with the addition of a set of Cadillac "sombrero" hub caps. I wonder if he had to buy a set of four?

The emphasis on speed was never as paramount with "customizers" so it would have been perfectly acceptable for "rods" like this to have kept all stock running gear beneath the smooth sheet metal. Maybe a set of Smitty mufflers would have been installed to give a noticeable "rap" to the tone of the flathead V8. Speed shops selling hop-up parts were rare in those days. So, if you wanted stuff, you were best to get it mail order from the small ads of the magazines of the time – as and when you could afford it!

MAKE:	Ford
BODY STYLE:	4-door Convertible
YEAR:	1939
ENGINE:	Ford Flathead V8
BUILD STYLE:	Traditional Custom
OWNER:	Mike Russo

▶ A custom white top both matches the whitewall tires and contrasts with the deep red paint on this '39 mild custom.

'38 Ford Woodie

I t takes a certain kind of rodder to take on a Woodie as a potential project, especially when starting with an original unrestored example. Not only have you got all the work involved in upgrading the chassis, suspension and running gear – plus the usual tasks of paint, upholstery and sheet metalwork – there is also the (often mammoth) task of restoring any rotten areas of the wood-framed body . On that basis, a cool Woodie like this is an even greater achievement as a finished car. It's a particularly fine example and is based on the '38 Ford front sheet metal and still runs the original Ford chassis under its all-new wood body.

The '38 in-a-crate Ford was put together using a tried and tested formula. There is a stock 350 Chevy engine up front with a TH400 transmission, while a '72 Chevy Nova donated its rear axle, springs and propshaft to complete the all-GM running gear. The front end is all Chevrolet Corvair, although the steering rack is from an AMC Pacer. The quality of the restored ash wood body is set of by the '77 Pontiac Red metallic paintwork, new black vinyl roof covering and polished American slot mags.

MAKE:	Ford
BODY STYLE:	4-door Woodie
YEAR:	1938
ENGINE:	Chevy 350 V8
BUILD STYLE:	Street Rod
OWNER:	Owen Purvis

▶ Few models look better when given the Resto-rod treatment than a classic Woodie. Somehow, a roof chop and wild body mods just wouldn't work on this kind of car.

'33 Willys Coupe

Not all hot rods are street legal. In fact, many are built solely for racing; and just about the most exciting are the "gassers." Gassers were originally street driven cars built to compete in the gas classes at the drag strip. But as cars got quicker, they became more radical in the suspension department, in order to gain better weight transfer when launching from the start line. This '33 Willys Coupe is a fine example of that style. The raised profile is obtained by installing a straight front axle between the hubs, thus pushing the chassis up higher than standard. These lightweight but powerful cars, with their short wheel base and high center of gravity, are very entertaining to watch – as they tend to be a bit unpredictable in the handling department.

This high-flying '33 is owned and raced by the owner of the Valley Gas Speed Shop. With it's highly-tuned, big block Ford V8, it regularly lifts the front wheels in the air when the driver mashes down on the loud pedal. The mesh screen in the side window is a safety item required in the rules, as is the parachute mounted where the spare wheel would have been on the original car. Inside, the car features a full roll cage and a no-frills aluminum panelled interior.

MAKE:	Willys
BODY STYLE:	Coupe
YEAR:	1933
ENGINE:	513 ci Ford V8
BUILD STYLE:	Nostalgia Race Car
OWNER:	Jimmy Hibberd

▼ As a purely race car, the only exhausts necessary are the large chrome headers exiting the engine compartment just behind the front wheels.

'47 Ford Club Coupe

As the US auto industry struggled to get back into the swing of producing passenger cars after World War II, pre-war designs from 1942 were re-hashed and sold to the public for a couple of years – until Ford was able to turn the tables with their all new '49 "Shoebox" model. Nevertheless, the Fords of the late 1940's, while similar, were still handsome cars – as exemplified by this fat-fendered '47 Coupe. This is a Club Coupe that has been given the classic (and always effective) paintwork treatment of straight black paint, coupled with bright red steelie rims, chrome caps'n'rings, and a set of wide whites.

Add to that a lowering job, with a few extra details, and you are ready to cruise in fine style. To clean up the front aspect of the '47, the owner has subtly dechromed the topmost grille bar and the hood trim and had then had them painted body color. The grille bars themselves have been detailed with red to match the wheels. On top of the hood is another old rodding trick, several rows of louvers have been punched; they look cool plus let heat out of the engine compartment at the same time.

MAKE:	Ford
BODY STYLE:	Club Coupe
YEAR:	1947
ENGINE:	Ford Flathead V8
BUILD STYLE:	Mild Custom
OWNER:	Gordon Maxey

◀ Mild customs like these would have been common high school cruisers for cash-strapped teenagers back in the 1950s – and they still look good today.

'36 Ford 5-window Coupe

From about 1936, Ford cars started to become more "Art-Deco" in design, along with current styling trends at the time. The more curvaceous and flowing lines lent themselves to a different school of thought for hot rodders – the art of the custom. For customizers, the look was everything and the period custom look on a 1930's hot rod is exemplified by the low lines of this – oh-so-cool – '36 Coupe. Apart from the obvious lowering job, the top has had a mild roof chop, just enough to improve the look of the car without being too obvious and over the top, and the running boards have been smoothed out too.

A subtle and period touch is the removal of the door handles and stock mirrors, with a subtle "peep" mirror being added instead. The hood has been deliberately left off to show the fully-detailed Chevy engine and those neat chrome carburetor stacks. The stock grille and fenders have been retained, and why not? Ford got that part right first time around.

MAKE:	Ford
BODY STYLE:	5-window Coupe
YEAR:	1936
ENGINE:	Chevrolet V8
BUILD STYLE:	Early Custom Rod
OWNER:	Melissa Limones

▶ Chrome hubcaps with large bullet centers and beauty rings give just the right custom flavor when used with painted rims and whitewall tires on this early style custom '36.

'36 Dodge Pickup

I s that enough red paint for you? Maybe because this truck is owned by a lady, it's painted Lipstick red – or maybe not. But either way, it's one hot contemporary truck.

The latest combination of tricks for a modern style hot rod are used here to great effect – with super straight bodywork, a strong single color to grab your attention and a sneaky low stance. Cap that off with an up-to-date set of Colorado Custom directional polished wheels, and you have the recipe for a potential show winner. Once again, we see a roof chop on a truck used to create the illusion of added length to the vehicle.

You would probably have to park a stock Dodge next to this one to appreciate all the subtle body mods – details like the molded grille and front fenders, the shaved door handles

and the smoothed and painted running boards. One thing is for sure, those rear fenders have definitely been widened to cope with the big 20's shod with Michelin rubber. Front wheels are 18s, also with Michelin tires. Lest we forget, there's a 350 Chevy small-block V8 under the hood coupled to a TH350 transmission.

▼ A '36 Dodge truck might have seemed an unusual choice for a rod a few years back. But with the right treatment, just look what can be achieved.

MAKE:	Dodge
BODY STYLE:	Pickup
YEAR:	1936
ENGINE:	Chevy 350 ci V8
BUILD STYLE:	Street Rod
OWNER:	Julie Dikes

'34 Ford Tudor Sedan

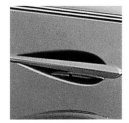

The finish on this super straight '34 Sedan took many hours of work to bring it back to life from the rusted and bent body that the project started with. Many of the panels have had to be replaced with fresh steel, rather than the owner attempting to repair the rusty and damaged originals. While the welding equipment is in use, another common custom trick on 1930's cars is to replace the canvas roof insert with a steel panel – and this has been skilfully carried out on this sedan. Check out the filled hood side panels featuring a custom chrome side trim. And while we are talking body mods, the roof on the rod has also been chopped 2^1/$_2$ inches.

A repro '34 frame was used underneath the car and all new suspension components have been installed, including a chrome dropped I-beam to get that front end down low. In keeping with the traditional flavor on this trick sedan, the car features a set of chrome reverse rims, with a set of Mercury hubcaps rather than alloy wheels. The whitewall tires on the car echo the owner-installed custom white pearl upholstery job too. Despite all this, the car was not built to win trophies, but to transport the owner Neil Tadman and his family to rod runs in real style. Neil freely admits he'd rather be driving it than parking it, and we don't blame him one bit!

MAKE:	Ford
BODY STYLE:	Tudor Sedan
YEAR:	1934
ENGINE:	350 Chevrolet
BUILD STYLE:	Traditional Street Rod
OWNER:	Neil Tadman

▶ If your business is trimming high-class hot rods, you better have a class act yourself, like this '34.

'34 Ford Victoria

Often considered to be one the prettiest body styles of a pre-war Ford, the Victoria – or "Vicky" as it's affectionately known – is a rare model, either stock or rodded. Characterized by the stylish sloping rear bodywork, the Victoria was available from a Model A through several model changes. Such is their appeal that it's nowadays possible to buy 'glass Vicky's from which to build street rods. This one is a real steel '34, however, and features all-stock sheet metal, including the factory 4-piece hood. Other details are the small cowl lights, opening screen, rubber running boards and the fenders.

The two obvious giveaways to the street rod heritage of this Vicky are the bright Richard Petty blue gloss paint and the polished 5-spoke Weld Star wheels (a very popular choice back in the 1980s). It bears the legend "Victoria" across the lower doors, just in case you hadn't spotted it. Despite its mild-mannered looks, this car has spent many days, with its owner at the wheel, at street events, courtesy of a very warm, small-block Chevy under the hood.

MAKE:	Ford
BODY STYLE:	Victoria Tudor Sedan
YEAR:	1934
ENGINE:	Chevy SmallBblock V8
BUILD STYLE:	Street Rod
OWNER:	Dick Morse

▶ The Massachusetts plate says "Relic," although the true blue Vicky looks pretty good to us.

'32 Ford 5-window Coupe

 efinitely a case of old meets new, both traditional and right up-to-date styling cues meet head on in this '32. What is more, the traditions work perfectly to create an exciting and cool Deuce Coupe. The filled grille shell, big headlights and flame theme say "yesterday," while the fully-polished independent front suspension from Heidt's Hot Rod shop and big diameter rims says "right now." The rear end of the fenderless coupe features a fully-chromed and polished independent Corvette unit. You can't see it – but trust us, it's there!

Those wheels are American Racing's 17-inch and 20-inch latest versions of their classic 5-spoke design – and are also fitted with spinner center caps and low-profile rubber band tires. The three-dimensional hot licks have been laid over a rich coat of Dupont Candy Blue gloss, which has also been applied to the chassis. But this car is not just a pretty face. Under the hood there lies a killer engine in the form of a stroked 355-inch Chevy small block, with a BDS 6-71 blower and dual Holley four barrels. You can guarantee that it's detailed to the max in order to match the rest of the finish on this fine 5-window.

MAKE:	Ford
BODY STYLE:	5-window Coupe
YEAR:	1932
ENGINE:	355 ci Chevy V8
BUILD STYLE:	Street Rod
OWNER:	Lee Getzelman

◄ Extra body details like the smooth hood sides and the custom air scoop add further interest to this cool coupe.

'41 Willys Coupe

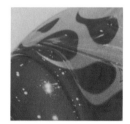

For years, the Willys Coupe was ignored by hot rodders who were looking for early street rod projects; and modified Willys were only to be found as gas class racers on the drag strips. Well, look who got all dressed up for the show! This is one '41 Willys with a perfected 21st century look. An Outlaw rod body and chassis package form the basis for this outstanding Coupe, the Outlaw ensemble being available with a fully-tubbed body and narrowed Pro-Street frame, ready to go. To this was added a narrowed Ford 9-inch rear end and a full package of Air Ride Technologies air bag suspension hardware.

Residing under that smooth hood, with its subtle custom scoop, is a 502 ci Chevy big block equipped with a Ramjet Intake. Transmission in the Willys is a 700R4. On the outside, the only stock Willys parts left are the headlights, but then their teardrop shape is hard to improve on anyway. A custom grille has been made for the molded aperture before the car was dipped in the candy vat – emerging with an Oyster pearl top over a Prowler Orange lower half with Gold Ice pearl highlighting. Also, the flame effect on the rear beltline works well to blend the colors together.

MAKE:	Willys
BODY STYLE:	Coupe
YEAR:	1941
ENGINE:	502 ci Chevy V8
BUILD STYLE:	Show Rod
OWNERS:	Bill and Sandy Baron

▶ Some serious Billet Specialties – 18-inch and 20-inch rims, respectively – fill the big Willys fender wells. The tires are by Nitto and are super-low profile.

'32 Ford Pickup

What at first glance appears to be an early Ford truck that's been lowered and had the fenders and hood removed, is actually a cool custom pickup with much trick metal fabrication to create this hardcore ride. Firstly, the cab, which has received a 4-inch channel, plus a 3¹/₂-inch roof chop to bring the profile back down to earth. Then we have the pickup-bed, which has also been shrunk in dimensions by being shortened in length and chopped in height (That's a lot of metal work right there). Additionally, a rolled rear pan has been constructed and fitted to the rear along with a pair of Maltese Cross taillights.

Judging by the front frame horns, the '32 chassis has remained unboxed – though sometimes, hardcore rodders box for strength where necessary, but leave the visible frame sections just as Henry intended for authenticity. The engine is a 283 ci Chevy with the minimum of razzmatazz – just a set of unpolished alloy valve covers to keep everything looking natural. Stock Ford parts make up the suspension, with split "bones" and an I-beam. Bias-ply whitewalls on steel rims once again keep the wheel and tire combo "old school." Interior comfort is provided by a favorite Mexican blanket!

MAKE:	Ford
BODY STYLE:	Closed Cab Pickup
YEAR:	1932
ENGINE	Chevy 283 V8
BUILD STYLE:	Hardcore Rod
OWNER:	"Slick" Rick Esposito

▸ These early Ford Pickups can be difficult to recognize by year, once a hot rodder has done his stuff on them. This '32 is hidden behind a later model 33-34 car grille.

'41 Willys Coupe

With over half-a-dozen specialist reproduction hot rod body companies out there, some body styles probably boast more fiberglass versions on the road than original steel ones.

When it come to Willys Coupes, we say "bring it on" – as there'll never be enough of these tough looking Coupes as far as we are concerned. This cute canary, done in the popular Pro Street style, features a one-piece flip front. This can be seen by the seamless join, where the hood meets the fenders. Stock headlamps and rims are fitted, as well as a stock reproduction '41 grille. Along the sides, contemporary mirrors have been fitted and painted in Viper Yellow gloss in order to match the body, and the door handles have been shaved to keep everything smooth and uncluttered.

Beneath the curvaceous hood of this '41 lives a serious little 327 Chevy engine, bored 30 over and equipped with an Edelbrock Tunnel-Ram manifold and Dual Quad carbs. A modern 700R4 4-speed auto transmission handles shifting duties and a Ford 9-inch rear axle running 3.57 gears has been narrowed and installed between the big wheel tubs.

At the other end, a Heidt Super Ride front end with tubular arms give the Willys a far superior ride than the old stock front end ever could have.

MAKE:	Willys
BODY STYLE:	Coupe
YEAR:	1941
ENGINE:	Chevy 327 V8
BUILD STYLE:	Street Rod
BUILDER:	Ron Pedro

▸ The set of highly polished Weld Pro-Star wheels were carefully chosen to suit to the Pro-Street style.

'37 Ford Highboy Coupe

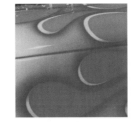

In general, hot rodders, have such an innovative streak within them that when they realize that Ford didn't produce a certain model, some enterprising soul will design and produce the "phantom" model in fiberglass. One such company is Minotti of Florida. A few years back they produced this '37 Ford 3-window Coupe which has proven popular with rodders ever since. This flamed stunner was put together as a fenderless coupe in order to compete for the famed Ridler award. What a car it turned out to be: super smooth hood sides blend the body work seamlessly from the grille back into the B pillars, with sculpted cutouts for the suspension. The rear body has been tubbed for the narrow axle Pro-Street look and the chopped top features a V-butted glass windshield.

A big-block, 502 ci Chevy V8 crate engine fills the under-hood area. Also, rather than go the multi-carb route, the builders decided to fit a Street and Performance high rise electronic fuel injection unit, an innovation that many hot rodders have taken to readily. To add more spice, a 500 hp pro-fog, nitrous-oxide system has also been added. All hardware and fuel lines have been chromed, polished and are visible through the cutout in the hood. Billet Specialties came up with the goods in the wheel department with a set of polished five spoke rims.

MAKE:	Ford
BODY STYLE:	Minotti 3-window Coupe
YEAR:	1937
ENGINE:	502 ci Chevy V8
BUILD STYLE:	Show Rod
BUILDERS:	Lenny Spallone and Dave Ellis

◀ Flames never go out of style with hot rodders – and there are plenty licking across the House of Kolors Tangelo pearl job on this '37.

'37 Chevy Roadster

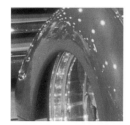

You need to compare the slick body on this custom '37 with Bob Delia's red one (see pages 290-291) in order to appreciate all the trick modifications. The list of changes are endless and overload the senses with the coolness of the fabrication involved. We'll attempt to list a few, starting at the sharp end with the custom fabbed grille with molded aperture, re-shaped front fenders, custom headlamp pods, smooth hood side panels, nosed and decked hood and trunk, custom front-to-rear side trim and smooth running boards. Of course, there are loads more, and you would need to see the car first-hand to appreciate all of them.

As you would expect, to get the car this low to the carpet, a set of Air Ride airbags has been installed, this method being the ultimate way to preserve a quality ride along with a cool profile, come show time. Those hood sides are fully removable and we can assure you the quality of fit and finish is as good under there as it is on the top sides of the car. Once again, we see the contemporary use of big-inch polished billet wheels being used on this '37 to great effect. Credit for the outstanding build quality goes to Ray Tourigny at Extreme Rod and Custom of Portland, Maine.

MAKE:	Chevrolet
BODY STYLE:	Roadster
YEAR:	1937
ENGINE:	Chevy LS1 V8
BUILD STYLE:	Show Rod
OWNER:	Fred Morrison

▶ The car has been built as a true Roadster, but had a hard top available to be fitted in rainy weather, hence no rag top visible behind the passenger compartment.

'32 Ford Victoria Convertible

Here is a real different take on the Ford Victoria body style – but done with a contemporary flair, of course. While the heritage of the lower half of the body is still recognizable, it's the radical top of the Vicky that turns it on its head. The 2-door Vicky phaeton body is readily available from several US manufacturers. For this, a severely chopped, Carson-style hardtop has been constructed as a lift-off roof, giving the owner the best of both worlds. The body has been smoothed over front to back, in vogue with current style, and both it and the frame has been treated to a coat of yellow and green pearl finish – along with the distinctive purple flame design.

The 350 Chevy engine is detailed all the way and features (by way of a change) a set of Weber downdraught carbs. (It's just a shame we can't see them in the pic.) A TH 350 transmission is installed, and so is a fully-chromed and polished Jaguar independent rear axle assembly, featuring inboard rotors and calipers to complete the show-quality running gear. A state-of-the art set of Budnik wheels grace all four corners, with the obligatory skinny rubber band tires – 20's on the back and 17s up front.

MAKE:	Ford
BODY STYLE:	Victoria Hardtop
YEAR:	1932
ENGINE:	Chevy 350 V8
BUILD STYLE:	Show Rod
OWNER:	Shane Baldwin

▾ Echoing the color of the Candy Purple flames, the interior of this eye-poppin' '32 is trimmed out in matching purple leather.

'33 Ford Roadster

▲ Not all flame jobs look as good as this
one's. It's easy to get the proportions wrong,
but orange on top of House of Kolor's purple
passion works great here.

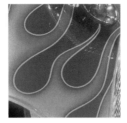

Some hot rods have a timeless style that does not reflect any particular decade. This flamed '33 is one of those. Look closer and you might find some custom parts that you know were only available at a certain point in history. Otherwise, it's truly timeless. The convertible top has been chopped 3-inches on the chrome screen posts and the door handles have been shaved, though this custom trick goes back decades. The '33 grille has been color coded to match the flame job and the running boards and hood sides have been smoothed. Otherwise, the body appears mostly stock.

A set of big ol' chrome King Bee headlamps are always the right choice for a '33 or '34 body style — and you can't fault the decision to equip this rod with Halibrand polished mags, either. That high-shine continues on the running gear, with a fully-detailed 350 Chevy between the frame rails, and also on the fully-independent Jaguar rear axle, which rodders first started to liberate from the British-imported sedans and sports cars back in the 1960s. They're not easy to find, but look great when all tricked out. Inside, the roadster, plenty of gray leather provides cruising comfort.

MAKE:	Ford
BODY STYLE:	Roadster
YEAR:	1933
ENGINE:	Chevy 350 V8
BUILD STYLE:	Street Rod
OWNER:	Deb Baldwin

'30 Chevrolet 3-window Coupe

This is a righteous little Chevy 3-window, really given the treatment. The 4-inch chop, plus 5-inch channel tells us that it's an East Coast car built with scant regard for anything resembling a fender, or even a roof insert. The rod is further camouflaged by the neat '39 truck grille and the swap-meet, find-early REO headlamps. But it's those parallel leaf springs sticking out in the breeze that give the game away, Ford never used that setup on a car frame. Black suede paint clothes the hot rod with a contrasting white firewall.

One of the coolest engines ever to come out of Detroit was the ohv Buick V8, otherwise known as the "Nailhead" due to the shape of the overhead valves. This engine featured a very strong bottom end and heaps of torque. They always look good in a hot rod, especially when dressed for the street, as is this one. This is a 364 ci block from a '60 Buick LeSabre and making a good engine even better is an Offenhauser manifold with three carbs. Four forward gears with a stick shift maximize the available fun, and an 8-inch Ford axle puts power to the pavement (sometimes resulting in a lot of white smoke!).

MAKE:	Chevrolet
BODY STYLE:	3-window Coupe
YEAR:	1930
ENGINE:	Buick 364 ci V8
BUILD STYLE:	Hardcore Rod
OWNER:	Pete Flaven

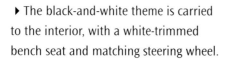

▸ The black-and-white theme is carried to the interior, with a white-trimmed bench seat and matching steering wheel.

'32 Ford 3-window Coupe

Sharing many elements of hot rod build inspiration with the East Coast hardcore crowd, this 3-window coupe takes the style to another level – with several buckets of high gloss red and almost as much chrome plating. Chopping and channeling gives the car an immediate cool presence. The chrome fine-spoke wires add an extra dash of flash too. Are they Buick Skylark numbers, or aftermarket? Either way, they look too cool with the wide whites. How about those bobbed fenders? Just enough to stay legal, officer! One concession to modern parts availability is the stainless steel spreader bar between the front frame horns, which also serves to house the front turn signals.

Somewhere, underneath all that chrome and polished metal, is a small block Chevy engine; but to see it you have to look past the Edelbrock valve covers and the braided hoses, not to mention the chromed-out firewall and cooling fan. A massive tunnel-ram inlet manifold dominates the engine and it has also seen a considerable amount of time on the polisher's wheel. Twin chromed, 4-barrel carbs with velocity stacks feed fuel to the engine, with the spark provided by a magneto. The chrome Lakes Style pipes are pleasantly "blued," indicating this rod gets to see plenty of road miles.

MAKE:	Ford
BODY STYLE:	3-window Coupe
YEAR:	1932
ENGINE:	Chevy Small Block V8
BUILD STYLE:	Street Rod
BUILDER:	Tom Clancy

◀ Front suspension is a fully-chromed out I-beam on a four-bar, which still retains its drum brakes. The grille shell has been filled and smoothed too.

'32 Ford Roadster

Originally built by Eugene Wentworth and his business partner Vernon Hoyt in their shop in Massachusetts, the cool '32 was entered and raced in the competitive "C" Roadster class at Bonneville, way back in 1951. It made many show appearances during the 1950s, but by 1959 it had been acquired by Eldon "Sy" Sidebotham. The extensive rebuild and subsequent feature in *Rod and Custom* magazine in 1959 earned forever this rod's place in the history books as "The Sidebotham Roadster." The car appears here in much the same guise as it did back then, the only significant changes were to the re-done interior trim.

Bodily, there are few modifications apart from a rolled rear pan, which dated back to its original build. A filled cowl vent and filled and peaked grille shell, plus '50 Pontiac

▼ The original Seabaker Auto body applied, hand-rubbed black lacquer still survives to this day; and, as you can see, still looks great.

taillights, were added by Sy. Whatever else, the main story on this car has always been its speed and performance. The flattie boasts 296 cubic inches on a '46 block and nothing but the best components were used to extract maximum horsepower from the V8. An Edelbrock intake lines up four Stromberg 97's in a row, all capped with Stelling and Hellings air cleaners for a classic profile. A '39 Ford trans with an Auburn Clutch transmits big torque power down to the '40 Ford rear, and with all this "go," the '40 Ford hydraulic brakes provide the "whoa!"

MAKE:	Ford
BODY STYLE:	Roadster
YEAR:	1932
ENGINE:	Ford 296 Flathead
BUILD STYLE:	Vintage Hot Rod
OWNER:	Dave Simard

'30 Ford Model A Coupe

Just one glance at this low-slung '30 will tell you that this is an East Coast A Coupe. The heavy channel job is a dead giveaway – and even if this is the first book on hot rods you've read, you'll soon recognize the style as you leaf through the pages. There is more to this coupe than a channel job though. The cowl and doors came from a similar year model 2-door sedan; and if you were thinking that the unchopped top was high in relation to the body, that's because the body also has had a 3-inch section job taken from it. Look at the height of the rear tire in relation to the deck lid, as this is where it is most noticeable. The chassis has been "z-ed" by some eight inches in the rear in order to get the car low – and it adds to this look.

A traditional approach to the suspension components is evident with split wishbones visible

▼ Two visible components indicate this car is a contemporary build of a nostalgic car. One is the chromed alternator sitting high on top of the engine, and the other is the use of modern radial tires.

MAKE:	Ford
BODY STYLE:	5-window Coupe
YEAR:	1930
ENGINE:	292 ci Chevy V8
BUILD STYLE:	Nostalgia Rod
OWNER:	Bob Flagg

under the car. Also, the frame and running gear are all detailed in white with red accents, even on the brake plates. Aftermarket chrome shocks have been used for an added touch of sparkle. Moving back behind the grille, a '62 Corvette gave up its small block for the project and this has been bored out to 292 cubes and fully detailed. Although the headers have been built with a flange for a full under-car system, they are blocked off – and what you see is what you get in the loud noises department. A TH350 transmission handles the shifting chores from the Chevy engine.

'32 Ford Roadster

Firmly back in hardcore territory, Paul Varley's roadster could never be mistaken for anything else other than a hot rod! The body is not mint, but at the same time it doesn't appear rusty or too beaten up – and with a good coat of dark gray primer applied it certainly looks like it means business. A nice detail is the white firewall and matching white grille insert. These Deuce grille shells are often referred to as "filled," but this one is un-filled, i.e., it still has the original Ford badge in place, sometimes referred to as a "spoon," because of the shape. The Duvall-type, swept-back screen always adds a classic look to a roadster, harking back to the racy luxury sports cars of the 1930's that probably inspired the design.

This '32 is Chevy-powered, by far the most popular choice for hot rod power plants. But instead of a small-block, we have here a legendary 409 ci – as in the Beach Boys' "she's real fine, etc." (Why don't they seem to write songs about car engines these days?) Anyway, the unmistakeable valve covers of this series of engines have been chromed and two 4-barrels feed the beast, while the block has been treated to a liberal coat of red paint. Front suspension on the roadster features a swap-meet-find dropped tube, with disc brakes and a four bar rather than hairpins.

MAKE:	Ford
BODY STYLE:	Roadster
YEAR:	1932
ENGINE:	Chevy 409 ci V8
BUILD STYLE:	TraditionalHardcore
OWNER:	Paul Varley

◀ The Duvall windshield has been installed in its raw brass finish rather than being first dipped in the chrome vat.

'30 Ford 2-door Sedan

Only one way to describe this high-stepping "dirty thirty," and that's hardcore! Imagine seeing this looming large in your rear-view mirror one dark night – scary, uh! Well, maybe; but definitely cool! The bare bones sedan body has been stripped of its fenders and splash aprons – giving a whole new meaning to the term "highboy" – and sits atop the stock Model A frame rails. A '26 T axle with Buick drum brakes and a high-arched transverse leaf give the front end some altitude, not to mention attitude! A massive chop has been achieved by whacking out nearly eight inches from the lid of the sedan, the factory visor adding even more menace to the windshield area.

The engine has been deliberately installed high on the frame rails. This is enhanced by the addition of an Offenhauser plenum tunnel ram and a Weiand intake manifold. On top of this is the 4-barrel carb and chrome induction scoop. The engine is a 302 Ford unit and is painted and detailed with polished valve covers. The drag-style, sweptback headers look loud without even firing up the car – though it is a common trick to fit motorcycle baffles to these to subdue them a bit. Whitewall tires on black-painted rims and a set of beauty rims provide just enough hardcore glamor in the wheel department.

MAKE:	Ford
BODY STYLE:	2-door Sedan
YEAR:	1930
ENGINE:	Ford 302 ci V8
BUILD STYLE:	Hardcore Hot Rod
OWNER:	Willie G.

▸ When a hot rod looks as mean as this one, a shot of gray suede paint is all you need. The car itself makes the statement.

'33 Ford Coupe

Built as a Show Rod by Dave Puhl's House of Customs back in 1961, this '33 Coupe displays many of the way-out body mods that were typical of the day – with no innovation deemed too wild to be included. This White Pearl beauty features a chopped top that is hardly unusual on a hot rod. But what about that wild grille treatment, looking as if it was inspired by the nose of a circuit racer. The firewall is completely smooth and molded, and the body also features an abbreviated running board that doesn't look like it was ever meant to be stepped upon! Odd that the door hinges are still in place, given that, these days, we are so used to seeing rods with hidden hinges.

Quite apart from the bodywork, the engine alone is enough to grab your attention. It's a '54 Chrysler Hemi, polished and chromed to within an inch of its life. Further, it is fitted with a Weiand 6-71 supercharger and dual Edelbrock four-barrels. The custom-made chrome headers end in neat, flared bellmouth tips. A chrome and drilled I-beam resides under the rod and classic Halibrand rims with spinners are fitted all-round. The car is obviously a restored re-creation of the original, judging by the billet aluminum door mirror and brake back plates. Hot rodding artistic license at work.

MAKE:	Ford
BODY STYLE:	3-window Coupe
YEAR:	1933
ENGINE:	Chrysler Hemi V8
BUILD STYLE:	Show Rod
OWNERS:	Dan and Denny DeLara

◀ The stunning pearl paint is set off by the passion purple fogged stripe with aluminum finish insert. The block is painted to match.

'30 Ford Model A Pickup

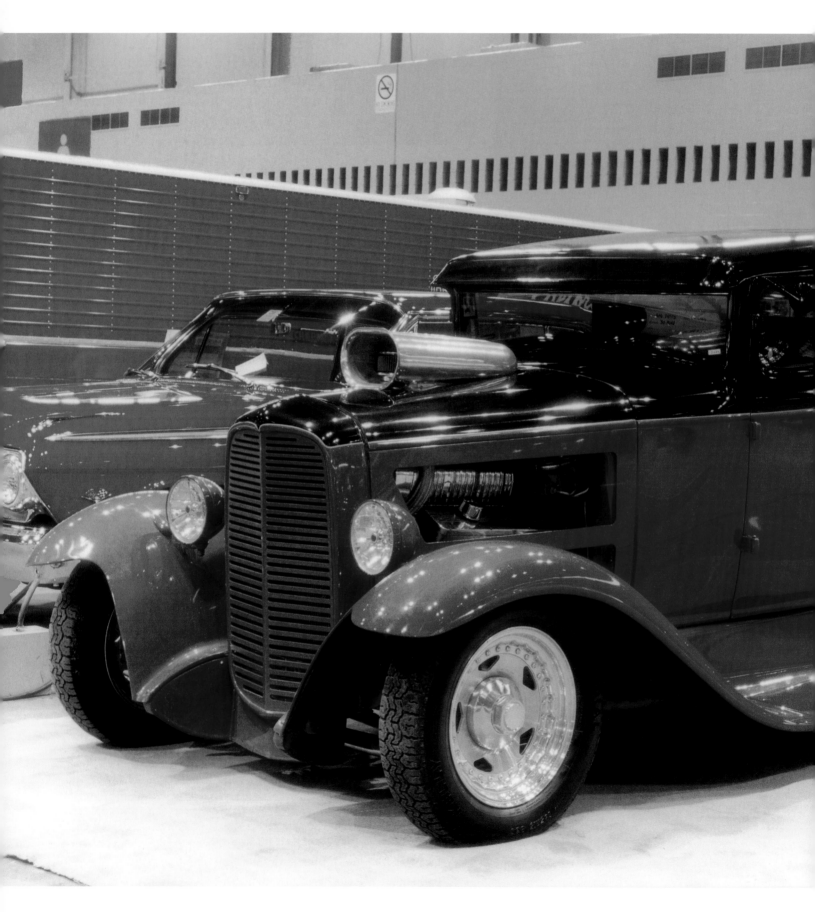

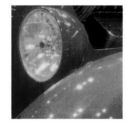

The Pro Street look really became popular on cars back in the 1980s, originally with the muscle car set and then spreading to the earlier hot rods. The intention was to give the car a look synonymous with the Pro Stock drag racing classes of the time. This meant big, race-inspired power plants under the hood. But more importantly, it also meant narrowed rear frames, allowing super-wide racing wheel-and-tire combinations to be squeezed under the stock body work. This Ford captures that look perfectly on a prewar body style. The chrome scoop and the big rear rubber confirm the race heritage of this style of hot rod.

A roof chop is obvious immediately and the Model A grille has been replaced with a custom deuce-style shell with molded insert and the hood sides are custom-built to show off the detailed engine within. That engine being, specifically, a dual-quad-equipped, small block Chevy, polished and detailed – and with a similarly polished B&M blower also installed. The polished headers lead to a short system, exiting in a large-bore pipe in front of the rear wheels. Talking of wheels, the fronts feature custom billet 5-spokes and the rears are a set of deep Convo-pro's.

MAKE:	Ford
BODY STYLE:	Closed Cab Pickup
YEAR:	1930
ENGINE:	Chevy Small Block V8
BUILD STYLE:	Pro-Street Rod
OWNER:	Emo Petito

◄ This style of contrasting split-color paint, with the heavier shade on top, was also very popular in the 1980's, tying in with the Pro Street build style of that era.

'33 Ford Victoria

First, you take one of the Downs Manufacturing's repro '33 Ford Victoria bodies. Then, have them create a custom lift-off top. Hey Presto! – you end up with a unique hot rod! This is the "Vickster." This Hollywood Torch red "slickster" features some of the very best tricks in contemporary hot rod design that are currently available. The suspension on the car features a fully independent system by well-known aftermarket manufacturer Kugel Komponents. Kugel is one of the top suppliers of these types of suspension units and their front I.F.S. setup is a sophisticated version of the popular Mustang II conversion. The rear system is Corvette-derived with Ford 9-inch internals.

Following the high-tech theme of the '33, the sedan is equipped with polished aluminum custom wheels from Billet Specialities. Billet aluminum, as a construction material, has become a key to a style of hot rods popular for many years now, with many and varied parts being replaced with items machined and polished from solid aluminum stock. The engine in this '33 features many such pieces, but standing out – literally – are the twin Paxton uperchargers fitted to the detailed small block Chevy.

▲ The hood sides of this '33 have been cut-out to give clearance to the twin Paxton superchargers protruding from each side.

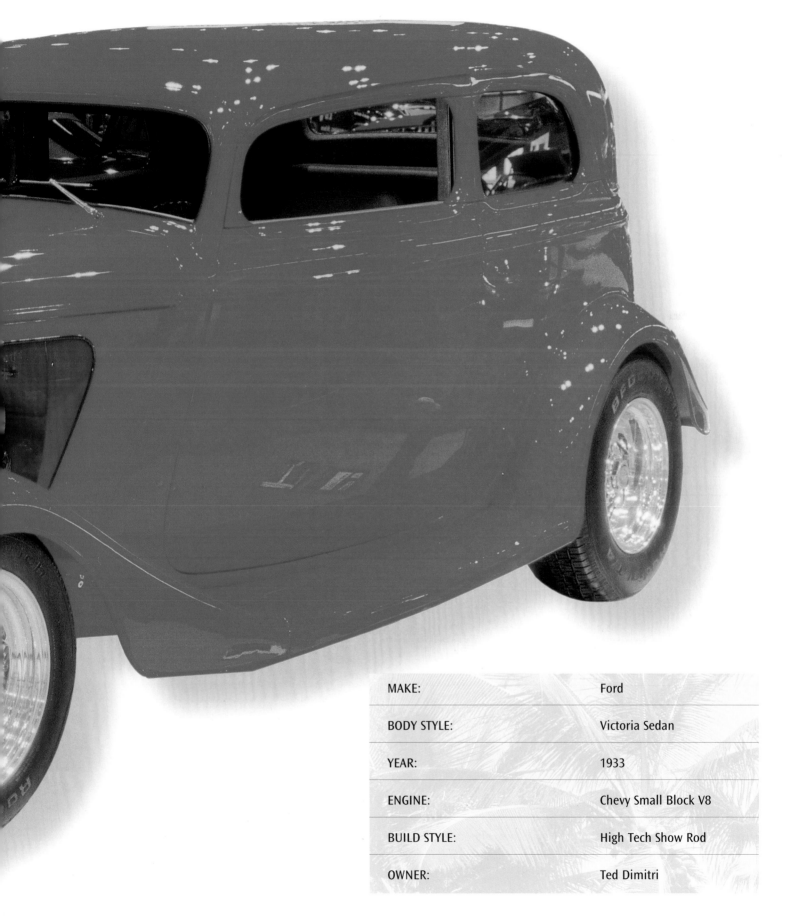

MAKE:	Ford
BODY STYLE:	Victoria Sedan
YEAR:	1933
ENGINE:	Chevy Small Block V8
BUILD STYLE:	High Tech Show Rod
OWNER:	Ted Dimitri

'37 Chevy Cabriolet

A '37 Chevy Cabriolet is a rare find in the hot rod world – but it is another one of those car designs that Detroit got right first time around, only needing a few subtle cosmetic changes to its overall design. As you can see, the sheet metal is virtually all stock in dimensions, save for a mild 1/2-inch chop to the windshield posts ready for the new top.

There's been some mild shaving of exterior doo-dahs to the doors and trunk lid – just to clean up the look – plus the fact that the running boards have been smoothed and painted. The stock headlights have been retained, but at the rear, '59 Cadillac taillights replace the usual small Chevy units. Porsche Guards red make the rod look even redder than a really red thing!

The stock chassis was boxed – and additional stainless tubing was added before the Ford 9-inch on parallel leaves was added out back. Then, Heidt Super Ride I.F.S., with dropped spindles, was installed at the front. The car is all Chevy, with a '70 Corvette mill displacing 350 ci and transmitting the power through a GM TH350 transmission. The 350 is dressed and detailed, with an Edelbrock High-Rise manifold and Holley 650 Double Pumper carburetor. A Crane Cam helps extract even more horsepower from an already potent engine.

MAKE:	Chevrolet
BODY STYLE:	Cabriolet
YEAR:	1937
ENGINE:	Chevy 350 ci V8
BUILD STYLE:	Street Rod
OWNER:	Bob Delia

◀ Highly-polished Budnik Gasser rims look great against the red Porsche paint. They are 16s on the front and 17s on the rear, with Good Year Eagle tires.

'31 Ford 3-window Coupe

We're not sure whether "Lucky's Speed Shop" is a real establishment or not; but we reckon you'd be feeling pretty lucky to be behind the wheel of this cool, fenderless Model A Coupe. The 5-window features a 5-inch chop and the roof insert has been left unfilled – or it certainly appears that way. The drilled sun visor is a nice touch, as early racers used to perform this trick to attempt to channel the air away from the flat windshield when the car was at speed. (Early aerodynamics at work?) The checker fire wall is another cool touch, although it's a painstaking job masking up all those squares! To dress up the otherwise plain steel wheels, this coupe runs a set of Oldsmobile Fiesta hubcaps, a style popular with rodders and early customizers alike.

The Chevy small block used here is a '64, 327 ci, with an Edelbrock tri-carb setup and a set of matching Edelbrock finned alloy valve covers. The chrome headers on the rod exit the engine T-bucket style – and rather than being capped and running to a full muffler system under the car, they end in the chrome turnout below the doors. Betcha it's loud!

A deuce grille shell adds interest up front, with the insert being painted white to match the whitewall tires. A set of '35 Chevy headlamps look good too.

MODEL:	Ford
BODY STYLE:	5-window Coupe
YEAR:	1933
ENGINE:	Chevy 327 ci V8
BUILD STYLE:	Traditional Hot Rod
OWNER:	Marc Olimpio

◀ The highboy look of this coupe is what you get when the body is left unchanneled on a stock A chassis.

▲ Check out the side-mounted gear shift lever outside the
body, and the chrome canister on the cowl, which is a
manually operated pump for maintaining fuel pressure.

'30 Ford Sprint Car

In some parts of the country, hot rodders sought inspiration from the weekly Sprint Car events held in their area. Running regularly from the 1920s onwards, such dirt-track races were the first introduction to grass roots auto racing for many young men. In the early days of the sport, the cars were almost exclusively powered by in-line 4's. In addition, much of the speed equipment for these long-stroke engines was developed for the Sprint scene. As was the case for most auto sports, the cars themselves suffered from a high attrition rate and few survived. However, this little Sprinter is a great example of the type of car that raced back then.

Often constructed on narrow Model T rails, the cars were built with single-seat aluminum bodies over traditional and readily-available early Ford running gear. This one seems to be running a Model A 4-banger with the stock cylinder head – although many companies, such as Ardun and Riley, offered overhead valve conversions for the Ford A and B engines. This one is fitted with a single Stromberg, but fitting twin jugs on a dual inlet was a quick way to hop up for more power. An alloy aftermarket finned side cover, with a tube breather, is also installed on this detailed 4-pot. The red finish on the engine is echoed on the vintage Kelsey Hayes wire wheels.

MAKE:	Ford
BODY STYLE:	Sprint Car
YEAR:	1930
ENGINE:	Model A 4-cylinder
BUILD STYLE:	Race Car

'31 Ford Model A Pickup

ere's a cool Model A pickup with an interesting story. It was originally built in 1961 up in Ontario, Canada, to compete on the North Eastern show circuit. That was until, for whatever reason, it was put into long-term storage. It was rediscovered some forty years later, still in its original show condition and is now enjoying a new lease on life on the road. A perfect snapshot of hot rodding during that period, it serves to show the way for rodders wishing to emulate that style. Just for a change, but popular back then for a spell, was the tall, unchopped look – although the fenderless rod still sits low, as the result of a substantial channel job.

Using white detailing to contrast the body color was a common trick too. Also, as well as plenty of white interior trim and whitewall tires, we see white used for the diamond-tuft roof insert and bed cover. The all-Ford running gear features, in the truck with a '46 Ford Flat engine equipped with Edelbrock cylinder heads, a 3-pot intake and three Stromberg 97 carbs. The engine drives through a '39 Ford transmission to a '40 Ford rear end on wishbones. Neat three-into-one, custom-made headers have been chromed and have survived well.

MAKE:	Ford
BODY STYLE:	Closed Cab A Pickup
YEAR:	1931
ENGINE:	Ford Flathead V8
BUILD STYLE:	Show Rod
OWNER:	Randy Kinville

◄ The original Sapphire Blue metallic still graces the exterior of this hot rod survivor – and note the custom insert to the Deuce grille shell.

'48 Fiat Topolino

 lsewhere in this book, there is a shot of a wild, street-driven Topolino. So, it seemed only right to show you the sort of car that inspired it. This little Fiat typifies what happens when you pass the point of no return for a street car and commit yourself to building a strip-only machine. The basic frame construction is very similar to many of the other cars in this book, and a traditional I-beam setup on hairpins provides more than enough stability for high-speed, quarter-mile runs. You'll notice though, that there are no front brakes fitted, as this class of car will use a parachute to slow it down on completion of its run.

A small block Chevy, with six deuces on top, shows that even drag racers can build nostalgia-flavored machines too. While almost too short to be called "headers," the exhaust gases exit unsilenced from the shortest pipes possible on each side. From the position of the steering wheel and roll cage, you can see that in a dragster like this, the car is constructed with a central driving position; no passengers allowed! Skinny magnesium 10-spoke, spindle-mount wheels are fitted up front, while wide 5-spokes are fitted at the rear with Mickey Thompson Drag slicks for maximum traction.

MAKE:	Fiat Topolino
BODY STYLE:	Replica Coupe
YEAR:	1948
ENGINE:	Chevy Small Block V8
BUILD STYLE:	Competition Altered
OWNERS:	Jack Brady & Jim Mahan

◀ While clearly a race-only machine, this Topolino Competition Altered can trace many features back to street-driven hot rods – and indeed, vice versa.

'32 Ford Roadster

So you want to know what a genuine East Coast hot rod would have looked like in the late 1940s? Well, here is the real thing. This '32 would have been a real hot shot in its day and its build style is a world away from what they were doing in California at the time. Built in 1949 by Shawmut Motors in Worcester, MA, the roadster features a very heavy channel over a 1940 Ford chassis, which seems to be relatively unaltered to receive its new light weight body. The doors have been welded up and feature cut outs to aid entry and exit – which also look to have been inspired by the British MG sports cars of the day that had the same shape door tops. Further European influence is evident in the shape of the windshield, although this is looks to be a raked item from a boat.

The Chevy 283 V8, with the Weiand 3-carb manifold, is obviously a later addition, as these engines weren't introduced until the 1955 model – some six years after this hot rod was put together. Judging by the virtually all-Ford content, it would almost certainly have been flathead powered back in '49. A stock '32 grille sits perilously close to the ground

and has probably scraped the asphalt more than a few times in its life! The rose metallic paint on the car seems to have survived well – and dig that ornate pin-striping design.

▾ Skinny black wall bias-ply tires are the same size on all four corners; and the wheels feature unidentified full chrome wheel covers.

MAKE:	Ford
BODY STYLE:	Roadster
YEAR:	1932
ENGINE:	Chevy 283 V8
BUILD STYLE:	East Coast 1940's Rod
OWNER:	Dick Kiusalas

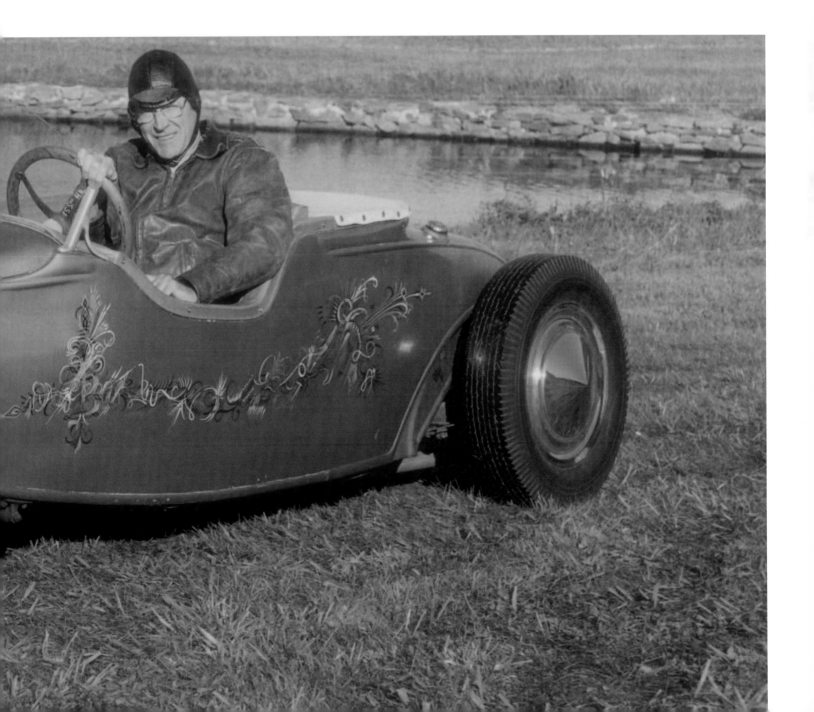

'27 Ford T Roadster

As long as hot rodders have known about the dry lakes out West, they've been building and taking their cars out to those wide expanses of salt flat in the quest for higher and higher top speeds. It started out with hopped-up, street-driven, Model Ts way back when. Then cars gradually became more and more race-prepped, until some evolved so far as to be barely recognizable from the original vehicle. This '27 is about midway in that grand scheme. It is still very much a '27 turtle deck roadster, but you wouldn't assume for a minute that it's a street-driven hot rod.

The T body sits squarely on a custom-fabricated chassis, with mounting brackets for the stainless hairpins locating the early style, dropped I-beam axle and transverse leaf. The engine is fully enclosed within an aluminum 3-piece hood, which, for aerodynamic reasons, is smooth and without any cooling louvers. Also, to aid top speed airflow, the cockpit is almost fully enclosed – save for the driver's seat and its safety loop. Up front, the Moon fuel tank is probably functional, unlike most street-driven cars, where it's usually just for show. A repro T-grille shell is almost the only chrome touch on the whole car.

MAKE:	Ford
BODY STYLE:	Roadster
YEAR:	1927
ENGINE:	Chevy Small Block V8
BUILD STYLE:	Lakes Racer
OWNER:	Bob Jepson

▶ The fully-enclosed Moon discs on the wheels are also aerodynamic aids and were first seen on Salt Lake cars – though they soon spread to street-driven hot rods.

'32 Plymouth Roadster

How many of you would have guessed at the origins of this cool little roadster? Did we say roadster? It actually started out as a '32 Plymouth Coupe, before having the top surgically removed by a very talented bodyman. Staying with the unorthodox build recipe, the body is sitting on a set of frame rails from a 1925 Dodge and this explains the very long front frame horns and the unusual parallel leaf front suspension. The grille shell is from a '33 Plymouth, and is the feature that probably first draws your eye to the car – well, that and those unique teardrop-shape headlights that appear to have come from a '32 Hudson.

As for the engine, no Chevy small block or flathead Ford for this baby. It is Caddy-powered by a '49 Cadillac 331 ci unit – one of the first overhead valve V8s to be mass-produced by Detroit – and it's fed by an Edelbrock 4-carb manifold, fitted with a quartet of 81-series Stromberg's. The engine is mated to a '53 Ford transmission, with an overdrive unit. In turn, this feeds the power down to what is probably the newest part of the running gear – the Ford 8-inch rear end. I guess even an unusual roadster like this had to have a Ford part in the mix somewhere!

MAKE:	Plymouth Coupe
BODY STYLE:	Roadster
YEAR:	1932
ENGINE:	Cadillac 331 ci V8
BUILD STYLE:	Traditional
BUILDER:	John Willis

◄ Not black this time, but a very dark coat of Washington Blue provides the understated finish – though it still goes great with the red rims and whitewalls.

'27 Ford T Roadster

There must be a hundred ways to build a Model T hot rod – and here's yet another. This low-flyer not only has the original body and cowl section, but also keeps the original sloping rear turtle deck body work. This hot rod has been built using a set of Model A frame rails, the original reason being that A rails were wider and so made a V8 conversion easier than on the narrow T rails. Early Fords had a wishbone-style suspension system that pivoted from a central point under the car; but hot rodders were quick to improve on this setup and "split" the wishbones, mounting each half on, and parallel to, the frame rails. You can see these clearly, painted red on this car.

An early Chevy 327 V8 provides plenty of power for this roadster; and it is another hot rod using an Edelbrock dual carb inlet, topped with a pair of Stromberg 97s. A set of shortie headers dump the gases out each side of the car. A Model A grille shell is used, painted suede black to match the low-key, low-shine finish on the car. The windshield posts are also painted black and a full size, early steering wheel is mounted on the column in the "cockpit."

MAKE:	Ford
BODY STYLE:	T Roadster
YEAR:	1927
ENGINE:	Chevy 327 V8
BUILD STYLE:	Traditional Hot Rod
OWNER:	Mike Karol

▼ Just enough red detailing is used on the engine and suspension to match the red steelies and whitewall tires. It was early cars like this that coined the phrase "hot rods" in the very first place.

'30-31 Ford Roadster

Pay attention gang, because this one is complicated. Rather than use an existing body, builder and owner Pete Flaven used the cowl from a '31 Ford Vicky and the rear body section from a '30 Ford Sedan (with the roof removed) to create this early style-modified roadster. The body, having been built, it was then set on a boxed Model A frame with an 8-inch kick-up added to the rear to get it sitting low. Once the body was in position, it was given a 7-inch channel to get it even lower. Using the rear section of a 2-door sedan meant there were no doors to weld up either. A one-off, custom windshield was made for the cowl, before the body work was shot with a cool, vintage, metallic gold color.

▼ Typically East Coast in style, the attention to detail and careful selection of period parts means that you'd be hard pressed not to know this car wasn't built back in its day.

Everything used on this car is either home made or constructed from existing old car parts, with nothing store bought! For example, the rear end is a '48 Ford Banjo axle with '36 Ford radius rods and a Model A spring; and the fuel tank mounted out back is from a 1930 Chevy with home-made mountings and hold-down straps. The owner also fabricated his own taillight stands too. Foregoing V8 power, this rod has a '55 Chevy six-pot installed with a 2-speed Powerglide transmission. Of course, the 235 ci six is adorned to the hilt with period dress up parts.

MAKE:	Ford
BODY STYLE:	Roadster
YEAR:	1930-31
ENGINE:	Chevy 235 ci In-line Six
BUILD STYLE:	Traditional East Coast Rod
BUILDER:	Pete Flaven

'32 Ford Roadster

This beautiful period '32 is recognized as one of the top surviving 1950s Show Cars on the East Coast and was originally built by Norm Wallace. Having said that, the car has always seen plenty of road miles as well. So, in terms of our categories, it's a true "Show and Go" all-rounder, since it's not short on hot performance goodies either. Displaying the typical East Coast, full-on channel job and Deuce grille shell, this roadster also features neat fenders on all four wheels, which sit pretty and snug to the tires. This is often a subtle indicator of a well-built car as any true hot rodder knows.

The car is loaded with neat details, including chrome nerf bars (front and rear), chrome I-beam and hairpins, plus many other chromed suspension components.

▼ Another neat touch that is easily overlooked is the trio of gauges let into the panel on the lower fire wall, just above the steering column.

The steel wheels are painted to match the body color and are dressed with a set of full-size Oldsmobile Fiesta hubcaps. We mentioned performance; and the '32's engine demonstrates the ultimate in Flathead speed equipment for a street driven hot rod in the 1950s. The V8 is fully maxed out and detailed – with a set of Edelbrock heads, a Scot blower fed by twin Stromberg's, and chrome everywhere. Truly, this is a piece of living history.

MAKE:	Ford
BODY STYLE:	Roadster
YEAR:	1932
ENGINE:	Ford Flathead V8
BUILD STYLE:	Show and Go
OWNER:	Larry Hook

Belly Tank Lakester

We couldn't bring you a book on hot rods without including at least one Belly Tank Lakester. These are just about the most minimal – and certainly the most aerodynamic – hot rods ever devised and were built exclusively for use on the salt lakes to achieve maximum top speeds. They consisted of a chassis constructed from chrome-moly round tubing and clothed in a streamlined shell of a military-surplus belly fuel tank discarded from the aircraft industry. This one debuted at Bonneville in 1951 with a 296-inch blown Flathead and ran 188.284 mph first time out. In this case, the body shell is from a World War II P-38 Lockheed Lightning 315-gallon tank that was lengthened by 14 inches – but a mere 36 inches wide – and had a custom fairing built to cover the driver's head.

This Lakester has had many engine combinations in its time on the salt, but this latest incarnation features an Oldsmobile 303 ci V8 that's been de-stroked to 260 ci and fitted with a Winfield cam and '57 Olds heads. Much of the build has been credited to Tom Beatty, who not only cast the aluminum manifold and designed the belt drive for the GMC 6-71 blower, but did the ground-up engine build as well. Six Stromberg 97s feed the Olds' engine and power is transmitted through a '56 Olds' 4-speed Hydromatic to a Halibrand V8 quick-change center section.

MODEL:	Oldsmobile
BODY STYLE:	Belly Tank
YEAR:	Timeless
ENGINE:	Oldsmobile 260 V8
BUILD STYLE:	Lakes Racer
OWNER:	Dave Simard

◄ This Lakester has run 243.438 mph, setting a record in the process for the B Lakester class back in 1962 at Bonneville.

'34 Ford Roadster

This very cool, 1950s-looking roadster has been built in the old-school style, but using the best of the brand-new traditional parts that are on the market today. Starting with a new chassis from Cornhusker Rod and Custom, a Super Bell dropped I-beam and hairpins were supplied by well-known rod shop Pete'n'Jake's, along with a set of So-Cal Speed Shops finned Buick drum kits that hide a conventional disc setup. Currie Enterprises supplied the 9-inch Ford rear end, which is hung on ladder bars and Aldan rear shocks. With an all-new rolling chassis under the car, it made sense to install a new engine too. So a Chevy ZZ4 crate engine was installed along with a Tremec 5-speed transmission.

The all-steel Ford body, meanwhile, has received a 2-inch chop and had the screen posts laid back before receiving the ten coats of midnight black gloss paint. A new white convertible top contrasts dramatically. Tasteful red-and-white pinstriping has been laid on, echoing the red-and-white theme set by the steelies and wide whitewalls. The '50 Pontiac taillights have always been a favorite with hot rodders, and this roadster has them. Finishing the deal is a tasteful, dark red leather upholstery job with rolled pleats – just like in the old days.

MAKE:	Ford
BODY STYLE:	Roadster
YEAR:	1934
ENGINE:	Ford Flathead V8
BUILD STYLE:	Traditional Hot Rod
OWNER:	Dave Helmer

◄ This awesome Roadster shows that it's possible to build a cool, traditional car using virtually all-new parts; such is the current appeal of nostalgia.

'36 Ford Coupe

There's nothing wild or fancy here, just the classic curves of one of Ford's classiest pre-World War II designs – the '36 Coupe. Elegant in its simplicity, the '36 retains its stock sheet metal right down to the hood trim, the mirrors and wipers, and the door handles – with just a lowered lid to add just the right amount of street credibility. The fenders are stock and so are the rubber running boards, so often smoothed over and painted on more contemporary rods. The Halibrand alloy slot mags have a classic look of their own. These were once one of the most popular styles of aftermarket wheels before the onset of a myriad billet designs.

The '36 Ford, with its styled grille shell blending into the hood and fender sheet metal, represents a real turning point in Ford's prewar styling. No more did the grille shell serve just as a housing for the radiator, it now seemed part of the overall design and immediately gave the car its character. It also began the short period of elegant "Art-Deco" styling that touched many areas of design in popular American culture. At this point in history, the USA led the world in car design.

MAKE:	Ford
BODY STYLE:	3-window Coupe
YEAR:	1936
ENGINE:	Chevy Small Block V8
BUILD STYLE:	Street Rod
OWNER:	Ralph Lisena

▶ This Coupe needs nothing more than the right suspension updates to get the right hot rod stance – plus wheels, tires and the roof chop to get the hot rod look.

'32 Ford 3-window Coupe

If ever a hot rod personified the immortal lyrics from the pen of Brian Wilson, then this one does. For this is most definitely "a little deuce coupe with a Flathead mill." Whether the builders of the '32 used that Beach Boys sung-about car for inspiration, we don't know; but it sure turned out that way. The chassis is the original Ford frame with many updates, including the hot trick of using a Model A front cross member which serves to mount the dropped and drilled – not to mention chromed – axle. All traditional, early Ford parts have been used to create this masterpiece in nostalgia – and far too many to list all of them here, unfortunately. But one can safely say that only the best has gone into this project, from the full-house '48 Flat engine to the '40 Ford rear axle.

Nash Bermuda Blue metallic gets the looks in the paint department and the white roof insert adds terrific contrast, as does the painted fire wall. The grille shell has been filled and a set of '40's Chevy taillights bring up the rear in fine style. If stance on a hot rod is everything, then this rod says it all, with the car sitting with just the right nose-down rake to mean business. We're used to seeing plenty of chopped '32s, so a stock height example done so well makes a refreshing change.

MAKE:	Ford
BODY STYLE:	3-window Coupe
YEAR:	1932
ENGINE:	Ford 276 ci Flathead V8
BUILD STYLE:	Traditional Nostalgia Rod
OWNERS:	Ray and Matt Kinnunen

◀ A set of unpolished American 5-spokes set the mood on this "Li'l Deuce Coupe" – and they look a million bucks when combined with the wide whites.

'32 Ford Roadster

Originally created in 1946 by young Californian Jim Khougaz, this roadster was built to compete both on the lake beds and be Jim's transport on the street. Competing in the SCTA's C Lakester class during the late 1940s, a best top speed of 141.95 mph was achieved with the car running on methanol fuel. To get this phenomenal speed from a street roadster, Jim employed many ideas ahead of their time, including much use of aerodynamics. To get the car as close to the ground as possible and in order to cheat the wind, the car was channeled a total of 7 inches over the frame and the chassis was kicked up 3-inches out back. In addition to this, Jim constructed a full-length, 11-piece aluminum belly pan to further streamline the underside of the car.

It was recently fully restored by Dave Simard and staff at East Coast Custom, Leominster, MA, to the standard that you see here. Of course, the restoration had to match the original quality of work that was well above the standard of the day when first completed. This meant that the rod just had to have a full-on '47 Mercury block filled with

goodies from Messrs Edelbrock, Winfield & Stromberg and a transmission full of Lincoln Zephyr gears as per the original. Front end was always a 4-inch dropped I-beam on '35 Ford split 'bones – and it was fully chromed too, even way back in the 1940s.

▼ It's difficult to appreciate the 500 man-hours that went into re-creating the full aluminum belly pan on this low flying '32, but you can see part of it under the front frame horns.

MAKE:	Ford
BODY STYLE:	Roadster
YEAR:	1932
ENGINE:	Ford Flathead V8
BUILD STYLE:	Lakes Hot Rod
OWNER:	Mark Van Buskirk

'33 Ford Roadster

When it comes to building a smooth, high-tech highboy, the '33 body style is always a favorite for innovative hot rodders. This car goes one step further, however, by using a Speedstar body from '33-34 specialists Rats Glass. The Speedstar is a stylized, slicked and stretched version of the Model 40, available as either a Roadster or Coupe body. The Speedstar was designed by innovative and talented rodder Bobby Alloway, who also built the chassis for this car. As a departure from the regular design, this black beauty uses a laid-back, stock chrome grille rather than the molded version that normally comes with this body. Check out the neat and discreet nerf bar protecting the lower edge of the grille shell.

For a high-tech hot rod, independent suspension is a must – and the '33 features a Heidt front end and a Zipper Motors unit at the rear, all polished to perfection. While name-dropping some of the industries high rollers, let's not forget the Boyd Coddington billet alloy wheels wrapped up in super low-profile rubber. Also, 502 cubes of big block Chevrolet power serves up the horses in the roadster, though only the polished headers are really visible under the stretched hood. The cream top installed on the car is a custom fabbed, lift-off number – a pop-top, as they've become known.

MAKE:	Ford/Speedstar
BODY STYLE:	Roadster
YEAR:	1933
ENGINE:	Chevrolet 502 V8
BUILD STYLE:	Show Rod
OWNER:	Jim Hubbell

◀ The Speedstar interpretation of the classic '33 Roadster is easily recognized by the stretched hood and the rounded windshield corners.

'32 Ford Coupe

Using the old hot rodders premise that you can never have enough horsepower, this Coupe takes that mantra to another dimension. It has not one, but two huge, polished GMC huffers mounted on a custom dual inlet – and a blower drive setup that can only be described as a work of art. On top of the each blower is, yet again, a custom manifold, angled to ensure the four-by-four-barrel carbs are mounted on the level. Somewhere underneath is a fully-detailed big block Chevy rat engine that even boasts polished aluminum cylinder heads! Meanwhile, two huge, hungry scoops suck vast quantities of air into the thirsty engine. Finally, an awesome pair of Funny Car-style "zoomie" headers are left to dispense with the unwanted exhaust gases.

The Electric Yellow high gloss finish extends from the grille shell, engine block and carb bodies, throughout the 3-window Deuce body work and right underneath to the Pro-street '32 frame. The detail of the hot rod's undercarriage can be appreciated by the strategically-placed display mirrors beneath the car. Thanks to these, the fully polished Currie Enterprises third member can be clearly seen, as well as the fully-chromed drive shaft. The unusual stylized flames on the sides would be best viewed with the car in profile, where they give the impression of being emitted directly from the headers.

MAKE:	Ford
BODY STYLE:	3-window Coupe
YEAR:	1932
ENGINE:	Chevy Big Block V8
BUILD STYLE:	Show Rod
OWNER:	Larry Gould

▶ Has anyone thought to ask the driver what the forward vision is like, while sitting behind this super-sized, supercharger setup?

'30 Ford Coupe

A traditional rod doesn't have to mean only cars built with a strong 1940s and 1950s image . The hot rods of the early 1960s displayed some very cool trends as well – as we can see from this cool Model A coupe. Radir Tri-Rib alloys are a hallmark of a 1960s influenced ride, especially when used with a set of whitewall "cheater" slicks and matching whitewall front runners. A well-proportioned chop and channel job provide a purposeful stance – and bring the A down out of the breeze and back to street level in Coolsville. A filled Deuce grille shell hangs between the front frame horns, adorned with some funky pinstriping, and a ribbed roof panel replaces the old fabric insert of days gone by.

A small block Chevy has been stroked out to 355 cubes in this Coupe, with chromed original equipment tin valve covers making a welcome change in engine "dress-up" items. The crowning glory, though, has to be the polished BDS 6-71 blower, topped with twin Holleys, and that wicked custom air scoop color matched to the House of Kolors green "flake" paint accented by simple but neat flames. A polished alloy fire wall panel finishes off a nicely detailed engine compartment. Talking of details, check out the pinstriping on the front frame rails too.

MAKE:	Ford
BODY STYLE:	Coupe
YEAR:	1930
ENGINE:	Chevy 355 ci V8
BUILD STYLE:	Traditional Nostalgia Rod
OWNER:	Dan Souza

▸ Harking back to the pin-up art of the 1940s, but not looking out of place for a minute, is the "Hot rod Bettie" with the car's moniker "L'il Whiner" on the cowl sides.

'32 Ford Roadster

Stand by your beds, men; wild paint is back with a vengeance! Especially if Ron Coco's swirly '32 is anything to go by. The fact is, there are plenty of great Deuce highboy's out there in showland, and if you want to get noticed you better think of something innovative to make yours stand out some. This smoothie achieves it with a red-and-yellow faded paint scheme reminiscent of a badly mixed Tequila Sunrise – but like the cocktail, it sure packs a kick. The smoothed-out body features neither hood louvers, handles or even side mirrors to avoid diverting your eyes away from the trick finish, which extends down and into the frame rails and also into the door jambs and shuts.

The suspension on the roadster is aftermarket and fully independent, both front and rear, ensuring the low slung rod handles as well as it looks. Billet Specialties wheels fit the bill, with 20-inch polished rims at the driving end and a set of similar 17s at the steering end. A Duvall-style screen keeps the wind out of the light tan, rolled leather cockpit, where Westach gauges fill the dash and keep the driver informed of vital signs. A small block Chevy provides the power and sends it out through a Phoenix-built 700 R4 transmission.

MAKE:	Ford
BODY STYLE:	Roadster
YEAR:	1932
ENGINE:	Chevy Small Block V8
BUILD STYLE:	Show Rod
OWNER:	Ron Coco

▶ Every once in a while someone builds a car with some wild innovative features to wow the troops. This '32 roadster is one of those cars.

'30 Model A Sedan

MAKE:	Ford
BODY STYLE:	2-door Sedan
YEAR:	1930
ENGINE:	392 Chrysler Hemi V8
BUILD STYLE:	Hot Rod
OWNER:	Jack Higgins

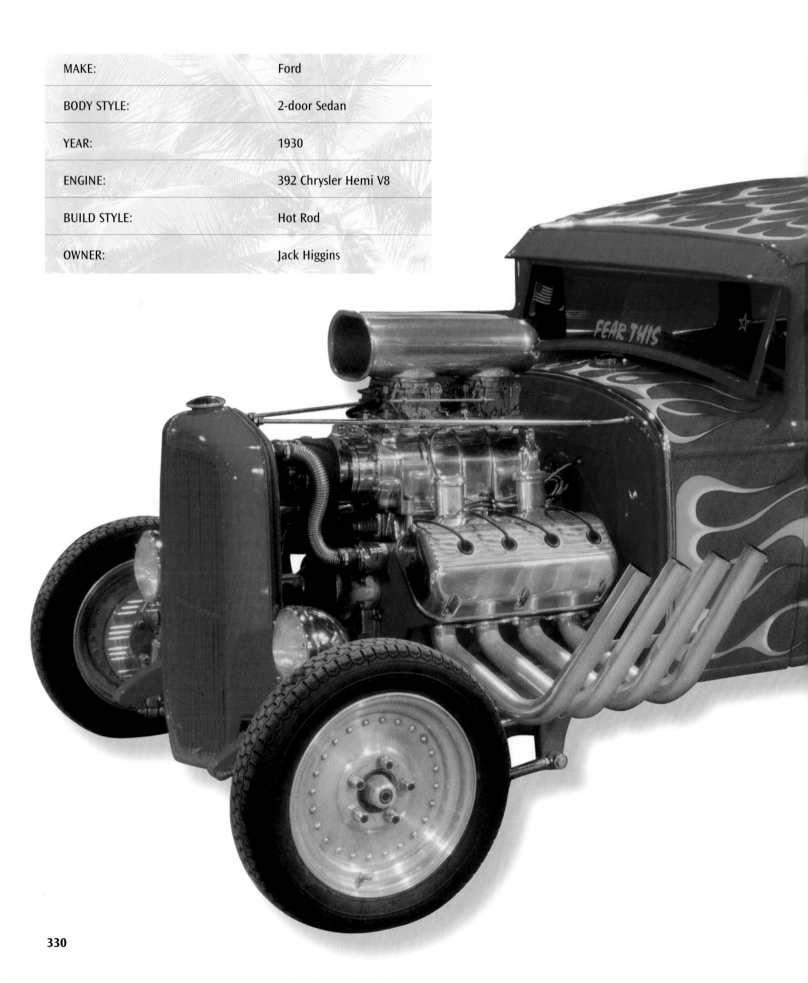

Here's a recipe for one wild sedan. Take a mild-mannered Model A body and hammer the top, hard. Then take same body and slam it down on the narrowed rear frame until well and truly channeled to taste. Baste complete body in Orange Twist for flavor, including '32 truck grille shell and chassis, and then turn up the heat until flames are licking at all sides including the top. Leave until it looks real cool and ready for some serious motive power. For presentation, add a set of competition-style centerline wheels, preferably skinnys up front and ultra deep dish at rear, wrap in new black rubber treads and serve. Magnifique!

Cordon bleu hot rodding aside, an engine that looks like it was lifted almost straight from a Top Fuel dragster is bound to get your hot rod noticed, and this dirty thirty is no exception. A big, bad blown 392 Hemi with a BDS compressor gets the job done with a pair of Edelbrock 4-barrels providing the juice. Spent gases exit via a radical set of custom zoomies packed with Harley-Davidson baffles to dampen down the decibels. Suspension details include a narrowed rear axle to tuck those big meats into the tubbed rear body, and a four-bar suspended I-beam at the front.

◄ A car like this is bound to attract attention from all sides. No wonder it was awarded a trophy at a local car show entitled "Car Most Likely to be Pulled Over."

'35 Ford 2-door Sedan

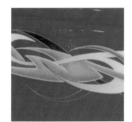

Overlooked for many years by early hot rodders, somehow the '35 model year Ford has neither quite the visual impact of the '33-34 Model 40 that came before, nor the smooth art-deco looks of the '36 that followed it. That's not to say that '35s don't make tasty street rods, as this super Sedan testifies. Several gallons of Fire Engine red cover this car, from the monochromatic grille, through the shaved doors and smoothed running boards to the trunk lid. The side panels of the hood keep their punched louvers, however, and a complex but cool graphic adds extra interest to, and breaks up, the acres of rouge. Custom mirrors have been added and painted body color and the only brightwork remaining are the chrome headlamps and the Weld Directional, 3-spoke billet wheels.

Power for the sedan is pretty standard street rod fare in the form of a warmer than stock 350 Chevy small block V8, TH350 transmission and an 8-inch Ford rear axle for comfortable and reliable long-distance cruising. The interior is a good place to be for a cross-country jaunt too, with air-conditioning installed in the custom dash, plus a pair of cloth-covered bucket seats trimmed in a pleasing tan color. Hot rods like this are built to cruise, and this '35 gets to many shows over the summer, judging by the NSRA and Goodguys membership decals on the windshield.

MAKE:	Ford
BODY STYLE:	2-door Sedan
YEAR:	1935
ENGINE:	Chevy 350 ci V8
BUILD STYLE:	Street Rod
OWNERS:	Dwight and Pauline Winter

▶ The monochromatic paint with graphics, tweed interior and billet wheels displayed on this '35 are typical rodding trends of the 1980s, but are still popular today.

'34 Ford Coupe

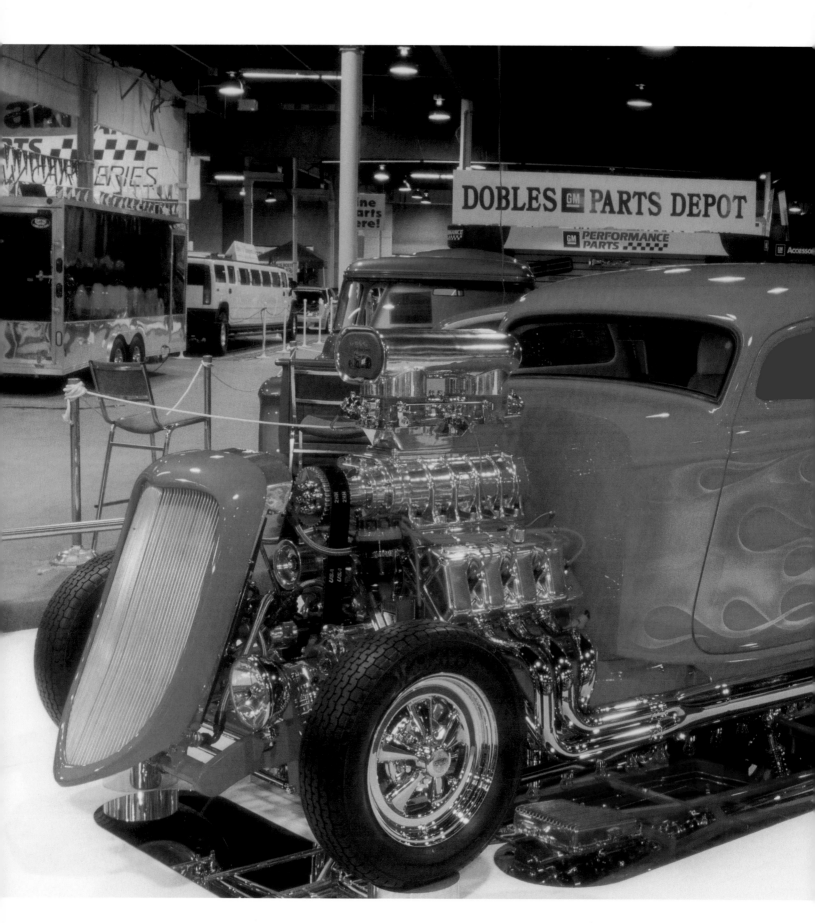

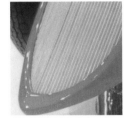On the show circuit, this jaw droppin' Coupe is known as "In Excess" and it's not hard to see why. Centerpiece for the '34 has to be the unusual and exotic choice of a big block Ford 429 engine. The 429 was introduced by Ford for use in competition in 1968 and featured canted over valves to create larger ports in the head. It was almost a Hemi and a close look at the valve covers hints at this design. The 429 here has not only been detailed to show standard but has been bored out to 433, before being endowed with a huge capacity 14-71 Huhl Blower and a pair of massive Holley 1050 Dominator carbs. To accommodate this huge engine and its beefy blower drive, the whole radiator assembly has been shoved forward, resulting in the smooth grille shell being stuck way out further than normal.

A custom tube chrome moly chassis has been constructed for the coupe and can be seen in the display mirrors. Front end is an independent setup featuring chrome coil over shocks on custom chassis mounts. A big engine means big horsepower, and this means fitting big tires! The fat Hoosier rubber in this case being fitted to a set of classic Cragar S/S chrome rims. Keeping it chrome, the four-into-one headers flow into long Lakes pipes, neatly filling the gap between the wheels.

MAKE:	Ford
BODY STYLE:	3-window Coupe
YEAR:	1934
ENGINE:	Ford 429 V8
BUILD STYLE:	Show Rod
OWNERS:	Pat and Laura Gauntt

◀ House of Kolor Tangelo Pearl is the finish of choice, with Silver Pearl for the flames blending in nicely with the base color.

'34 Chevy Coupe

Chevrolet were somewhat up against the ropes in the volume market sales stakes in the early 1930s. This was because Ford had recently introduced their popular and affordable Flathead V8, while Chevy stuck to their guns with their "Stovebolt" six, which would continue for a couple more decades. Chevy did steal a march on Ford, however, by introducing independent suspension in 1934, although the solid axle remained an option until 1940. Harley Earl and his designers also revamped the range, resulting in the crisp – if somewhat conservative – design seen here.

This classy '34 keeps the flag flying for the Bowtie brigade in the prewar street rod class, the "Cheebie" retaining its original features like stock height top, roof insert and cowl vent – but making up for it with high gloss red paint, smooth running boards and pinstriped hood sides with those three long side vents each accented by a single pinstripe. The front end has been cleaned up with the removal of the fenders and hood emblem and turn signals now live where the fender irons used to extend from the front frame horns. A few "go-faster goodies" on a 350 Chevy small block with '63 'Vette Powerglide transmission keep this rod all GM.

MAKE:	Chevrolet
BODY STYLE:	3-window Coupe
YEAR:	1934
ENGINE:	Chevy 350 V8
BUILD STYLE:	Street Rod
OWNER:	Ed Paraday

◀ Is there a car out there that doesn't suit Cragar S/S 5-spoke rims? If there is, it certainly isn't a red '34 Chevy Coupe.

'32 Ford Coupe

Many rods are built as nostalgic pieces. These are the cars that take their owners back to a simpler time. Some are the hot rods they dreamed about in school, but never got to build – but this one is the real thing and is still true to each last nut and bolt. Even the tires are the originals. As the Don McLean song told us, the tragic plane crash terminating Buddy Holly's career was sad news to rock'n'roll fans, back in 1959, when this cool '32 first hit the street and drove to the levy. Apart from the small block Chevy which was still relatively new (and so rare in the wrecking yards), the hot ticket was a big Oldsmobile V8, which was already 10 years old and famed for its power and tuning potential.

Joe Englert's '32 3-window runs just such a engine and – true to its day – is hopped up with an Edelbrock 3-hole intake and three Stromberg 97s. The V8 is dressed with chrome air cleaners and chrome tin valve covers. But that's as far as it goes, as even the stock Olds cast-iron exhaust manifolds are still on there. In true East Coast style, the body features a hard channel over the frame rails, coupled with a major slice out of the roof pillars. A filled Deuce grille shell completes the body work on the fenderless period piece.

MAKE:	Ford
BODY STYLE:	3-window Coupe
YEAR:	1932
ENGINE:	Oldsmobile V8
BUILD STYLE:	Traditional
BUILDER:	Joe Englert

◄ It's a source of constant amazement to old school rodders how many original old hot rods survive unmolested from several decades back. How many more are out there?

'36 Ford Coupe

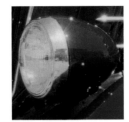

The year of 1936 was the last in which Ford built their Coupe body in a 3- or 5-window style for the home market. But why was that? They resumed the business coupe body style for 1940 onwards, as we well know. Anyhow, the true-blue, 5-window right here is a fine example of Henry's handiwork. The body work on this baby is as stock as a rock and as cool as they come – the reason probably being that the owner Dave LeFebre has owned the car since 1959 and hasn't the heart to cut it up, thank goodness! When you look at the straight body and the deep reflection in the side panels, you just know that it was the right thing to do.

Don't let the mild exterior fool you, though, for under the hood of this Coupe is a tarmac-ripping, Buick Nailhead, with 425 cubes of torquey horsepower. To keep the Nailhead's thirst quenched are two Holley four-barrels, easily mounted on the stock manifold since the Buick came with dual quad's from the factory anyway. Dave regularly bangs gears courtesy of a Muncie 4-speed transmission, which sounds like fun to us. Interior comfort is well catered for with a stunning white hide interior and headlining.

MAKE:	Ford
BODY STYLE:	5-window Coupe
YEAR:	1936
ENGINE:	425 ci Buick V8
BUILD STYLE:	Street Rod
OWNER:	Dave LeFebre

◀ All that's needed is set of highly polished American Racing Equipment 5-spokes and a lowered stance to trick out this '36 for the street.

'32 Ford Sedan Delivery

Due to being used-and-abused commercial vehicles back in their day, Deuce Deliveries are rare models to find. So, what to do? Well, you could create your own from an unloved 4-door sedan, as has happened here; no kidding I mean, can you see the join? Once you're done welding up the rear doors, save yourself some time and install a pair of 2-door sedan front doors to keep the proportions right too. The reworked body sits high on a stock height frame and I-beam, which has been detailed just enough in lime green gloss to match the grille insert and the wheels.

A "Ford in a Ford" is the mission here, and a small block from Henry's stable is installed between the frame rails, the block being painted in the same Lime Green as the other details on the car. A 600 cfm Edelbrock carb is all that's needed to keep this high-revving engine humming, and an old set of alloy valve covers is good enough for engine dress-down. Big stock headlights are mounted off the chassis at the front, and there are some neat bullet turn signals of unknown origin mounted to the grille shell. Brightwork on the suede body is limited to the door handle, the wiper arm and the solitary aftermarket peep mirror.

MAKE:	Ford
BODY STYLE:	Sedan Delivery
YEAR:	1932
ENGINE:	Ford Small Block V8
BUILD STYLE:	Hardcore
OWNER:	Jack Murphy

▶ Tall steelie rims wear '42 Ford hub caps, and that lime green sure looks good against the wide whitewall bias ply tires.

'40 Ford Sedan

When Henry Ford uttered his famous words about black-painted cars, we doubt that he was thinking about, or envisaged, a mean black Ford quite like this bad boy '40 Sedan.

It takes a brave man to attempt to whack a large slice of metal out of a car so successfully, with such a curved roof as one of these, and still get the proportions right. But the builder of this Sedan managed it. Using many tricks from the customizers handbook, the car was also nosed, decked and shaved of all emblems and trim. The screen has been V-butted too, for a clean look. Also, body parts that are normally bright but couldn't be shaved (we're talking about the grille and headlamp rims mainly here), have been de-chromed and painted instead.

Obviously, some major frame and suspension work has gone into this car to get the nasty, low stance right on this Ford. The favorite method has to be one of the many excellent aftermarket front units based on the Mustang II setup and that provide superior road holding and ride characteristics necessary for a big cruiser like this. A set of Centerline Auto-Drag wheels are an inspired choice, adding a heavy competition image to the tough 2-door. Inside, we can tell you that a cool, gray tweed interior indicates that this was a car built in the 1980s, maybe early 1990s, when such trims were at their most popular.

MAKE:	Ford
BODY STYLE:	2-door Sedan
YEAR:	1940
ENGINE:	Chevy 350 V8
BUILD STYLE:	Street Rod
OWNERS:	Paul and Dorothy Horton

▶ An interesting variation on the flame theme is the simple red belt-line design applied to the black sedan, running front to back, then tapering down the rear quarters.

'48 Austin Devon

These diminutive British imports, with their light weight and short wheel base, made them popular choices for the gasser racers of the 1960s – until different class rules and fiberglass replacement bodies virtually ended the traditional gas classes. It was inevitable that some of these cars would end up as street rods; maybe this '48 4-door Devon Sedan is one of them. Now adopting a much more contemporary and mean Pro-Street stance, the Austin chassis is long gone and is now replaced with a full custom tube frame. The body has been fully tubbed out in order to take the big Mickey Ts; and an all-new floor and fire wall have been built too.

To accommodate the Chevy small block that now powers the little Austin, the driving position had to be moved rearward; notice the position of the seat in the photo. The 350 concerned has also benefited from a Holley carb on an Edelbrock Victor intake, a Crane Cam and Mallory ignition. A Turbo 400 sits between the new frame tubes, and links to a severely narrowed 9-inch rear end. Front suspension is now a 4-inch drop tube with 40 Ford spindles and Vega steering. Much of the body work, prep and paint were carried out by the owner in his home garage.

MAKE:	Austin
BODY STYLE:	Devon 4-door Sedan
YEAR:	1948
ENGINE:	Chevy 350 V8
BUILD STYLE:	Street Rod
OWNER:	Kevin Robbins

▸ A rare Street Rod, even on its home soil in the UK, these little Austins make for truly cool hot rods.

'38 Ford Convertible

The Ford model year of 1938 was very similar to the '37 models, but without the more clearly defined grille design. Maybe because of this, '38s are not as common as hot rods as the 39-40's and, latterly, the '37s. This convertible custom gets around this by use of a novel, yet subtle, custom grille treatment. The topmost bars of a '38 extend back into the hood sides anyway, but this one goes further by blending them way back – almost the full length of the hood. By painting them body color, as per the factory finish, you'd swear that they were always that way! The sign of a good custom modification is something that stops and makes you ask the question – and this purple pavement prowler does just that.

▾ Wild flames lick all around the hood, fenders and sides of this pearl purple paint job; starting off white, they fade into yellow and red with blue highlighted tips. Cool.

The late great '38 has a maximum chop windshield with V-butted glass and is nosed, decked and shaved. Otherwise, chrome body details have been color-coded, such as the side mirrors and headlamp rims. The iron holes have been filled and running boards smoothed and small aftermarket turn signals have been added to keep it all legal.

The only chrome visible is the baby moon caps and beauty rings on the red-painted steelies and a super-low stance completes the custom rod.

MAKE:	Ford
BODY STYLE:	2-door Convertible
YEAR:	1938
ENGINE:	Chevy 350 V8
BUILD STYLE:	Traditional Custom Rod
OWNER:	Bill Cooper

'39 Chevy Master Sedan

Proving that it's just as possible to make a killer-looking hot rod from a fat fendered "stovebolt" Sedan is this hot '39. The big cruiser has had a wicked chop top to the curved roof and the V-butted windshield has been laid back at a less steep angle. Custom hood sides have been built, with the trademark Chevy bowtie emblem incorporated in the sides; and the running boards have been smoothed with cut outs made for the exhaust. The fenders, handles and emblems have been shaved but the stock headlamp buckets remain. The complete car has been covered in PPG Brute Yellow, with wild flames added fading between orange and yellow.

Big Centerline Convo-Pro rims, with the unique ribbed dished rims, pack out the rear arches of this Pro Sedan, thanks to a narrowed rear frame, tubbed body and narrowed 9-inch Ford rear-end. A common chassis upgrade for the front of these bigger rods was the fitting of a complete front "clip" from a Camaro or similar GM car, providing – at a stroke – modern disc brakes, power steering and engine mounting hardware. These days, aftermarket independent front suspension units are available to do the same job, but are an even easier swap. A big sedan needs a big power and a blown Chevy rat engine coupled to a TH400 transmission is installed in this one.

MAKE:	Chevrolet
BODY STYLE:	2-door Sedan
YEAR:	1939
ENGINE:	Chevy Big Block V8
BUILD STYLE:	Pro Street Rod
OWNER:	Bob Sapienza

▶ A big hot rod already, this Chevy sedan looks even bigger – thanks to the bright color – and longer, thanks to the radical roof chop.

'33 Ford Coupe

If you are well versed in your hot rod history, there will be no prizes for guessing where the inspiration came from for this radically chopped and stream-lined Lakes-style coupe.

Both the So-Cal Speed Shop and the Pierson Brothers, also of Southern California, ran similar '34 Coupes at the lakes in the early 1950s – though only as competition cars; their window apertures were even smaller than this street driven version. Having said that, the lid is as low as legally possible – allegedly the height of a dollar bill on end – and the minimum allowed. Both of those cars ran a Kurtis "track nose" grille. This one has that too, although the grille is slightly taller to increase cooling capacity to the engine.

Four double rows of louvers are punched into the deck lid for that old timey race car feel, and the car runs a Halibrand quick-change rear axle for further authenticity. Obvious concessions to modern driveability are the telescopic and coil-over shocks fitted front and back, plus disc brakes and a full lighting system. These considerations aside, the use of painted steel wheels, bias ply tires and the overall stance are enough to be a respectful homage to those famous race cars. Actually, considering their fame, surprisingly few hot rods have been built in this street car style, so it's refreshing to see this one.

MAKE:	Ford
BODY STYLE:	3-window Coupe
YEAR:	1933
ENGINE:	Ford Flathead V8
BUILD STYLE:	Traditional Lakes Coupe
OWNERS:	Roger and Linda Pythila

◀ Although its heritage is obvious, the Deep Purple metallic paint is individual enough to state that the builder wasn't trying to build a copy or clone with this car.

'27 T Roadster

Now, this is the sort of old Ford your grandpappy would instantly recognize as a "Jalopy," as a '27 T body on a set of '32 rails. It is one of the oldest hot rod double acts going. Guys were slinging these light weight "Tin Lizzie" roadster bodies onto V8 frames in search of the ultimate speed machine back when dinosaurs ruled the earth (well, maybe not quite that long ago, but you get the idea!). Dig the full-height windshield and red oxide paint, with racing number, on this roadster re-creation from the first half of the 20th century.

A vintage V8-60 period piece powers the T, complete with finned Edelbrock cylinder heads, a 2-pot intake and a pair of Stromberg jugs size 81 to go! We're willing to bet there's Potvin or Harmon and Collins bumpstick in there as well. The finned cylinder on the firewall is an early custom alloy coil cover, a popular dress-up accessory – as are the pair of Stelling and Hellings chrome air cleaners. A simple, upswept Lakes pipe takes the gas away from the 3-branch exhaust manifold on the block. A dash of color is provided by the red-painted Kelsey-Hayes wire wheels, with early bias-ply tires.

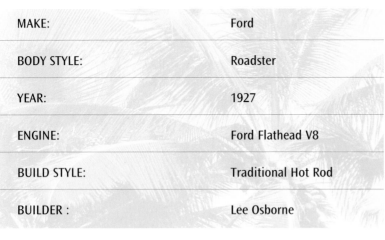

MAKE:	Ford
BODY STYLE:	Roadster
YEAR:	1927
ENGINE:	Ford Flathead V8
BUILD STYLE:	Traditional Hot Rod
BUILDER :	Lee Osborne

▸ A small detail, yet absolutely correct for this car, is the S.C.T.A sticker discreetly placed on the firewall of the Lake Style T.

'49 Chevy Pickup

These fat Chevy pickups are really popular with both hot rodders and the custom pickup crowd They were made from the late-1940s through to 1954 and since we don't know the exact year of this one, we'll let it under the wire and call it a '49. Truth is, there's been so much custom work on this truck that it doesn't matter what year it is! Where do we start? A full custom smooth truck bed has been built, incorporating molded rear fenders, and this blends into the cab body that looks like it's had a roadster conversion done and now uses a fabric soft top. Smooth running boards replace the old ribbed ones and the front fenders have been opened up and reduced to swoop the lip down to the front fender edge.

Just about everything on the body has been smoothed and filled, until only the Chevy's five bar grille remains as an original bolt on fixture. Late-model, semi-elliptical headlamps have been molded in place of the old ones. These look possibly like Mercedes-Benz units that have recently been adopted by some customizers. To finish off, there is the truck's radical treatment; a scorching yellow paint job has been applied with black and orange accents. Subtle it ain't!

MAKE:	Chevrolet
BODY STYLE:	Pickup
YEAR:	1949
ENGINE:	Chevy 350 V8
BUILD STYLE:	Custom Truck
OWNER:	Derek Martindale

▶ We're willing to bet there's a set of air bag's hiding under those fenders, dropping this truck way down over its big billet rims.

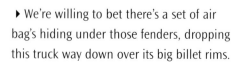

'34 Ford Coupe

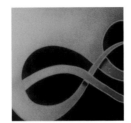

A world away from some of the high-tech '34s that grace these pages, this all-steel, 5-window is, instead, just pure bad boy attitude. Basically, anything that wasn't necessary on this car to make it run hard and fast has been junked. The top has been chopped 3 inches and the body slammed down over the frame too – with the lack of fenders and splash aprons turning it instantly into a wicked highboy coupe. The '34 grille covering the radiator almost looks like an afterthought, although the car would lose some of it's identity without it. Certainly, the car is well turned out; but something about it lets you know that it was built to be driven – hard.

Halibrand slot mags provide virtually the only polished bright-work, apart from the detailed small block. A big set of Hoosier rear tires give the coupe a wide footprint on the street. That small-block up front is dressed up with a set of polished alloy valve covers and a street-tough Weiand blower. Carburetion is via a pair of chrome Holley's, with a matching shiny air-scoop. Just visible behind the Cooper front tires are a set of wild zoomie headers pointing skywards.

MAKE:	Ford
BODY STYLE:	5-window Coupe
YEAR:	1934
ENGINE:	Chevy 350 V8
BUILD STYLE:	Hot Rod
OWNER:	Dave Anderson

◄ Aah – black 'n' flames! Some things just never go out of style on hot rods, and this car will still look as cool in another 25 years at least!

'35 Ford Roadster

When there's a rod shop with your own name above the door, you better have something special as your own ride, in order to "wow the troops" and to serve as a rolling testimony to your own special skills. Down at Tucci Engineering in Marcy, New York State, they have this wild '35 "Phantom" roadster to fly the family name. A fiberglass body is wrapped around a steel tube frame, with hand-made aluminum stretched around front end hood and side panels. The running boards are steel for strength, and the stretched and laid back '35 grille is also hand-formed stainless steel. Can't place those headlights? Well, they're Harley-Davidson V-Rod units, the sloping lens blending in perfectly with the overall design.

With a super smooth body devoid of any mirrors, handles or anything else for that matter, it's left to the big-inch rims to provide the "bling" on this slick puppy. The 20s and 17s, respectively, are a one-off design made especially for this car, and they ride on a set of Falken rubber bands tires. Air Ride Shockwaves provide a remotely controlled wireless suspension system, hence that ground scraping stance. A brand new Ford Motorsport 351 mated to a Tremec T5 transmission provides the power for Tucci's copper creation, and this turns the Lincoln Mark VIII rear end between the back wheels.

MAKE:	Tucci/Ford
BODY STYLE:	Phantom Roadster
YEAR:	1935
ENGINE:	Ford 351 V8
BUILD STYLE:	Smooth!
BUILDER:	Dave Tucci Jr. and Co.

▶ In a true case of East meets West, the finished body was shipped out to Seattle for the Candy Copper paint by Rich Thayer of RJ Customs and the upholstery, in black, was stitched by Jamie McFarland, also of Seattle, Washington.

'34 Ford Coupe

There's a tendency in life to look back at the past in black and white or other muted tones, since much of the images we see from those times are presented that way. Many traditional rods, when built, almost reflect this with black, red oxide and gray suede, etc. But hey, they did have colored paint back then, too – such as the Sikkens Pale Blue finish here, that although flattened to lo-shine or no-shine, makes a refreshing change. The stock height rumble seat coupe has been channelled 6-inches, but otherwise appears pretty much as Henry intended, less a few fenders, etc. The Frenched aerial on the rear quarter is a nice period custom touch.

A '50 Ford has given up its Flathead for the nostalgic Coupe, stopping only long enough in the workshop to receive a detail job, an Isky Jr. camshaft to bounce those side-mounted valves around and a Weiand triple intake manifold with three Stromberg 97 carbs. A simple but cool Lakes pipe exhaust looks great, with some white high-temp paint and a chrome tip. Back in the day, a 3-speed would have shifted the cogs, but since you can't see it, a T-5 transmission does the job here without spoiling the old school image.

A Ford 8-inch rear end and a set of '48 Ford brakes are also included in the package.

MAKE:	Ford
BODY STYLE:	5-Window Coupoe
YEAR:	1934
ENGINE:	Ford Flathead V8
BUILD STYLE:	Traditional Hot Rod
OWNER:	Al Lemieux

▸ A set of '40 Ford "ripple" hub caps set off the cream painted steel rims and the wide whitewalls. Not just cool, but triple cool!

'29 Model A Sedan

A traditional style A sedan set up in the style of the late 1940s, but with a definite modern attention to detail and finish. (Were they ever this clean, back then?) Very definitely not channelled, this 2-door is sitting up there on its rails just as pretty as you please. A tan roof fabric replaces the original top, a feature that often gets replaced with fresh steel on more contemporary cars. In timeless fashion, a Deuce grille shell sits up front along with a spun ally Moon tank. A few louvers have been added to the hood top in case this sedan ever runs with its hood side panels in place. The cowl has been filled too; the original fuel tank on a Model A was behind the dash, with the fuel filler in front of the windshield.

A set of Offenhauser finned aluminum cylinder heads dress up and improve performance from the Flathead. Further, and true to the period, the favorite hop-up item, the 3-pot intake for a multi-carb setup is here. The exhaust headers finishing in a long, polished cone tucked in to the chassis rail – a neat and very cool touch on this A-bone. The running gear stays with the early theme, through to the Halibrand quick-change rear axle and unsplit rear wishbones. Ford hubcaps and bias-ply tires set just the right mood on the axle sets.

MAKE:	Ford
BODY STYLE:	2-door Sedan
YEAR:	1929
ENGINE:	Ford Flathead V8
BUILD STYLE:	1940's Traditional
OWNER:	Randy Dalaiso

▶ In harking back to the era when whitewalls were mainly only found on luxury cars, the tall black wall tires are definitely the way to go.

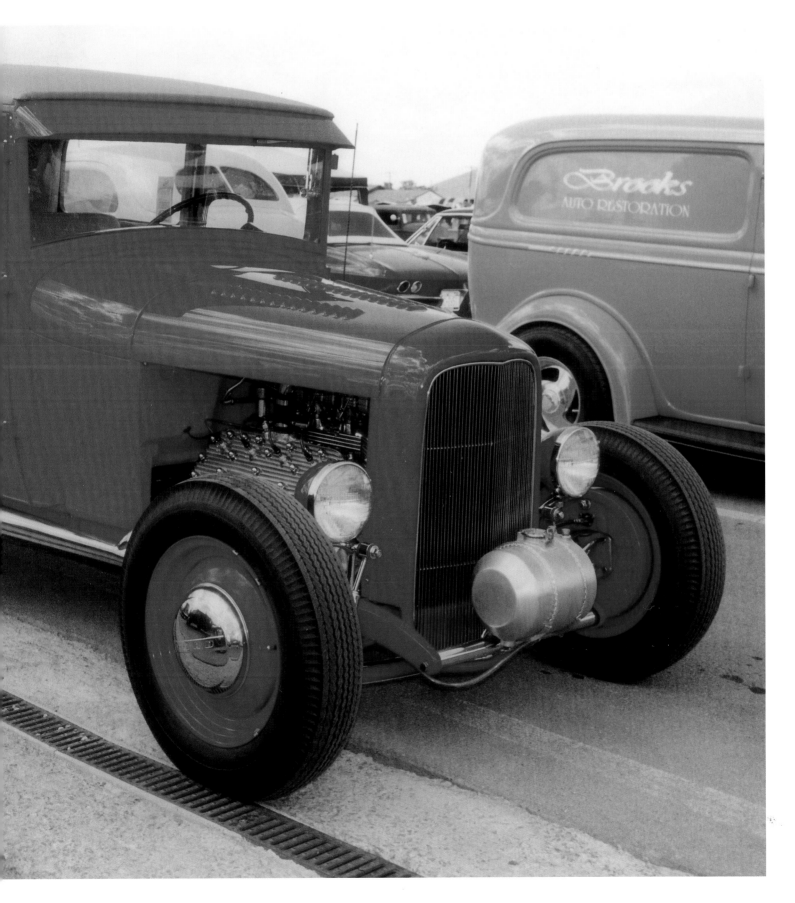

'27 Ford Roadster

The "27" racing number on the door of this Lakes T roadster not only hints at its competition past, but also indicates the year of manufacture – though any true rodder would know that! This is a restoration of a well-known car that spent much of its life out West on the dry lakes and salt flats. It was restored back in the early 1970s. That's well ahead of the current nostalgia craze for bringing back from the dead significant early hot rods and race cars. It looks like someone was well ahead of the game!

As you'd expect from a genuine early Lakes car, the T runs a full-on Flathead Ford V8 with Offy cylinder heads, with the three scoops poking through the hood indicating the usual three-carb setup. The "no nonsense," homemade Lakes pipes relieve the engine of its spent gases. Demonstrating early concessions to aerodynamics, the body is channeled over the frame, which is completely hidden from view thanks to a fully louvered belly pan. A track nose gives this rod a distinctive look; these racy front panels were usually hand-formed from aluminum. This one has a neat grille installed – but of unknown origin.

MAKE:	Ford
BODY STYLE:	T Roadster
YEAR:	1927
ENGINE:	Ford Flathead V8
BUILD STYLE:	Traditional Lakes Roadster
BUILDER:	Bud "Flathead" Jones

▸ Coral paint work sets this roadster apart from the crowd and a half-height T windshield, headlights and nerf bars complete the "street trim" for this dry Lakes old timer.

'29 Ford Roadster

This gorgeous '29 Roadster is not only right on the money in respect of looks and finish, as it also runs an early Hemi, which would have made it a car definitely not to be messed with back in its day! The Dodge engine is a Red Ram V8, just as fitted to many big-finned sedans throughout the 1950s. Take it out of a 2-ton car and drop it into a light-weight roadster like this, and you have one wild ride. The big V8 is fully detailed with chrome valve covers and carbs, plus a Vertex magneto and Offy three-carb intake. A cool power plant indeed!

The flawless Teal metallic body sits on a similar matched '32 frame, pinched at the cowl to match the lines of the Model A cowl. The bulkhead is painted white in typical 1950's style. This always looks good, with white interior trim and wide white tires. A filled Deuce grille shell completes the look. Underneath the frame, early Ford running gear is evident in the form of un-split wishbones and lever-arm shocks. The dropped I-beam front axle is fitted with Ford juice drum brakes and big 16-inch steel wheels wear tall bias-ply treads.

MAKE:	Ford
BODY STYLE:	Highboy Roadster
YEAR:	1929
ENGINE:	Dodge Hemi V8
BUILD STYLE:	Traditional Hot Rod
OWNER:	Bob Jepson

▸ The construction and finish on this '29 is well thought out. For example, the gold paint on the engine is also used for the running gear underneath the car.

'32 Ford Coupe

Here is another veritable blast from the past. This '32, 5-window was built (as its style suggests) back in the late 1950s. It was used and shown for a few years before going into storage in 1964 and wasn't seen again until 2003, when it wowed the crowds at the Ty-Rods Old Timers Reunion on the East Coast. With a really heavy 11-inch channel job and a 4-inch slice from the roof, this rod's profile runs well below the radar. Narrow bias-ply whitewalls run on chrome reverse rims all-round, with whitewall Cheater slicks fitted out back – of course! Mercury hub caps provide a un-fussy clean look to the rolling stock.

As if this wasn't enough vintage eye-candy, how about the '49 Cadillac overhead valve V8 nestling between the frame rails. The big GM engine is detailed to the max, and fed by six carbs on an Offenhauser intake manifold. Polished valve covers and a chrome water pump add extra interest to the Caddy mill, which is reflected in the polished fire wall on the cool coupe. The Maroon red lacquer on the hot rod is the original and, although cracked and aged, looks all the more genuine because of it.

MAKE:	Ford
BODY STYLE:	5-window Coupe
YEAR:	1932
ENGINE:	Cadillac V8
BUILD STYLE:	Traditional
OWNER:	George Veracka

◀ This must have been quite a show-stopping car in its day, with its attention to detail. Take, for instance, the interior featuring period white trim with red buttons to match the exterior theme.

'40 Ford Coupe

Once again, proving how cool a '40 Ford Coupe can be with just a few mild custom touches is this fine flaming forty. Simple, but classic, yellow flames fade to orange and contrast against the lipstick red gloss and are separated by a fine pinstripe. Most of the original brightwork trim is retained on this car, though the fenders are plain. The 1940's models often had fender guards or "over-riders" either side of the centrally mounted license tag. Here, the plate has been moved to the right-hand iron. A chrome peep mirror is an aftermarket piece added to the door pillar.

The fiery rod is greatly enhanced by its lower stance indicating chassis and suspension work has been carried out to get the car lower than stock. The stock rims have been replaced with some chrome reverse numbers sporting baby Moon hub caps, with white bands. Inside, an aftermarket, dash-mounted rev counter hints at than a performance capability greater than the flathead that would have been originally fitted. Staying on the inside, the car is upholstered in black and red rolled pleats for added cruising comfort.

MAKE:	Ford
BODY STYLE:	2-door Coupe
YEAR:	1940
ENGINE:	Chevy V8
BUILD STYLE:	Traditional Street Rod
OWNER:	Donna Mondello

◂ In case you were in any doubt, a subtle script mounted on the grille confirms that this is indeed a hot rod. The license tag confirms the owner's initials and the model year of the Coupe.

'23 T-Bucket

A real Model A chassis was selected as the basis for the frame for this T, the owner spending many hours narrowing, shortening and boxing the rails in order to get the correct dimensions for the body to be mounted. A full-height screen and original-style cowl lamps add to the vintage look. Some T-buckets run fenders, some don't; it all depends on the local state vehicle building regs. In this case, J.C. Whitney items came straight out the catalog to conform with the regs. A custom grille surround was constructed to enclose the '56 Chevy radiator used to keep the Chevy engine cool and give the T its unique look. A 42-48 Ford axle has been drilled and chromed and installed up-front, suicide style, while a '57 Chevy does the job out back.

There's a strong "bowtie" theme running throughout this car, with a '59 Chevy 283 providing motive power – although it's been taken out to 292 cubes by being bored .060 over. A solid lifter cam, '55 Corvette spec has been fitted, with a Mallory dual point providing the spark. Apparently, the owner of this car has many induction combinations available to fit to this car, but it's shown here with an Offenhauser six-deuce intake fitted with half a dozen Holley 94's. Unusually, the hot roadster runs a stick-shifted, three-speed transmission from a '56 Chevy. The shifter itself is a rare piece; a vintage vertical-H shifter. Such a shame that we can't see it here.

MAKE:	Ford
BODY STYLE:	T-Bucket Roadster
YEAR:	1923
ENGINE:	Chevy 292 V8
BUILD STYLE:	Street Rod
OWNER:	Carl Libucha

▶ Whitewalls mounted on chrome reverse rims add flash to the red and white detailed running gear on this '23 T.

'32 Chevy Coupe

No-one said that just because you have a boxed Model A frame at hand that you had to use a Model A body for your hardcore hot rod. Why not install a perfectly good '32 Chevy body instead? You'll still end up with a cool ride, as we can see here. Just chop the top as you would have done anyway and give it a channel as well. The difference is that this body was massaged back in the 1950s, before finding a new lease on life on the street in the 21st century. The vintage steel body also features a '27 Chevy truck fire wall and a '38 Ford truck grille just to keep the early parts spotters busy!

Adding to the list of donor vehicles is the Rocket engine from a '51 Oldsmobile, equipped with the perennially-favorite Edelbrock 3-pot manifold – this time equipped with a trio of Ford 94-series jugs on top. A short set of Lakes pipes end where they stop for maximum loudness and presence. The engine is nicely detailed in red and white along with the chassis and suspension details too. A '40 LaSalle transmission shifts all three gears down to a '57 Chevy rear axle. The newest parts of this hot rod are the oil in the engine and the fuel in the tank!

MAKE:	Chevrolet
BODY STYLE:	5-window Coupe
YEAR:	1932
ENGINE:	Oldmobile V8
BUILD STYLE:	Hardcore Hot Rod
OWNER:	Roger Miret

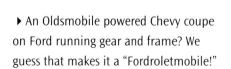

▶ An Oldsmobile powered Chevy coupe on Ford running gear and frame? We guess that makes it a "Fordroletmobile!"

'34 Ford Coupe

Packing plenty of vintage race car features, and more louvers than you can shake a stick at, this cool coupe is a well-known hot rod up in the North East. The awesome nostalgic attitude, plus the distinctive "She Bad" license plate, makes sure that this car is "once seen, never forgotten." The 5-window Model 40 features a roof chop that's radical enough to turn the screen into a letterbox aperture – although the screen still winds out for some early air-conditioning. The grille shell has been filled and once resided on the front of an old fire truck before being radically re-worked with a Lakes-style louvered insert instead of the stock mesh. The chassis has been "z"-ed at the back to create that wicked rake.

The front end features Buick finned drums on Ford brakes on a very low dropped axle. Then, a Frankland quick-change rear end makes the back view of the hot rod as cool as the front one; there's a two piece louvered belly pan under there too. A more unusual feature is the tubular nerf bars in front of the rear tires. These are more often found on sprint cars or dirt trackers, but look right at home on this '34. In addition, note that the door hinges, while still on the outside, have been streamlined and blended into the body and, keeping with the competition theme, expensive aftermarket wheels have been forsaken for this car, in favor of a set of classic Moon wheel covers.

MAKE:	Ford
BODY STYLE:	5-window
YEAR:	1934
ENGINE:	Ford 302 V8
BUILD STYLE:	Traditional Hot Rod
BUILDER:	Sam Samson

▶ The bright orange color makes sure this car stands out in any line up, the red flames and red detailing on the frame adding an exciting contrast.

'34 Ford Coupe

If this car looks familiar, it's because it has been built to closely resemble a very well-known alcohol burning race car, known as the "Mooneyham and Sharp" coupe. The stance, choice of parts, as well as the wheels and the paint color, all pay homage to the original. However, so as not to be a complete clone and to add his own identity to the car, the rod's lettering clearly states that this is Charlie Padula's '34 – and, of course, it was built by Charlie's own rod shop. Also, the original bore the race number 554, instead of 334. The car was so cool, however, that this particular re-creation is a very welcome sight at any rod gathering.

It doesn't look like it would take much to put this car back on the street, only the lack of headlights and street legal tires defining it as a strip and show only car. (We also happen to know that there's another just like it on the street in the UK, but that's another story.)

A chopped top and plenty of louvers in the trunk lid are the only obvious body mods, although a hole has been carved in the hood for the chrome air scoop. A drilled I-beam is located by a cool set of stainless hairpins, and the headers exit the engine compartment just behind the hairpin brackets on the chassis. A set of wheelie bars are installed out back to maximize hard launch potential.

MAKE:	Ford
BODY STYLE:	5-window Coupe
YEAR:	1934
ENGINE:	Chevy 406 Rodeck V8
BUILD STYLE:	Replica Race Car
OWNERS:	Charlie Padula

▸ The unpolished American 5-spokes are tougher than tough, especially when wrapped in Good Year Eagles and M&H rubber, front and back.

'30 Model A Roadster

The great thing about the hardcore movement of late is the ability of those involved to scrounge up parts from wherever and put together a real cool car on a limited budget, using know-how and canny swap meet skills. By using original old parts that other high buck rodders discard, some real sweet rides are hitting the black top, if hardcore is your thing. This A-bone roadster is as simple as it gets in its construction and concept, but in itself is as cool as they come. Fenderless and proud of it, it wears an unfilled deuce grille shell – and who needs a hood anyway! So the steel wheels are different colors, is that going to stop you grinning from ear to ear as you zip down the street in this jalopy? I thought not!

The small block Chevy engine will guarantee that the roadster certainly does "zip down the street," it'll probably leave a couple of black lines at the stop light too. The engine is decidedly un-detailed and the alloy parts are "as found" in finish. Of course, you still got to have three "deuce" carbs on a three-jug manifold, anything else just wouldn't cut it, well, except for maybe even more carbs! Interior comfort is limited to a pair of oxblood colored, well-worn bucket seats and a set of rubber mats. Once again, what else do you actually need?

MAKE:	Ford
BODY STYLE:	Roadster
YEAR:	1930
ENGINE:	Chevy V8
BUILD STYLE:	Hardcore Hot Rod
OWNER:	Jared Brouillette

▶ A couple of swap meet finds adding interest to the roadster, are the period "Guide" headlamps, and the big diesel truck horn on the right-hand frame rail.

'31 Ford Roadster

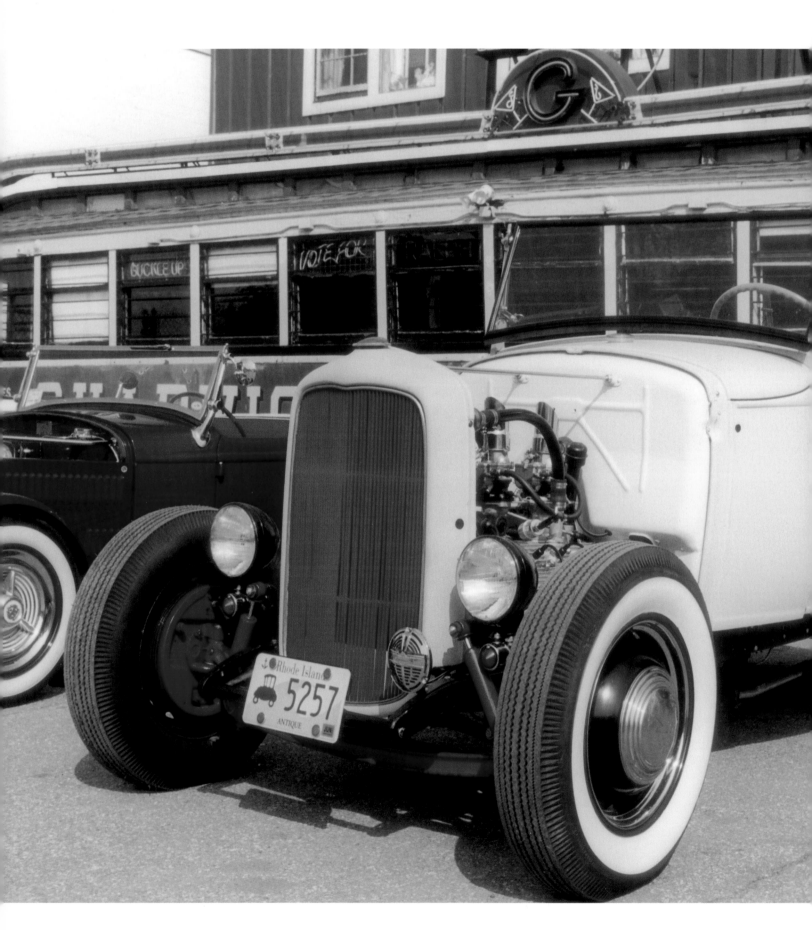

'31 Ford Roadster

When folks talk about old houses and properties, they often talk about "olde worlde" charm – it's an indefinable term that means more than just "old" and encompasses a good feeling and warmth about the subject. This terminology is not often applied to vehicles; but if it were, then this Model A "Jalopy" would have it in spades. Not sure if it's the cream anti-gloss finish or the tall tires, but this late-1940's-style roadster just makes one long for time gone by, spent hanging out at a postwar root beer stand or working Saturdays at the local gas station. Strangely, this even applies even if you weren't old enough to have actually been there!

Romance aside, this nifty roadster is more than just a pretty picture of days gone by. With a V8-60 power plant equipped with Edelbrock finned aluminum heads, and an Eddie Meyer intake with a pair of Stromberg 81s, this car was built to haul in fine style. Everything chassis-wise sits at stock height and the Henry-designed original wishbones remain un-split. The tall, bias-ply whitewalls contrast with the black rims and Ford hubcaps. But what happened at the back? Reckon he had a flat on the way to the show and had to fit the spare?

MAKE:	Ford
BODY STYLE:	Roadster
YEAR:	1931
ENGINE:	Ford Flathead V8
BUILD STYLE:	Traditional Jalopy
OWNER:	Koby Borodkin

◄ A Deuce grille shell with painted insert is typical of the era; but did you spot the 1940's Harley-Davidson horn mounted on the front frame rail?

'32 Ford Roadster

Originally purchased in 1951 for $35, this real-steel '32 took teenager Fred Steele around four years to build into the sweet ride it still is today. What's more, he still owns it. The 6-inches that measure the amount of channel on the body is also the same amount taken out of the windshield posts and the grille shell, and these are just some of the reasons the proportions on this roadster are so "right." Of course, even back then, an expert choice of the best parts money could buy helps lots too. A dropped Dago axle on unsplit 'bones, later Ford hydraulic brakes and Houdaille shocks all make up the running gear on the early hot rod, most of this hardware having seen the inside of a chroming vat before installation.

Despite the above-average finish and attention to detail for the period, this isn't just a good looker. It has the brawn to match the beauty. This comes in the form of a full bored and stroked, ported and relieved '48 truck block with all the goodies. A full race Iskenderian cam keeps the valves jumping and a Sharp intake with two Stromberg 97s feeds the flattie. Harman-Collins provide the dual coil ignition system, while a '40 Ford sideshift trannie puts the power down to a Columbia two-speed axle. Although the purple lacquer has faded slightly with the years, the original show finish has now taken on the pleasant mellow patina of age.

MAKE:	Ford
BODY STYLE:	Roadster
YEAR:	1932
ENGINE:	Ford Flathead V8
BUILD STYLE:	Traditional Period Hot Rod
OWNER:	Fred Steele

▶ With two magazine features under its belt, and two first place honors at major car shows soon after it's debut, this roadster's history and reputation has been well earned.

'36 Ford Roadster

Street

★ ★ ★ ★ ★ ★ ★ ★ ★ ★ ★ ★ ★ ★

Every once in a while, a car is built that stops the hobby in its tracks, the originality and innovation just catching everyone on the wrong foot. This is one such car. It was conceived and executed, way, way back by one Sebastian Rubbo, a man with a decidedly different take on building his dream roadster. Starting with a '36 body, he dropped it over a full '40 Merc chassis, channeling it by 6 inches before welding the body and frame as one. A later Mercury gave up its flat engine for the project and was punched out to 286 cubes before being filled with all the trick stuff. A Halibrand quick change replaced the stock Mercury axle, ensuring that Sebastian had a bulletproof drive train for his rod.

To set the car apart from the usual roadster crowd, the rear fenders were wrapped in custom fender skirts, while the front end had its own unique treatment in the form of a sectioned '37 Ford truck grille, two-piece hood sides and separate cycle fenders for the front wheels. This was wild stuff, especially for the early 1950s. Having built the car, Sebastian never sold it and over the years attended events all over, clocking up over 450,000 miles, before his passing in the late 1980s. Now that's a real hot rodder! The car is still wowing new generations of fans today.

MAKE:	Ford
BODY STYLE:	Roadster
YEAR:	1936
ENGINE:	Mercury Flathead V8
BUILD STYLE:	Street Rod
OWNER:	Lenny Biondi

◄ An already famous hot rod, the car was treated to a well-earned full restoration in the late 1990's by its new owner, an old buddy of Sebastian. The legend lives on!

'23 Ford Roadster

Just when the traditional T-bucket theme was beginning to wear a little thin, with many rods almost becoming catalog cars with little variation, along came Lady Luck II. Drawing on a definite nostalgic theme with its chopped Deuce grille shell, laid back screen and wide whites, suddenly T-buckets were cool once again. Old met new with a decidedly up-to-date drive train in the form of a dyno'd and balanced big block Corvette motor. Not content with one of the biggest cubic bent-eights in captivity and in such a light weight car, the motor was then hogged out to 465 inches while also incorporating a big Competition Cams camshaft, stainless steel valves, Keith Black pistons and an Edelbrock Dual-quad, with two same make 650 carbs. Hmmm, I wonder if it's quick?

A custom tilt-removable Carson style top looks good and helps keeps the weather off of the gray diamond tuck upholstery and Stewart Warner "Winged" gauges installed in the dash. Paint finish is light lavender pearl gloss and is themed thru the car with the motor, frame and top, all finished in the wild shade that only the mis-informed ever refer to as "Pink." The top drawer T-bucket has certainly gained itself a cool reputation, with numerous magazine articles and many prestigious show appearances across the country, including an art gallery appearance as part of a Kustom Kulture exhibition. Looking at the picture here, it's not hard to see why.

▼ With its whitewalls on color-coded steelies and other nostalgic cues, this 1950s-themed T Roadster set a new standard for T-bucket building and has inspired many copies.

MAKE:	Ford
BODY STYLE:	Street Roadster
YEAR:	1923
ENGINE:	Chevy 454 V8
BUILD STYLE:	Street Rod
OWNERS:	Chuck and Kim Vranas

'32 Ford Roadster

So many '32 roadster hot rods adopt the stripped-down, fenderless highboy look, whether sleek high-tech smoothsters or hardcore jalopies, that it's a pleasure sometimes to check out a fully-fendered version. Right up there ranking as one of Henry's nicest ever designs, all it needs is a vibrant attention grabbing color to stand out in the crowd, as this one right here does. Having got your attention, your eye is then drawn to the neat but subtle modifications that make it a hot rod and not just a red '32 Ford. Details such as the chopped windshield, filled grille shell and lowered stance. No smooth running boards here; these are stock rubber and are fully functioning too!

It is actually entirely possible these days to build a complete '32 using all reproduction parts, including the body in either fiberglass or even steel. This one is a gennie steel one, however, with a repro '32 frame underneath it. You can see that the front dropped axle is located with a four-bar setup, which was extremely popular for awhile. At the moment, hairpins are currently in favor, using a single mounting point on the frame – unless the car is going real old style and using split wishbones. It's great to see that this Deuce still keeps the stock-style bumpers too, to add a little more chrome.

MAKE:	Ford
BODY STYLE:	Roadster
YEAR:	1932
ENGINE:	Chevy 350 V8
BUILD STYLE:	Street Rod
OWNER:	Tom Baker

◄ With an unfinished roadster in the background, this workshop shot could almost be an example of "before and after" rod building.

'40 Ford Coupe

If you're going to race a 40s coupe hot rod on the strip, there are more ways than one to accomplish it. You could build a traditional high-riding gasser, or you could go the other way and build a unique low-slung coupe like the "Jade Buggy." The old '40 body has been channeled hard down over the frame for a super low start line stance, and all stock sheet metal forward of the fire wall has long since been discarded. This has been replaced with a commercial Deuce grille shell and custom hood top, complete with louvers. The arrow-straight bodywork is finished in the same pearl jade color that gives the car its distinctive name.

"Hemi Powered" proclaims the legend on the hood, and it tells no lie. An injected Hemi Chrysler provides the motive force for this quarter-mile coupe, although it has been set much further back in the frame than is usual. In fact, even in a profile shot of the car, you can't see the engine under the hood. Instead, a Moon fuel tank installed in a north-south configuration occupies the space above the axle. The wide front axle in question is located by a four-bar setup; and the skinny front runners contrast enormously in comparison to the huge rear racing meats.

MAKE:	Ford
BODY STYLE:	2-door Coupe
YEAR:	1940
ENGINE:	Chrysler Hemi V8
BUILD STYLE:	Competition Coupe
OWNER:	Bob Schneider

◄ The "Jade Buggy" is just about as radical a hot rod as you can get while still retaining a recognizable factory body.

'48 Chevy Coupe

When you read books containing all the old class regulations regarding the gas coupes of the 1960s, you soon begin to understand why you saw less of these big late 1940s coupes racing than you'd expect. It was all about wheelbase dimensions and weight and we won't go into it here, but free of those restrictions, we see some great contemporary interpretations of the gasser style. Case in point is this wild '48 Chevy coupe – mean and green and packing plenty of attitude. A drilled I-beam is mounted on chrome parallel leaves, giving it the appearance that it's about to jump straight over the perimeter fence! Some neat custom-chromed ladder bars locate the 9-inch rear axle and are visible beneath the rocker panel.

The "Strip Teaser" features a seriously straight paint job in Cactus pearl gloss with some classy artwork on the doors for good measure. Does that say "12.0 Best" on the glass in racers shoe white? If so, that's a respectable time for a car on street tires. The chrome five-spokes are classic Cragar S/S, front and back, which is totally the right choice for this high stepping, 1960s hot rod. The chrome scoop atop that long hood hints at the high horsepower 350 Chevy engine under the hood, which has received, a 0.030 over bore.

MAKE:	Chevrolet
BODY STYLE:	2-door Coupe
YEAR:	1948
ENGINE:	Chevy 350 V8
BUILD STYLE:	Street Gasser
OWNER:	Brian Russell

▶ A rare, but very welcome, treatment of a late 1940s fat fendered stovebolt coupe, the "Strip Teaser" is an instant classic!

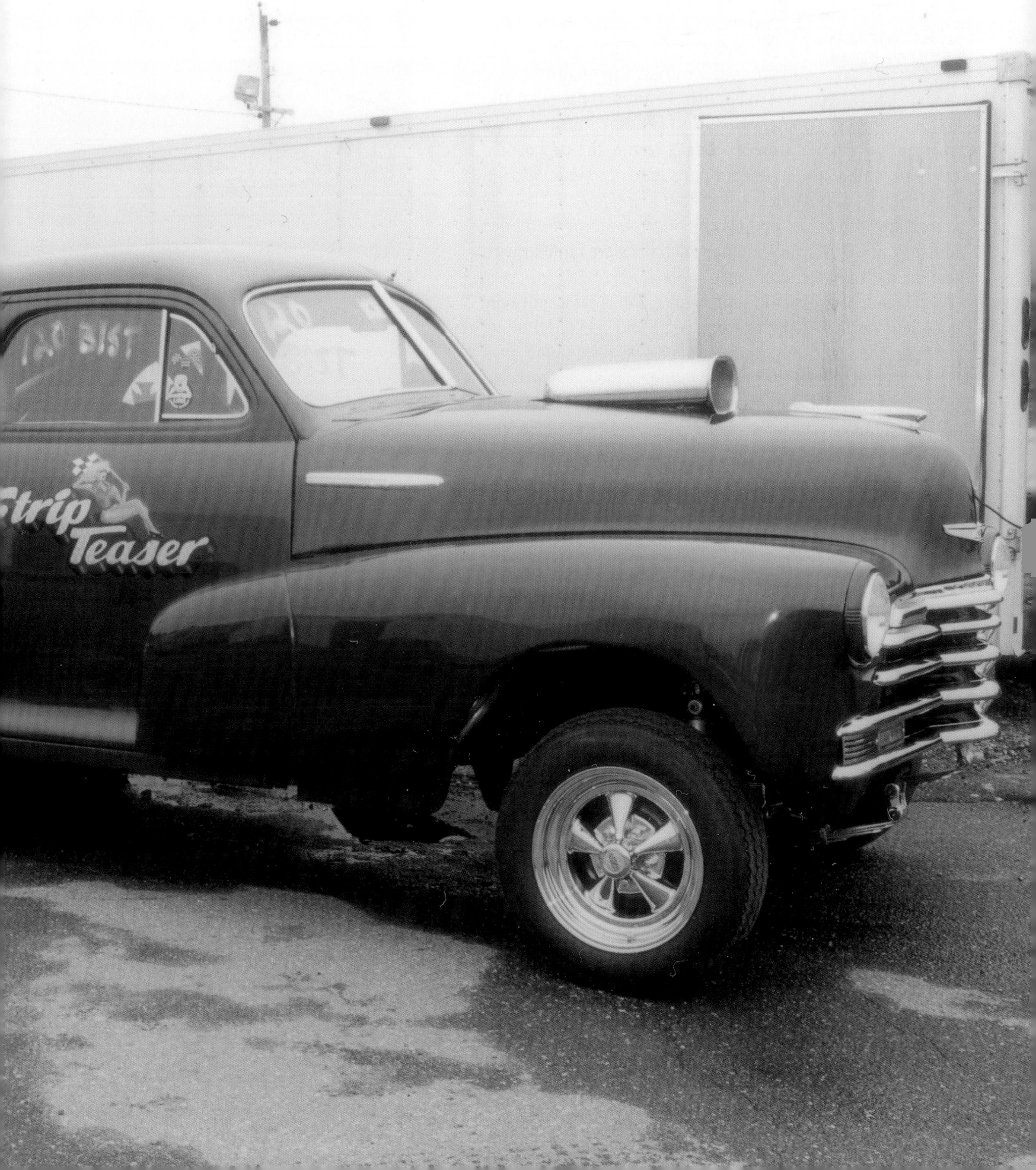
Strip
Teaser

'28 Ford Cragar Special

Auto racing really came into its own in the late 1920s-early 1930s, when oval dirt tracks sprang up all over the country, at county fairgrounds and purpose- built venues. This was the domain of the single-seat sprint car like this one. Built on a narrowed Model T frame, the cars used a variety of readily available Ford parts, such as Model A axles and driveline and Model B 4-cylinder engines, all heavily "souped up" of course. By now the aftermarket performance industry was in full swing and names that we are familiar with today began to make their mark.

As the name suggests, the performance of this car was heavily dependent on the Cragar cylinder head and pressured oiling system on the 200 ci, four-banger engine. As if he didn't have his hands full handling the heavy steering on the loose surfaced tracks, it was up to the driver to maintain the required oil pressure to the engine via a manual pump that was mounted to the outside of the cockpit on the left-hand side. Dual Winfield carbs on a dual plane manifold helped extract up to 125 bhp from the engine, the exhaust exiting through a single megaphone pipe mounted on the right-hand side.

MAKE:	Ford Sprint Car
BODY STYLE:	Single Seat Racer
YEAR:	1928
ENGINE:	200 ci Ford 4 cyl.
BUILD STYLE:	Dirt Tracker
OWNER:	Owls Head Museum

▶ A true dirt tracker, complete with a Cragar head and that wonderful, megaphone exhaust – and just look at those red painted linkages and wheel arrangements, both front and rear.

'31 Chevy Coupe

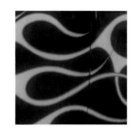

Just by way of a change, here's a cool little Chevy Independence Sports Coupe, which is refreshing in several ways. There is not only the fact that it's a non-Ford, but that it also runs a stock height profile. The straight body is all steel, with fiberglass fenders. Deep Sapphire Blue Pearl on its own would have looked great with the Silvertown whitewalls alone, but then there's that wild flame job. Hot rods with flames aren't in any shortage, but the color scheme chosen here really works well with the white Pearl licks ending in yellow and orange, which then matches in with the Tangerine Pearl steel rims.

The original Chev frame is boxed and front suspension is home-brewed independent, using Mustang II hubs and brakes. The rear is an Oldsmobile limited slip on an original GM four-link, one Chevelle coil spring was cut to make two short hot rod ones! A 330 hp Chevrolet crate engine was mated to a 700R over-drive transmission, this being dressed with a polished Edelbrock intake and a 650 Edelbrock carb. Built for comfort, the Chevy also features full air-conditioning, cruise control, and power windows.

MAKE:	Chevrolet
BODY STYLE:	3-window Coupe
YEAR:	1931
ENGINE:	Chevy 350 V8
BUILD STYLE:	Street Rod
OWNER:	Bill Doherty

◂ The cool combination of colors used on this Chevy three-window really draw attention to the already rare stock height coupe.

'48 Anglia Sedan

An unremarkable car by any standards in stock form, these English Fords were powered by a miniscule 4-cylinder engine and didn't even feature juice brakes as standard – mainly because of the British governments horsepower tax which continued post World War II for awhile. However, cars like this found a new lease on life in the gasser classes of the 1960s, where their short wheelbase and light weight bodies proved killer on the strip, especially when stuffed with a mighty lump of Detroit iron V8 between the frame rails. The little Fords were instant crowd pleasers, with their wheel standing antics and squirrelly handling.

This example of an English Anglia is actually an old campaigner from the 1960's gasser wars. Though it's ride height is not as extreme as some of the straight axle equipped examples around, it's sitting at pretty much stock height now. No mistaking those period, unpolished old slot mags and Mickey Thompson rear slicks though. This car has seen some serious quarter-mile action in its time. These days it's powered by a Hilborn injected V8 Flat engine for a real nostalgic flavor.

MAKE:	Ford Anglia
BODY STYLE:	2-door Sedan
YEAR:	1948
ENGINE:	Ford Flathead V8
BUILD STYLE:	Traditional Gasser
OWNERS:	John Linville and Dick Edwards

▶ With a fiberglass flip front and tangerine pearl paint, I wonder why DJ's Louver Service hasn't punched any into in this particular Anglia!

'31 Ford Coupe

Satin black and bad to the bone is the only way to describe this moody-looking A coupe. Seeing as the photo was taken in the staging lanes of a local drag strip, the car also walks the walk too. A nice roof chop is just enough to give the '31 some serious attitude, as if the tunnel-rammed engine on full view didn't do it already. The full fendered, 5-window features super-straight body work and a filled deuce grille shell replaces the tall model A one. A pair of non-Ford headlamps are mounted on the dropped headlamp bar, giving a slightly different look to the front aspect.

Just one glance at the engine tells you this hot rod was born to run – and you need to have a pretty hot engine if you intend to run a tunnel-ram and dual carbs on the street. Bolt this set-up on to a stock engine and you'll probably feed the engine more gasoline than it can reasonably handle in normal driving conditions. No mistaking that it looks the total business, however, and would make plenty of folk think twice about choosing off this bad boy at the stoplight. A set of polished American five-spokes look even brighter when contrasted against the anti-gloss paint.

MAKE:	Ford
BODY STYLE:	5-window Coupe
YEAR:	1931
ENGINE:	Chevy 350 V8
BUILD STYLE:	Hot Rod
OWNER:	Ken Barry

▸ The numbers on the glass written in shoe white indicate the best times the car has run on this particular day at the track. This information enables the officials to run the car in the correct class.

'16 Ford Speedster

RAJO

When you leaf through this book and look at the outstanding cars, remember this page, for this is just about where it all began. Almost as soon as cars became mass produced, thanks to Henry Ford (and not just the play things of the idle rich), a performance market sprang up to fuel the ever increasing "need for speed." All over America, early enthusiasts dismantled Model Ts and tinkered with the components to improve performance. Once a modification was proven, it was marketed in the cottage industry that was the early speed business. These early cars, when replaced with minimal two-seat body work on shortened frames, were known as Speedsters.

This fine example, owned by the Owls Head Transportation Museum in Maine, sports all the hot tricks of the day. The 176 ci four-banger is bored and stroked and features a Model B RAJO cylinder head with sparks fed by a Bosch magneto and a Zenith carburetor – and it was good for all of 45 bhp! This equates to an easy top speed of 65 mph, which – without the paved road network we have today – was really flying! Bear in mind that these simple hop-ups actually doubled the factory power output, so we are talking serious 1916 hot rodding! Running gear updates include a Ruckstall rear end, Laurel front suspension and Houk wire wheels.

MAKE:	Ford
BODY STYLE:	2-seat Speedster
YEAR:	1916
ENGINE:	4-cyl. 176 ci Flathead
BUILD STYLE:	Restored Race Car
OWNER:	Owls Head Museum

◄ With its shortened frame and minimal body work, the humble Model T soon took on the appearance of a real honking race car!

'29 Ford Roadster

Every dude tooling around in an anti-gloss finished hot rod, like this cool A, regularly has to put up with questions from the uninitiated, such as "when are you going to paint it?" Well, by showcasing how cool some of these cars are in this book, we can maybe educate a few more as to the error of their ways. I mean, could a shiny paint job really make this car any cooler? We doubt it. The classic retro combo of a '29 on Deuce rails lives on here, especially with a Deuce grille shell with red insert. The red-painted theme continues on the split, early Ford wishbones and on the early lever-arm shocks, as well as the engine itself.

The engine is, of course, a 24-stud Flathead running a Tattersfield dual intake, with a pair of Stromberg 81s. The carbs are dressed with a pair of chrome air cleaners courtesy of messrs Stellings and Hellings. Transmission is a '39 Ford with a 1932 Ford rear axle. Like we said, a classic combo all-round. Front end maintains a cool ride height, thanks to the filled and dropped Dago axle with early drum brakes. While all these features yell "1950s Hot Rod," the owner has sneaked a set of early 1960s Radir Tri-Rib wheels with spinners and original Mickey Thompson bias-plys, for a little vintage update – and why not indeed?

MAKE:	Ford Model A
BODY STYLE:	Highboy Roadster
YEAR:	1929
ENGINE:	Flathead V8
BUILD STYLE:	Traditional
OWNER:	Wayne Leach

▸ Check the cool skull shifter sneaking a peek though the windshield on this way-cool A Roadster on Deuce rails.

'38 Oldsmobile Coupe

OK, own up! When was the last time you even saw a '38 Oldsmobile Coupe, much less, a cool rodded one like this one? The big, fat-fendered Coupe looks almost menacing with its jet-black paint and super-low stance. Perhaps it's the aggressive chrome grille that makes it look scary, like the ribs on a skeleton, in fact! Halloween coupe, anyone?

But seriously, taking on a job of rodding a rare car like this Olds can be quite a challenge, since it's unlikely that any after-market chassis brake and suspension components are available for it (unlike those for most manufacture years of Fords). Being a GM product, it's possible that parts from other models can be adapted to fit – and this where hot rodders excel.

It's highly likely that the builder of this Oldsmobile has used the trick of installing a complete front clip from a later model GM car. With that replacing the original front chassis, it would get the car down low, while also providing a fully workable steering, suspension and brake package all in one go. Another challenge would be to locate all of the original stainless and chrome trim for the body, as this too is unlikely to be available off the shelf. It looks like the builder of this handsome '38 did pretty well, assuming he didn't want a front bumper anyway.

MAKE:	Oldsmobile
BODY STYLE:	2-door Coupe
YEAR:	1938
ENGINE:	Chevy 350 V8
BUILD STYLE:	Street Rod
OWNER:	Tom Dwyer

▶ As ever, polished American mags compliment the straight black gloss on this '38 Olds – a classic combination that's hard to beat.

'34 Ford Roadster

ow we don't know for sure, so don't quote us, but it's a fair bet that this '34 rod was built back in the early 1970s. It definitely has the air of a resto-rod about it, as this trend for all the correct original parts over an updated drivetrain was especially popular at that time. For example, you don't often see the 'glass wind wings on hot rods these days, much less with original cowl lights and rear view mirror. The roadster also retains its hood emblem on top of the grille shell, plus original tail lights and rear fender. Another giveaway detail is the bronze two-tone paint, as contrasting fenders were also a popular paint scheme at that time.

The resto-rod style was swept away in the 1980s when, suddenly, billet aluminum parts were the thing to have – along with super smooth monochrome bodies, with a distinct absence of brightwork and chrome. To be fair, that style has lasted well and there are plenty of cars still being built in this vein. However, it's still good to see a roadster like this that has escaped unscathed from that period of hot rodding. Maybe we are on the verge of a resto-rod revival?

MAKE:	Ford
BODY STYLE:	Roadster
YEAR:	1934
ENGINE:	Chevy 350 V8
BUILD STYLE:	Street Rod
OWNER:	Wayne Page

◄ Brown diamond tuck interior and five spoke "Daisy Mags" also point to a seventies flavor on this resto-rod '34.

'40 Ford Pickup

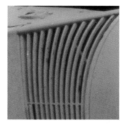 lthough totally hardcore in appearance, this truck may be a work-in-progress. In fact, since when this photo was taken, the truck had just hit the street with its 18-year-old owner behind the wheel! Talk about starting them young. Tom Guditis had owned the truck since he was 11 and, with help from his dad, just got it built. The paint job features red oxide detailing, and a red oxide primer over a red oxide primer basecoat! Cool or what? A 3¹/₂-inch chopped top sets the hot rod flavor on the otherwise stock, but straight, bodywork. The lack of hood means that you can see the recessed firewall, installed to accommodate the small block Chevy that now calls the truck home.

The lowered hot rod truck stance has been achieved with the use of a Mustang II front end that is a snap to install onto the original frame rails on a truck like this. At the rear, a Chevy 10-bolt rear end has been fitted to handle the new V8 power – again another fairly straightforward installation for a newbie rodder. Painted steel rims with plain chrome caps are just fine for this primero, primered truck.

MAKE:	Ford
BODY STYLE:	Pickup
YEAR:	1940
ENGINE:	Chevy 350 V8
BUILD STYLE:	Hardcore Truck
OWNER:	Tom Guditis

◀ Its always good to see a new generation getting into the hot rod thing, and many events run trophy classes for the under-21s. Building trucks like this '40 is a great way to get into old cars.

'32 Coupe and
'38 Chevy Truck

When hot rodding runs in the family like it does with the Osburn crew, it can be hard to separate the results, so we're not going to even try. Instead, we'll just show you both cars owned by the Osburn brothers. First check out Terry's fine '32, 3-window coupe, which runs a dropped tube front end and a healthy tunnel-rammed, dual-carbed small block Chevy with a yellow painted block and polished detailing. A Moon tank and a Hilborn style street scoop further add to the Deuce coupe's tough street image. Polished slot mags complete the picture and contrast with the black paint.

There's two ways to skin a cat, right? So while Terry's coupe stays down and dirty, brother Rick gives his '38 Chevy truck a real bad attitude by aiming it skywards, courtesy of a gasser style straight axle on twin leaf springs. The truck features such neat details as a trick aluminum firewall, raw 5-spoke Americans and fender well headers. Like the Coupe, Rick's truck runs a tunnel-rammed small block Chevy engine with a similar induction set-up. He also runs a Moon tank up front, perhaps they got a discount at the parts store for bulk purchasing!

MAKE:	Ford
BODY STYLE:	3-window Coupe
YEAR:	1932
ENGINE:	Chevy 350 V8
BUILD STYLE:	Hot Rod
OWNER:	Terry Osburn

▲ There's definitely a theme running through this family. The Osburns like their hot rods satin black and Chevy powered with plenty of attitude!

MAKE:	Chevrolet
BODY STYLE:	Pickup
YEAR:	1938
ENGINE:	Chevy 350 V8
BUILD STYLE:	Gasser Truck
OWNER:	Rick Osburn

'48 Fiat Topolino

Yikes! Is that thing street legal? Well, in fact, yes it is! The Topolino (Italian for "little mouse" and what they call Mickey) was a diminutive, post-war, 2-door Coupe, whose lightweight body quickly became popular as a lightweight body for clothing the frame of a dragster in the competition Altered class. Few have ever made it to the street as hot rods, but here is a notable exception. Most Fiat bodies like this are one piece fiberglass replica's these days, as this one is, and as such are molded already chopped and without doors but with a large open roof panel. We presume the owner flips the lightweight body up Funny car style to get in and drive it!

The wild street dragster is based on a race car style full tube frame, and utilizes a drop-tube front axle mounted on a four-bar link. Out back, the rear axle would have to have been narrowed drastically to tuck those super-wide treads in close to the body. The ten-spoke narrow front wheels are typically what you would expect to see on a car like this, be it on the street or the strip. Probably the biggest concession for road driving apart from fitting a radiator is the exhaust collectors, which are funneling the spent gas back under the car.

MAKE:	Fiat
BODY STYLE:	Coupe
YEAR:	1948
ENGINE:	Chevrolet V8
BUILD STYLE:	Race Style Hot Rod

▲ In case you were wondering where the lights are, they are there, we deliberately took the picture so they were hidden behind the wheel for maximum dramatic effect.

'37 Ford Sedan Delivery

Despite the fairly low survival rate of pre-World War II commercials, if you can find one worth saving, they make great looking and practical street rods. Obviously, there's going to be a lot more intensive body work involved to get the large sheet metal panels massaged to the sort of condition where they'll do justice to a quality Burgundy Pearl finish like the one on this truck. However, once done, the results speak for themselves, as you can see. There's a definite contemporary smooth theme going on here, with painted running boards, slick custom door mirrors and an absence of door handles. The screen has been V-butted too, adding to the modern street rod style.

Just enough brightwork has been left, however, with the stock hood vent trims, headlamp rims and the neat custom quarter fenders. The grilles on 37s were always painted body color though, so no change there. Classic Halibrand slot mags feature a high polish finish and are set off with a set of spinner center caps. Low stance is achieved with an aftermarket independent front end of which there are several on the market, most based on the Mustang II unit. The spacious interior is finished in light tan leather with bucket seats for driver and passenger.

MAKE:	Ford
BODY STYLE:	Sedan Delivery
YEAR:	1937
ENGINE:	Chevy 350 V8
BUILD STYLE:	Street Rod
OWNER:	Jim Klering

◄ The Sedan Delivery body style is based on the passenger car frame of the same model and it makes a cool and practical street rod.

'33 Ford Pickup

To give you some idea of how much custom work went into the creation of this very cool, 1950's-flavored truck, compare its stance and dimensions with the stock example of a similar model in the background. The all-steel truck, which was originally built into a hot rod back in 1961, has had a huge 9½-inch channel over the frame, plus a 4½-inch roof chop to bring it down and give it a much sneakier profile. The filled Deuce grille shell has also been dropped down between the frame rails in order to maintain the correct proportions. Behind the cab, the once load-carrying pickup bed has been shortened by 10 inches for the same reason. A cool red and white tarp now covers the bed area.

Those three vertical carb stacks suck clean air into the three Rochesters mounted on an Offy 3-pot intake, nestling in the valley of the Chevy 305 V8, and fuel is delivered to the Rochesters via a firewall mounted fuel block. Minimal engine dress-up is used, but it does wear the asset of early, finned alloy valve covers with chrome T-bar hold-down bolts. The satin anti-gloss is worn with pride on this little '33 hauler, and there are a few places on the truck where the pin striper has employed his craft. Check out the neat spider web on the cab visor.

MAKE:	Ford
BODY STYLE:	Pickup
YEAR:	1933
ENGINE:	Chevy 305 V8
BUILD STYLE:	Traditional 1950's Hot Rod
OWNER:	Tony Muscatella

▶ The chrome smoothies and wide whites are a recent addition to this '33 pickup but add the right amount of period "eye candy" to the old truck.

'27 Ford Roadster

Just when you think you've seen every possible different treatment of a certain body style, someone comes along and pushes the boundaries once again. Take this suede black '27, for example. There's nothing on the car that hasn't been done before, somewhere, but the overall style of the T still looks fresh and exciting. The Hallock-styled split-screen, so reminiscent of 1930's luxury sports tourers, gives a real racy feel to the low-slung roadster. Further, the inspired choice of adapting a '35 Ford grille, with its similar backward-leaning slant, is a stroke of genius.

Not for this car any overkill of chrome and glitz. Rather, the '27 takes on the air of a street Stealth Fighter, with black-painted suspension components like the drilled I-beam, hairpins and front shocks. The black theme is continued on the normally polished screen frame too. It's left to the polished, American 5-spokes to provide some high shine against the satin anti-gloss finish. After all, you must have some contrast somewhere. The three air cleaners poking through the hood feed three carbs beneath them, which, in turn feed a mighty Chrysler Hemi that undoubtedly just roars through those cool Lakes pipes.

MAKE:	Ford Model T
BODY STYLE:	Turtledeck Roadster
YEAR:	1927
ENGINE:	Chrysler Hemi V8
BUILD STYLE:	Lakes Hot Rod
OWNER:	Peter and Linda Calaguiro

▼ This '27 was definitely built for speed and not comfort – but that doesn't stop the owner from regularly driving it long-distance!

'35 Buick Coupe

A few years back, the hot rod press coined the phrase "Dare to be different." This was an appeal urging rodders to try taking off their blinkers and look further than Ford for potential new material from which to build unusual and innovative hot rods. To their credit, many rodders took up the challenge – but it's still rare to see a '35 Buick given the smooth treatment. With similar lines to a mid-1930's Ford, especially in the fender design, this Buford lends itself to some contemporary styling with ease. Body mods remain subtle, with a general cleaning up of unnecessary trim and barbs. The flush-fit, late-model door handles are a particularly nice touch and the door mirrors also work well with the overall theme.

Under the sheet metal, the car remains strictly General Motors, although most of it is Chevrolet-Corvette-inspired hardware, with America's favorite sports car donating both front and rear independent suspension to the project, as well as a Tuned Port Injection LT1 V8 and a 700R4 transmission. Skinny, low-profile rubber keeps this Buick close to the blacktop, and the polished Billet Specialties wheels compliment the superb Gunmetal Gray exterior perfectly. A sumptuous gray leather interior provides a level of comfort to match the ride and performance.

MAKE:	Buick
BODY STYLE:	3-window Coupe
YEAR:	1935
ENGINE:	Chevy 350 LT1 V8
BUILD STYLE:	Street Rod
OWNER:	Keith Samrany

▸ With all Corvette running gear under classic '35 Buick bodywork, this car could easily be called a "Buvette"!

'35 Chevy Roadster Pickup

There are Chevy trucks, and there are Chevy trucks; but nothing else quite like this kind '35 Chevy roadster pickup. While the front-end sheet metal is clearly recognizable as a vintage bowtie product, albeit with custom steel hood sides featuring sculpted cooling vents, the hand-fabricated pickup bed is something else again. Featuring a smooth wraparound rear end, which utilizes late-model taillights, an aerodynamic spoiler curls around the edge of the lip of the bed, with a cutout for the four tail pipes. A hydraulic ram-lifted hard deck covers the load area. Door handles have been shaved and the running boards are smooth. The whole car is finished with gallons of House of Kolors Burgundy Kandy pearl paint, so deep you could almost fall into it!

The ground-scraping stance is possible as a result of an independent front end, while, at the rear, a Ford 9-inch is more than enough to handle the power put out by the stroked Chevy small block that now displaces 406 ci. The engine is fuel-injected with a late-model TPI unit and also benefits from a set of aluminum cylinder heads. The transmission is a 700R4 unit for relaxed freeway cruising. Hi-tech 3-spoke billet wheels, with BF Goodrich rubber, support all four corners of this innovative concept pickup.

MAKE:	Chevrolet
BODY STYLE:	Roadster Pickup
YEAR:	1935
ENGINE:	Chevy 406 V8
BUILD STYLE:	Concept Rod
OWNER:	Gary Schweikert

◀ What looks like convertible soft top is actually a hard top covered in black fabric in order to preserve the Roadster pickup look on this '35 Chevy.

'33 Ford Coupe

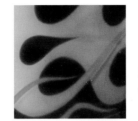

If someone should ever ask you, "Just what makes an old car a hot rod?" then just show them the picture of this funky, 5-window. It should tell them everything they need to know.

Just about all the hottest tricks are here, from the chopped, filled and louvered top to the killer engine. The trunk lid has also been punched full of louvers; and both the body and frame have been covered in wild purple pearl paint. As if that wasn't enough, custom hot licks blaze down both sides, the fenders nothing but distant memories on this coupe. A polished alloy firewall is installed to further mirror the awesome engine installed up front; and ahead of that, the stainless 33 grille appears to float mid-air with no sheet metal to surround it.

As ever with a car like this, it's the engine, which is the focal point of the onlooker's attention. In this case, it's a big-block Chevrolet, detailed to the max with polished aluminum heads. A highly polished supercharger gleams in the sun, while on top are three Holley's and a chromed, Hilborn-style street scoop to dazzle and delight. The chromed headers bunch together and then flare out into separate megaphones so as to turn the engine note into sweet V8 music!

MAKE:	Ford
BODY STYLE:	5-window Coupe
YEAR:	1933
ENGINE:	Chevy 454 V8
BUILD STYLE:	Performance Hot Rod
OWNER:	Stu Paer

◄ With no visible lug nuts on the polished Halibrand wheels, we can only assume these are spindle mounts on the front of this '33.

'39 Ford Roadster

If a hardcore Model A Coupe with rustoleum finish represents one end of the rodding spectrum, then this concept '39 Ford Roadster, with its futuristic body, must be way up at the other end. Manufactured by Coast to Coast Street Rods in fiberglass, it represents a stretched and stylized interpretation of a '39 Ford Roadster for those who like their rods truly "cutting edge." While mostly owner-built, no expense has been spared in the construction of this example. It boasts a narrowed '98 Corvette independent rear suspension, a '92 'Vette front and an Air Ride Technologies Shock Wave air bag system to slam the car down on the floor when not in motion.

The sharp end of the hood features a custom and color-coded grille – and although it's a '39, the '37 head lamps look right at home in the front fenders. Big-inch billet wheels are the only way to go on this kind of ride, and Boyd Coddington came up with the goods in the form of some 17- and 18-inch diameter custom wheels. A 347 ci Chevy V8 from a C5 Corvette is dressed to impress and is used with the Corvette rear-mounted LSI 6-speed transmission. Coast to Coast also supply the custom frame for these roadsters from which to mount all the necessary hardware.

MAKE:	Ford
BODY STYLE:	Coast-to-Coast Roadster
YEAR:	1939
ENGINE:	Chevy 347 V8
BUILD STYLE:	Street Rod
OWNER:	Rick Smith

◀ The oh-so-smooth body is finished in vibrant Corvette yellow, which is very fitting, since the '39 runs nearly all 'Vette running gear.

'29 Ford Roadster

While this isn't the only example of a '29 on Deuce rails within these pages, there won't be many with more hot rod history than this one. Originally built in Southern California as a hot rod back in '42, this car has run on the dry lakes of both El Mirage and Muroc in its time – as well as at the Morrow drags. For some of that time, it ran the hot ticket in the form of a '49 Oldsmobile Rocket V8. While much of the car retains the original parts, the engine now fitted is an Edelbrock and Tri-power equipped 283 Chevy V8, which retains its early "rams horn" exhaust manifolds.

Everything on this roadster is state-of-the-art 1940's hot rodding. The axle on split wishbones, with '40 Ford brakes equipped with Buick-finned drums, is the classic setup for the front end. The transmission and rear end is no less period correct, with a '39 Ford manual transmission and '39 banjo rear end. The red-detailed steel wheels match the chassis detailing and engine block, looking cool against the pale yellow body color.

The car would not be complete without the classic touches of a Deuce grille shell and a set of Guide headlamps.

MAKE:	Ford Model A
BODY STYLE:	Roadster
YEAR:	1929
ENGINE:	Chevy 283 V8
BUILD STYLE:	Traditional Early Hot Rod
OWNER:	Dick and Sherry Mellott

◀ With over fifty years of hot rodding history to its credit, this '29 Roadster has a list of credentials as long as your arm.

'37 Ford Cabriolet

Resplendent in a really fetching shade of Harvest Sunset Amber Mist Pearl (who thinks up these names!), this '37 is typical of some of the class act street rods being built in America today. Subtle modifications enhance the car's lines, rather than distract your eye. One way or another, this is definitely a case of "less is more." A subtle roof chop of just $2^1/2$ inches is enough. Also, a favorite modification on '37's – the windshield – has had the central divider removed and the new glass bonded together with a V-but cut. Solid hood sides give the car smooth flanks with matching smooth running boards and shaved door handles. Where as '37's normally have painted steel grilles, this one reverses the situation with the addition of a stainless aftermarket item with extra shine provided by the chromed quarter bumpers.

The cool Cabrio sits on a full TCI repro frame – which features fully independent front and rear suspension – and a Currie Enterprises, nodular 9-inch rear end with disc brakes.

Everything is fully detailed and the rod rides on a set of 16- and 17-inch Budnik billet wheels. A Corvette LSI V8 lights the fire under this particular '37 and this is linked to a 4L60E transmission to complete the running gear.

MAKE:	Ford
BODY STYLE:	Cabriolet
YEAR:	1937
ENGINE:	Chevy LSI V8
BUILD STYLE:	Street Rod
OWNER:	Fred Tugend

◄ A light tan top compliments the buff leather interior on this smooth, contemporary '37 Cabriolet.

'41 Willys Coupe

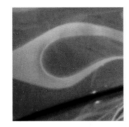

Here is another ex-race car that's been tamed for the street. This '41 Willys Coupe has been cherried out, cleaned up and had all that sticky rubber cleaned out from the rear fenders, to start a new life on the street. Those rear wheel wells have been fully tubbed out to accommodate the big race-style rear tires. The rod may now feature a fully carpeted trunk, but the racing heritage is still apparent with the full roll cage and bracing still in place. By the way, the car regularly used to run sub 8-second times in the quarter-mile time when in full race trim.

Although the Willys sees more street duty and exhibition halls than it ever used to, it still retains plenty of bhp under the hood, in the form of a big block Chevy engine displacing 468 ci. A Weiand Team G tunnel ram intake is sandwiched between the detailed and polished engine and the twin Holley Dominator 1050 carbs. Stainless steel fenderwell headers route the waste gas through street-legal mufflers and out of the custom exhaust just ahead of the rear wheels. Talking of wheels, they're a set of polished Weld Draglites under those bulbous fenders. The Willys is finished in a deep Candy Red with multi-hued flames courtesy of House of Kolors.

MAKE:	Willys
BODY STYLE:	2-door Coupe
YEAR:	1941
ENGINE:	Chevy 468 V8
BUILD STYLE:	Show and Go
OWNER:	Mike and Teresa Needle

◄ With a full tan interior now surrounding the race-style bucket seats, this is one born-again '41 Willys race car.

'31 Ford Coupe

As you leaf through these pages, you'd be forgiven for thinking that the only way to build a Model A hot rod is traditional or hardcore style, with a chopped top and Deuce grille. Well, just to prove that is not the case, take a look at this super-straight sweetie. While the lines of an earlier car are maybe not as slick as the late 1930's models that are often favorites for the contemporary look, this cool Coupe is a neat car and looks great. The filled roof is just about the only modification to the body, but it certainly looks like the Coupe is wearing a set of oversize rear fenders to accommodate the big 20-inch Centerline wheels, with a pair of 17s feature up front to match.

Harking back to an earlier period of hot rodding are the 'glass wind wings attached to the leading edge door pillars, and the cool nerf bars ahead of the stock '31 Model A grille.

The engine, with its front-mounted distributor, is probably a small-block Ford engine complete with polished intake and an Edelbrock 4-barrel carb. A chromed High-Tech air filter is used for under hood clearance, using twin K&N filters.

MAKE:	Model A Ford
BODY STYLE:	5-window Coupe
YEAR:	1931
ENGINE:	Ford 302 V8
BUILD STYLE:	Street Rod
OWNER:	Rick and Lisa Lord

▶ Proving that Model A Ford's can look good in a contemporary style as well as traditional, this Coupe looks great in its Aquamarine Pearl paint.

'40 Chevrolet Coupe

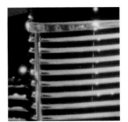

While the nose-high gasser stance was popular on drag strips all over the land in the 1960s – with racers looking to transfer weight and traction to the rear end – there was also a brief period where the sky-high look was used on the street, just for the sheer outrageous "wow" factor. Using straight or beam axles up front and radically re-arched rear springs (and sometimes re-positioned axles) out back, the car was often lifted both ends in order to sit high, wide and handsome. Mainly popular with the street machiners, a good few earlier cars were built with this attitude too. This bad-looking Chevy Coupe certainly reminds us of that period.

The big Coupe uses a drilled I-beam on parallel leaves to get that front up there in the breeze, with the rear springs set up so as to lift the back end by a similar amount. Interestingly, the rod retains most of its original stainless and chrome brightwork, including the wide hood spears and the stock front bumper. The bumper is usually the first thing to get tossed out, the absence of it making a raised car look even higher. The hood sides however, have been removed so that onlookers and admirers can check out the GMC 6-71 blown 396 ci big block Chevrolet engine. The muscle car engine is further enhanced by a pair of Dual quad carbs and a wicked Mr Gasket, bug-catcher-style, scoop poking through the hood.

MAKE:	Chevrolet
BODY STYLE:	2-door Coupe
YEAR:	1940
ENGINE:	Chevy 396 V8
BUILD STYLE:	Street Gasser
OWNER:	Manny Viara

◄ Chevrolet Rallye wheels with original center caps and polished rings keep this Chevy strictly "bowtie" throughout.

'32 Ford Roadster

'32 Ford Roadster

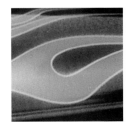

Probably the No. 1 on most hot rodder wish lists, the '32 Ford Highboy never fails to turn heads and draw admirers wherever fans gather. It's a rod that works well, no matter what its build style. Tech or trad, high or low, it will always have a loyal following. Add a bunch of flames to a black example like this one, and you'll be beating them back with a stick! A chromed, dropped I-beam on hairpins is the classic setup used on this one, and the polished American 5-spoke big'n' little combination of blackwall tires can't hurt either. A highboy just has to have Lakes-style pipes, right? Well that's OK. as this one's got those too.

A neat, black, folding top keeps the cool, white and rolled upholstery job in the shade, although the red-and-yellow flame job, with checkerboard detail ,keeps the heat turned up on the outside. Under that smooth louver-less hood, with lakes pipes cut outs, is a Chevy 350, fully dressed and backed up with a TH350 transmission. With such a winning combination, this hot rod comprises a whole bunch of "must-have" parts for any rodder, a sure-fire hit! Flames, fire, etc. Get it? ...Oh, never mind!

MAKE:	Ford
BODY STYLE:	Highboy Roadster
YEAR:	1932
ENGINE:	Chevy 350 V8
BUILD STYLE:	Street Rod
OWNER:	Richard Chilton

◄ Red flames on black – and on a '32 Roadster Highboy – surely at the very top end of any hot rodder's wish list?

'35 Plymouth PJ Coupe

"Welcome to Mopar Country" proclaimed the advertising slogan some years ago. Well, here is a picture of a Mopar actually in the country; a 1935 Plymouth Coupe, to be exact. The fine, 5-window Chrysler product features a perfect resto body with just about all the original trim, plus original opening screen and rubber running boards. The only non-stock additions are the turn signals on the fender irons, the peep mirror on the door and (of course) the patriotic bow on the grille shell! Naturally, the cool and low stance on the rod points to some major chassis updates having been carried out in the name of street rodding. A set of Centerline wheels fills the fenderwells perfectly.

Not only does this Coupe represent a fine example of a non-Ford resto-rod, the Old Gold metallic bodywork, with contrasting Chestnut metallic fenders, hide a combination of mechanical updates that's Mopar through and through. Starting at the front, we find a Chrysler 318 V8 running the show, but ably backed up with a 904 automatic transmission and a Chrysler 8½-inch rear axle. A Lokar shifter adds a period feel to the coupe's interior and a further touch of class is found in the Plymouth's wood dash.

MAKE:	Plymouth PJ
BODY STYLE:	5-window Coupe
YEAR:	1935
ENGINE:	Chrysler 318 V8
BUILD STYLE:	Street Rod
OWNER:	Terry Badman

▶ There must be an added kick in turning up at a show in a rarer model rod like this '35 Plymouth, especially when it could easily be the only one in attendance.

'41 Ford Pickup

'41 Ford Pickup

Sometimes, it turns out that the custom modification that takes the most work to carry out becomes so subtle on the finished car that it is often overlooked. A good example is the bodywork on this fine '41 Ford truck. It takes a keen eye to notice that both the cab and doors of the pickup have been stretched a full 4 inches to add extra interior comfort to the otherwise close confines of the stock cab. Other fine bodywork details include shaving the door handles and filling the fender holes, plus many others. The finished truck has been coated in a wild House of Kolors Tangerine Pearl that positively glows in the summer sunshine.

Fully-independent front suspension gives the truck its low Street Rod stance, while a stout Ford 9-inch rear axle is necessary out back to take the increased power from the Chevy V8 installed under the hood. The Chevy engine in question is a Crane roller-cam-equipped 350, fully detailed and polished, and fed by a Street and Performance Electronic Fuel injection system. These EFI units are becoming more and more popular with street rodders who looking for increased power along with maximum engine efficiency.

A set of Centerline directional billet wheels do the job on this outstanding '41.

MAKE:	Ford
BODY STYLE:	Half-ton Truck
YEAR:	1941
ENGINE:	Chevy 350 V8
BUILD STYLE:	Street Rod
OWNER:	Bill and Linda Yorker

◀ Ford half-ton pickups make great street rods and can create just as much impact as their passenger car cousins.

'34 Dodge Pickup

While it's perfectly possible to walk into your local Dodge dealership and sign on the line for a red Dodge pickup, with a chrome grille and a high horsepower engine, we guarantee it won't look as sweet as this li'l red wagon right here. Yes, even way back in1934, the Dodge Brothers were turning out a pretty nice line in pickup trucks, but we bet they never envisaged how good this one would look seventy-plus years later. The body on this vintage hauler is flawless, with its high shine red gloss and swoopy chrome grille. The running boards have been smoothed and painted too, and the fenders shaved to keep everything clean and simple.

Matching the grille shine-for-shine are the cool Cragar rims, the front ones mounted to the hubs of the Mustang II independent front end, and the rear ones bolted up to the Ford 8-inch rear axle. Under the hood is the tried and tested combo of a 350 Chevy crate engine and a TH700R4 automatic transmission – and you can bet your boots it's not covered in oil and rust straight from the junkpile! The truck even gets driven to work on the daily commute alongside all those brand new, red, slab-sided Dodge pickups!

MAKE:	Dodge Brothers
BODY STYLE:	Half-ton Pickup
YEAR:	1934
ENGINE:	Chevy 350 V8
BUILD STYLE:	Street Rod
OWNERS:	Moe and Pat Therrien

▶ The swoopy red paint on this Dodge Brothers truck makes it easy to forget the many hours it takes to massage old vintage tin into the condition you see here.

'41 Willys Coupe

Everyone dreams of finding their dream car someday – something that's been hidden away for years, all genuine and full of history that just needs the rodder's touch to put it back on the street. This is one of those cars, a real steel '41 Willys Gasser, that was hidden away for years, way up in Nova Scotia. It used to campaign regularly in the C/gas class in the North East back in the 1960s, but has now been fully restored to period-perfect condition to truly reflect "the way we were." Care has been taken to use as many correct-era parts in order to maintain its authenticity as a resurrected quarter-mile hero. It even has the original racing lap-strap seat belts fitted.

A drilled I-beam on parallel leaves maintains the ol' gasser's stance, with a set of classic 10-spoke ETs on the front and a set of American 5-spokes standing well clear of the rear fenders. After all, who needs wheel tubs anyway! The '57 Olds axle with its 3.55 gears is mounted on mile-long ladder bars and easily handles the copious amounts of torque produced by the built 350 small-block up front. The engine spec includes a set of Edelbrock aluminum heads, with same-make intake and 600 cfm carb which is plenty enough for street duty. A set of Mickey Thompson valve covers and an early Corvette air cleaner add extra period details to the engine.

MAKE:	Willys
BODY STYLE:	Coupe
YEAR:	1941
ENGINE:	Chevy 350 V8
BUILD STYLE:	Traditional Restored Gasser
OWNER:	Mike and Margaret O'Connor

▶ An original all-steel Willys gasser like this one is a rare find these days, as race cars are often dismantled and parted out when they are no longer competitive.

'32 Ford Coupe

Whilst being resplendent in its coat of Porsche Guards Red, if it wasn't for the color, this 5-window Coupe would almost be understated. Having said that, the fenderless Ford has "hot rod" written all over it, oozing class and attitude all at the same time. The red paint covering the body and chassis, plus all the chassis components not polished or chromed, is interrupted only by the three rows of multiple louvers in the hood side panels and the custom air scoop on the hood top. A chromed drop tube axle is located by a stainless 4-bar link with chromed shocks at the front, while a 9-inch Ford rear end is similarly located by a 4-bar and Panhard rod at the rear.

Just looking at the red rod, you know there's something special under the hood. You'd be right, as the engine compartment is completely filled by a Weiand 6-71 blown 454 Chevrolet big block V8, the mammoth engine being fed the fuel through a pair of Carter competition four barrel carbs. A 700R4 behind the big block transmission handles the shifting duties with ease and makes for relaxed highway cruising. Once again, we see a set of polished American 5-spokes being put to good use on this very cool Coupe.

MAKE:	Ford
BODY STYLE:	5-window Coupe
YEAR:	1932
ENGINE:	Chevy 454 V8
BUILD STYLE:	Street Rod
OWNER:	Dave Carpenter

◄ A classic style of '32 Ford. This style of fenderless 5-window will never date or go out of fashion.

'32 Ford Roadster

There is no doubt that today, with the money and resources available, modern recreations of period hot rods are actually finished to an even better standard than they were back in the old days. This is not to take anything away from the early rodders, who often did the best they could with somewhat limited resources. In fact, some of those guys are now building the car they always wanted to back then but couldn't afford to. So, we end up with hot rods like this stunning late-1940s Deuce Roadster. No stone has been left unturned in sourcing some of the rarest of vintage speed parts in order to recreate the "dream rod" of the 1940s.

We just do not have the space to do full justice to this car in a couple of paragraphs. However, just to give you an idea, we are talking a 59Z Flathead block displacing 304ci with an original S.Co.T polished blower, Eddie Meyer heads, a brace of 97s, Harman & Collins ignition; the list goes on and on. Super-rare Kinmont "Safe Stop" brakes are used and under the back end is a Halibrand quick-change with polished center section. But it's not just the big stuff, incredible attention to detail means that even the smallest items match the exacting criteria of the perfect 40's era Deuce Roadster.

MAKE:	Ford
BODY STYLE:	Roadster
YEAR:	1932
ENGINE:	Ford Flathead V8
BUILD STYLE:	Traditional 1940's Dream Rod
OWNER:	Ken Gross

▸ This incredibly authentic '32 is topped off with a faithful recreation of a classic chopped Carson top, with every detail included.

'48 Chevrolet

It used to be so easy. Hot rods were, generally, early cars stripped down for speed and performance, while Customs were heavier, later model cars built for more show than go. These days the lines are completely fuzzed, especially when you have a total custom makeover applied to a pre-1949 car like this '48 Chevy. Professionally built, through and through, this car displays every trick in the book – and then some – so much so that its stunning image completely conceals the Chevrolet beneath. Over 3700 hours of custom metal fabrication went into its construction, including chopping the top 5 inches and raking the screen back, while turning it into a pillar less Coupe at the same time. The car has also had a complete "section" job that involves making two cuts right around the car's beltline and removing a band of metal to lower the depth of the body panels. It is no mean feat and only a task for the very brave!

The front end is completely custom-fabbed with a custom grille and flush fitting Mercedes headlamps. The interior features a complete wraparound custom dash and console that has to be seen to be believed. A full custom chassis was built for this wild car and this features full air suspension from Airlift Co. The huge billet wheels are by Colorado Custom. Under the hood is a 355 Chevy small block and Turbo 350 – although this almost seems incidental to the awesome amount of unreal body modifications, which kind of takes us back to that earlier custom definition.

MAKE:	Chevrolet
BODY STYLE:	Pillar-less Coupe
YEAR:	1948
ENGINE:	Chevy 350 V8
BUILD STYLE:	Custom Rod
OWNER:	Pat Keating

◀ When you build Street Rods and Customs for a living, you need something just a little bit special to call your own! This is Pat Keating's '48 Custom-Rod.

'32 Ford Coupe

The reflection in the pure black paint shows just how straight the body is on this traditional Deuce 3-window Coupe. The understated, low-profile hot rod relies on its simplicity of style to make its nostalgic statement. The top is chopped in a time-honored fashion and a hard channel over the frame gives it plenty of attitude. All that's needed is a sudden burst of color to grab your attention – and this is provided by the bright yellow, early Ford steels with caps and ribbed rings. A set of painted King Bee headlights flank the filled grille shell.

Chevrolet power features up front in the form of a detailed small block V8 with a 3-carb, tri-power setup, which, in turn, wears three chromed Stelling & Hellings vintage air cleaners. A set of polished no-name finned covers help dress the engine further, whilst a chromed alternator is a modern concession to reliability – on a chromed mounting bracket, naturally. More chrome covers the dropped I-beam and front suspension, which also features a set of Buick finned drums.

MAKE:	Ford
BODY STYLE:	3-window Coupe
YEAR:	1932
ENGINE:	Chevy 350 V8
BUILD STYLE:	Street Rod
OWNER:	Ron Carson

▶ Although built in a nostalgic style, like many others this Coupe incorporates useful modern features, such as radial tires and an alternator

'32 Ford Coupe

The color may remind you of a hook-billed wading bird, but we know which we would prefer to see on our front lawn when we walk out the door! This 1950's style, 3-window is really cooking in a combination of Tropical Rose gloss and white. The body sits on the frame right where Henry intended, showing off the swage-lined stock chassis in the same color as the body. The white detailing is picked out on the firewall, the suspension components and on the fine detail pinstripe accents. It was common to name one's car back then in the old days, and this one wears its deck of cards and "Full House" on the lower cowl with pride.

Nothing but a full-house Flathead engine would do for this 3-window, and this one has the works. A set of Weiand after-market heads grace the old V8, which features a tall, polished Thickstun 2-carb intake, with a pair of Stromberg 97s topped with a finned alloy air cleaner. There's a beehive oil cleaner in there somewhere, as well as plenty of chrome. A '39 Ford stick shift bolts up behind the flattie, as this hot rod has three pedals on the driver's floorboards. The tall bias-ply whitewalls, as ever, look great with the 'caps and rings.

MAKE:	Ford
BODY STYLE:	3-window Coupe
YEAR:	1932
ENGINE:	Flathead V8
BUILD STYLE:	Nostalgia Hot Rod
OWNER:	Michael Manno

▸ The white detailing theme on this 1932 style 3-window is echoed in the white trimmed interior.

'32 Ford Roadster

Before you dismiss this rusty jalopy for having a total lack of shine and no chrome, look a little closer. We guess you could almost call it a piece of living history. The aged body has certainly seen better days, it's true, but you couldn't buy a finish like that with all the money in the world. At some point in the Deuce's long history, the body has been grafittied with the names of many old New England hot rod clubs from days gone by. As well as that, many of the members of those clubs have signed the trunk lid. The car truly is caught in a time warp, and while it's valuable as a real steel '32 Roadster ripe for rodding or even restoration, it would be a shame to lose the hot rod history inherent in this car.

The old Roadster has had more taken away from it than has had added, but much of the car remains original '32 Ford. However, the Flathead V8 is by no means the original engine. In fact, it's a severely hopped-up replacement unit that has seen much race action back in the late 1950's. Indeed, at one time, it was in a record-holding race car at the Sanford Drags in Maine. Whatever you think of it, its future remains a dilemma. Does it warrant rebuilding? Or does it belong in a museum? Only the owner can decide for sure.

MAKE:	Ford
BODY STYLE:	Roadster
YEAR:	1932
ENGINE:	Flathead Ford V8
BUILD STYLE:	Original Hot Rod
OWNER:	Paul Aldrich

▶ A true piece of New England hot rodding history, no doubt this old '32 Roadster could tell a few stories.

'41 Willys Coupe

Echoing his racing past, the owner of this fine '41 Gasser-style Willys built this one to be a street legal re-creation of the car he used to race in anger over thirty years ago. Back then, the race car was powered by a hulking great fuel-injected Oldsmobile engine. However, since this modern version was to be primarily street driven, a tamer – but no less fun – 350 Chevrolet was chosen, coupled to a Turbo 400 transmission with a Ford 9-inch rear axle. Helping to get the air into the engine is a healthy-sized, chromed induction scoop protruding through the sharply-pointed hood. As with any self-respecting Gasser, the huge fenderwell headers are visible up behind the front wheels.

A customized, perforated and chromed grille fills the space in the front panel where the original vertical-bar Willys version used to live. A few, choice and race-inspired decals adorn the smooth, Candy red body. "Milodon" refers to well-known maker of drag race engines, whilst on the lower front bumper, "Cal Automotive" were responsible for producing the one-piece fiberglass front hood and fender assemblies that were used on many Willys race cars. Polished Halibrands are the wheels of choice for this Gasser style hot rod, which – like the line from the TV movie says – "rises up like a cutter through ice!"

MAKE:	Willys
BODY STYLE:	Coupe
YEAR:	1941
ENGINE:	Chevy 350 V8
BUILD STYLE:	Street Gasser
OWNER:	John Clark

▶ The appeal of this '41 is that it looks like it belongs on the track, but actually gets driven almost every day by its owner.

'32 Ford Coupe

"So clean, you could eat your dinner off it" is a saying we've often heard – though the exclamation is usually uttered by un-cool non-rodders, and we doubt the owner would welcome any spaghetti sauce anywhere near this show-quality 3-window Coupe!

The classic lines of this Deuce are left largely uninterrupted. They were good from day one, anyway, save for the rodders favorite custom trick of the chopped roof. A filled grille shell, along with a little extra cleaning up of body details, like the door handles and the running boards, has been carried out. An after-market billet mirror has been added and color-coded to the Deep Purple pearl paint with cool, complimenting-checker-themed graphics for added interest.

In keeping with its show car standard, this '32 goes its own way in the suspension department. No drilled I-beam or hair-pins here, but a fully independent set up incorporating an Air Ride suspension system. This allows the car to settle right down over those big 16- and 18-inch Budnik wheels, shod with super low-profile Pirelli rubber bands. A fully-detailed Chevy small block dazzles the eyes with its high-shine finish, its genuine gold-plated pair of Holley 4-barrels sitting high on top of a well-buffed blower. A Hilborn-style chromed scoop caps off the mill in fine style. Inside, cool white leather provides sumptuous luxury for anyone driving or riding in it.

MAKE:	Ford
BODY STYLE:	3-window Coupe
YEAR:	1932
ENGINE:	Chevy 350 V8
BUILD STYLE:	Show Rod
OWNER:	David DePaulo

◄ With gold-plated carbs featuring in the engine, this '32 Coupe, known as the "The Outlaw", is certainly blessed with the Midas touch.

'34 Ford Roadster

A recurring theme that you might notice on early cars throughout this book, is the practice of updating both Model A and T hot rods with the later Deuce grille shell. Well, this Roadster reverses that trend, with a filled and peaked '32 shell on a later '34 car. The channeled East Coast car features solid hood sides – and has done for the best part of fifty years, long before the current trend for smooth sheet metal. The unusual "peek-a-boo" cut out in the hood top is also unique to this car. A chopped windshield keeps the profile low and, as an especially nice touch, it sports discreet cycle bumpers on all four corners.

The front end hunkers down low over an original I-beam axle, with a set of chromed front shocks being the only bright work to be seen, with everything else painted in functional black. The rod has seen several engine and trans' combinations over the years. However, in this shot, it's running a big 455 ci Oldsmobile V8 equipped with a tri-power carb set-up. You can just see the individual chromed air cleaners lurking down under the hood. The engine puts the power down through a Turbo 400 transmission and down to an Olds rear axle. Thin white band radials wrap the chrome slot mags on the front, with a set of B F Goodrich raised white letter tires on similar rims at the back.

MAKE:	Ford
BODY STYLE:	Roadster
YEAR:	1934
ENGINE:	Oldsmobile 455 V8
BUILD STYLE:	Traditional Roadster
OWNER:	Jere Sheehan

◀ This classic East Coast '34 roadster has belonged to the President of New England club the Cam Snappers since the early 1950's.

'32 Ford Roadster

Almost looking like a stock example of a '32 roadster to the uninitiated, this California-built Roadster is both nostalgic and understated, yet as cool as you like. What's more, it has an interesting history, having once belonged to the Twentieth Century Fox Studio in Hollywood, where it appeared in the movie *Guess Who's Coming to Dinner*. Since then, both West and East Coast hot rod "names" have worked their own magic on the car – including a chassis by Pete Eastwood, a one-off polished stainless steel floor by Don Borsch and bodywork by Don Thelan, Paul Gamache and Dave Simard.

Underneath that flawless black lacquer finish, which took the owner 14 coats to get to that standard, is a winning combination of hot rod hardware. A '74 Corvette was once home to the 350 Chevy under the hood, although it is now fully-detailed throughout, with period dress-up parts and featuring a pair of '61 Corvette cylinder heads. A TH400 transmission puts the small block's power down to the 4.11:1 gears, contained within the 9-inch rear end that once resided beneath a '57 Ford station wagon. A red leather job by Steve Pierce of OTI makes the interior a comfortable place to be.

MAKE:	Ford
BODY STYLE:	Roadster
YEAR:	1932
ENGINE:	Chevy 350 V8
BUILD STYLE:	Traditional Hot Rod
OWNER:	Ray Kinnunen

▶ Even a Hollywood history doesn't eclipse the fine workmanship that makes this cool '32 such a cool hot rod Roadster.

'32 Ford Roadster

Yet another approach to building a '32 Roadster is this channeled but full-fendered example. The low-slung Deuce employs a number of well-established trick features, without conforming to any one hot rodding stereotype, and still looks real cool doing it.

The heavy channel over the frame is echoed by the chopped roadster screen, while the smooth body, the frame, plus the filled grille shell and the big headlight buckets, are all color-matched in a wild shade of Coral Pearl paint. The weed-eating stance and fine wire-spoked wheels almost give it the air of a European sports car, especially with the "knock-off" centers. Wire wheels like these were always standard on a vintage Jaguar, Ferrari and on other foreign exotica – while back home, they were found on 1950's Chryslers and Buicks.

The open engine compartment shows off the fully-detailed flathead engine complete with Ardun ohv conversion cylinder heads and polished BDS 4-71 blower, with three carbs, the bodies of which have also been color-matched to the body. A Vertex magneto serves to light the fire to the unusual but eye-catching choice of power plant; and polished Lakes pipes spit the gases out in two ways; either uncapped past the cowl, or for more civilized driving, through the muffler system under the car.

MAKE:	Ford
BODY STYLE:	Roadster
YEAR:	1932
ENGINE:	Blown Ardun V8
BUILD STYLE:	Street Rod
OWNER:	Jerry Ash

▸ This '32 Roadster brings together a mixture of hot features into one unusual, but impressive, style of its own.

'29 Ford Sedan

This slick red '29 Sedan, displayed at an indoor show, features modifications very much in the contemporary smooth style with which street rodding has finished up the 20th century, and slipped into the new millennium. The 2-inch roof chop is self-evident and, as is common practice on As, a new steel roof panel has been grafted on. Model A's also have a windshield visor as standard equipment, but this one has been expertly blended into the roofline. To further clean up the body, the handles have been shaved and a new steel Rootleib hood matches the curve of the cowl to the filled Deuce grille shell. The visible hood latching mechanism indicates that the car normally runs hood side panels when not on static display.

A chromed and dropped tube axle adds extra shine to the red front view – while, in profile, it relies on the billet slot mags, the design obviously having been inspired by early Halibrand wheels. The open hood sides reveal a fully-detailed Chevy 350 and this is backed up with a TH350 transmission. Other cool features include the beige tan leather interior with high back bucket seats and the Porsche Guards Red solid paint – with barely visible ghost flames licking along the sides.

MAKE:	Ford
BODY STYLE:	2-door Sedan
YEAR:	1929
ENGINE:	Chevy 350 V8
BUILD STYLE:	Street Rod
OWNER:	Joe Gulla

◄ In a show or on the street, this red Model A sedan can't fail to grab your attention with its very red paint and smooth style.

'27 Ford Track T

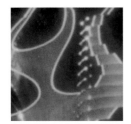

The tradition of building Model T hot rods in the circle track style goes way back. Nevertheless, it has always been there "on the fringes" of mainstream hot rodding. Whilst they certainly never caught on as a style in the way of T bucket or Fad Ts, there was somewhat of a groundswell of interest in them in California back in the mid-1970s. This led to noted rod builder Andy Brizio commissioning a frame from L'il John Buttera with whom to build his own version. This is that same car, several engines and several famous rod-building owners later, each of whom has left his own automotive statement on the car. With metalwork by Ron Covell and paint by Don Varner, this one is possibly the best example of a Track T that it's possible to behold.

Originally built and run by Brizio with a Mazda Rotary engine (a long story, so don't ask!) the 2.3-liter Ford Capri V6 and C4 Auto was substituted by subsequent owner Don Varner. He also made one-off alloy valve covers for the engine, as aftermarket ones weren't available. A 4-barrel carb on an Offy intake feeds the V6, which is squeezed into the narrow engine compartment that is so tight that there is no space under there for any air cleaner. The paint is a re-creation by Don of the original Rod Powell design, with flames and pinstripes licking around the many louvers in the Ron Covell-built nose and hood.

MAKE:	Ford
BODY STYLE:	Roadster
YEAR:	1927
ENGINE:	Ford 2.3-liter V6
BUILD STYLE:	Traditional Track Roadster
OWNER:	Dick Carroll

▸ The low-slung stance and wide track of the cool T indicate that this style owes its roots more to circle track racing than anything else.

'40 Chevy Coupe

Want to grab some attention at a car show? Then take on big, fat-fendered bowtie Coupe from the 1940s, chop it, pro-street it, and then paint it a real loud color. Looks like the formula worked beautifully on this one. The fat '40 looks even chubbier, with the top turret lowered a few inches to accentuate the long hood and wide bumpers. A lot of work has gone into removing all the stock trim and in filling and smoothing out the body, especially at the front, where the bumper has been removed and all holes filled for a real clean look. At the same time the old customizer's trick of frenching the headlamps has been used to great effect.

A big car needs a big engine, especially when it's had the full back-half chassis treatment for the maximum Pro-street look. Somehow, a 4-cylinder Pinto engine just wouldn't do here. Just as well, as this heavy Chevy has an awesome 541 ci big-block Bowtie engine under the hood. It is fed by a dual, quad-equipped 8-71 blower, meaning that the chromed scoop on the hood is totally functional. A set of high-shine Centerline Auto Drag wheels fill the bumpers arches – and check out the exhaust tips notched into the running boards ahead of the rear wheels. House of Kolors Tangerine Pearl makes this one a Chevrolet that's anything but subtle in execution.

MAKE:	Chevrolet
BODY STYLE:	2-door Coupe
YEAR:	1940
ENGINE:	Chevy 541 V8
BUILD STYLE:	Show and Go
OWNER:	Bill Sheridan

▼ Cool, multi-hue graphics splash more color down the sides of this very heavy Chevy Coupe.

'28 Ford Roadster Pickup

These days, custom trucks are an acknowledged part of the overall automotive scene. You can even buy factory custom special editions from your local dealer – but it was hot rodders who first saw the potential in a stripped-down, hopped-up hauler. This Model A Roadster Pickup has long left its farm roots behind, having been built into this so-cool fenderless "peek-op" back in the 1960s. The body and bed now sit on a set of pinched '32 rails with a filled '32 grille shell, all of which also sport some period pinstriping accents over the true-blue metallic squirt-job. A black rolled bench seat provides comfort to the minimal interior.

Most of the front suspension components have seen the inside of a chromer's vat, including the dropped I-beam, shocks and brake back-plates. Rear suspension is early Ford, with unsplit 'bones and a quick-change; and the un-dipped running gear has been detailed in a fetching shade of Baby Blue. This includes the block of the early Chevy V8 that has been equipped with an Offy Tri-power intake and trio of Stromberg 97s. Chrome headers, finned valve covers and a chromed generator cover keep the nostalgic-looking power plant gleaming.

MAKE:	Ford
BODY STYLE:	Roadster Pickup
YEAR:	1928
ENGINE:	Chevy 327 V8
BUILD STYLE:	Traditional 1960's Hot Rod
OWNER:	Alma Conforth

▶ This 1960's-style, Model A Pickup is a welcome variation on the traditional theme of nostalgic open-top hot rodding.

'40 Ford Coupe

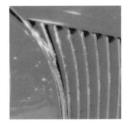

RRED! says the license tag, and we agree that it does exactly what it says, with PPG red gloss almost covering every inch of this fine Forty Coupe. This car is almost a family heirloom, the owner having owned it since he was in high school back in 1957. It's probably been through quite a few changes since then, but this is its latest incarnation. Much of the stock trim is left intact – or, perhaps, more likely, been replaced, including the door handles and mirrors. More red paint covers the smooth running boards. A set of 15-inch Boyds Billet wheels look cool under the fenders both front and back.

Though the rod appears to sit quite level, a 4-inch Bell dropped axle is fitted up front, with a disc brake conversion of unknown origin. An 8-inch rear end does the job out back and handles the power from the 355 ZZ4 Chevy stroker engine under the hood, all via a four-speed shifted manual transmission. For a combination of power, economy and reliability, a tuned port EFI unit feeds the fuel air mixture to the engine in finely-measured doses. The car is a typical example of the kind of quality Street Rod found at rod runs all over the country.

MAKE:	Ford
BODY STYLE:	2-door Coupe
YEAR:	1940
ENGINE:	Chevy 355 V8
BUILD STYLE:	Street Rod
OWNERS:	John and Ginny Urdi

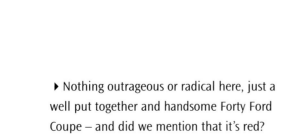

▶ Nothing outrageous or radical here, just a well put together and handsome Forty Ford Coupe – and did we mention that it's red?

'37 Ford Coupe

While an awful lot of '37 Coupes met their fate on the stock car tracks, here's an all-steel one that survived to make a tough Pro-Streeter. A complete custom chassis was fabricated and has been channeled 4-inches for a superb tough stance. This accentuates the fully-tubbed back end that boasts a total of 4-feet of rubber across the back. Front suspension is a mix of custom parts and Heidt's components based on the Mustang II design. Body modifications include filled fender mounting holes, plus sculpted hood sides and smoothed running boards – with Frenched '50 Pontiac taillights at the rear.

Under the hood, with its small custom-fabbed hood scoop, the Coupe is taking no prisoners. There's a 396-ci Chevy big block boasting 375 hp, care of a Demon carb on an early Corvette hi-rise intake. There's a very lumpy cam in there too; and the engine breathes out via a set of Hedman headers. The transmission is a Turbo 400 short shaft 'box with a shift kit. In turn, this rotates a narrowed 9-inch rear, filled with 4.11 gears. Not for nothing is this called a "Business" Coupe – and this '37 means it. Plus, to cap it all, the car was completely owner-built.

MAKE:	Ford
BODY STYLE:	Business Coupe
YEAR:	1937
ENGINE:	Chevy 396 V8
BUILD STYLE:	Street Rod
OWNER:	Steve "Schlos" Schlosberg

▶ Due to their popularity on the stock car tracks way back, all steel '37 Coupes are quite a rarity, the Pro-Street approach totally suits this particular survivor.

'27 Ford Roadster

The humble '27 T roadster, originally built and conceived as basic 2-seat, 4-wheeled transport for the masses, was never a particularly stylish or graceful car. In fact, rolling way up there on big old wooden-spoke wheels, they looked downright awkward. Yet, with hindsight, we generally regard old stockers as "cute" – but that's at best. Sorry, if you own one and disagree, but there you are. However, when you give them the full-on hot rod look, as the early hot rodders did, they take on a completely different image. This 1940's-style T is probably the most sinister looking one around, with its chopped top over a DuVall style screen and channeled body.

A custom-fabricated, track-style nose, more commonly found on dirt track racers of the period, sets the mood. Then, when coupled with a set of Jordan headlights (much sought after by early hot rodders), it couldn't look less like a Ford "Tin Lizzie" if it tried. A fully-built flathead powers the low-slung Roadster and includes a pair of Baron cylinder heads and manifold, with four downdraft Weber carbs that certainly don't look out of place. Baron Engineering is a company dating back to the 1930's, but now remanufacturing Ford-style Flathead speed equipment.

MAKE:	Ford
BODY STYLE:	Model T Roadster
YEAR:	1927
ENGINE:	Traditional Ford Flathead V8
BUILD STYLE:	Early Hot Rod

▶ Such is the authenticity of this car that if you saw a black-and-white photo of this T Roadster, maybe creased and a bit tatty, you'd swear it was taken some time just after World War II.

'32 Ford Pickup

Any pre-World War II hot rod truck that's been whacked this much is always going to draw a crowd, especially when it's driven daily and regularly parked up in the street. This Deuce Pickup has not only had major surgery, in the form of a healthy roof chop, but also features a hard channel over the frame. Resplendent in matt black anti-gloss and owner-scribed flames, this truck wears its finish – not to mention a few battle scars – with the pride of a truck that gets used as, well, a truck! The filled grille shell rides a little low, but looks great anyway. The headlamps are bolted direct to the fenders without the need of a headlamp bar.

The 355 small block is built Chevy Tough, with a lumpy cam installed. It provides the right engine idle note through the home-made Lakes pipes, which disappear through the running boards and back again to run along upside the pickup bed. The engine also features a tasty 3 x 2 Tri-power carb setup and a set of early finned valve covers. Banging though the gears is maximum fun in this hardcore hauler, thanks to the 5-speed manual transmission. Chromed reverse rims feature a set of hand-ground wide whites.

MAKE:	Ford
BODY STYLE:	Closed Cab Pickup
YEAR:	1932
ENGINE:	Chevy 355 V8
BUILD STYLE:	Hardcore Pickup
OWNER:	Dave Paras

▼ How else could you describe this truck other than by referring to it as a "hardcore hauler".

'32 Ford Coupe

Looking at the picture of this cool blue 1950's-style Deuce Coupe, it's hard to believe that it has remained unchanged since it was built in Lincoln, Nebraska back in 1958. It's even harder to believe that the car wasn't built by an experienced rodder, but by a 16-year-old at the time. The young Gary Peterson did a good enough job, however, for it to take a "Best in Show" trophy at a local event back then. This was probably due in part to the fact that it was powered by a 331 ci Hemi, which would have been pretty radical stuff in those days. Having said that, a Hemi-powered Deuce Coupe would still draw a crowd even today!

The big Chrysler V8 is fully chromed and detailed It puts the power down to a '39 Ford transmission with stick shift and a '40 Ford rear end, all of which is still in the car. The Coupe is painted in the original Bahama Blue metallic finish with white firewall and running boards; and you'll notice that the underside of the fenders are also detailed in white, a popular touch back then. Bias belt whitewalls wrap around shinny steel rims are finished off with a set of original Dodge Lancer hub caps.

MAKE:	Ford
BODY STYLE:	5-window Coupe
YEAR:	1932
ENGINE:	Chrysler Hemi 331 V8
BUILD STYLE:	Traditional 1950's Hot Rod
OWNER:	Wayne Martyniak

◄ The front license tag says it all. What could be more hot rod than a '32 with a Hemi!

'24 Phantom Touring

▸ With custom fabrication wherever you look, and with over 500 louvers, this Phantom '24 Touring is about as rare a hot rod as you will ever see – anywhere!

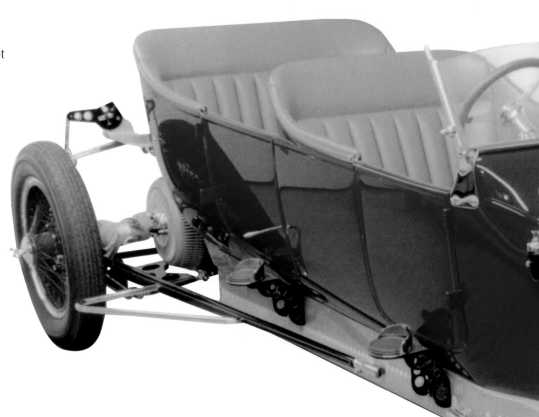

Just where do you start describing this one? It is totally unique. Built around a 10-inch narrowed 1924 Ford 4-door Touring body, it is mounted on a custom 3x1-inch rectangular tube chassis built especially for this car. The suspension treatment is just as imaginative, with a Bell chromed front tube mounted on home-made quarter ellip-tical springs, with '35 Ford rear wishbones and home made friction shocks. At the rear, a '40 Ford rear features a Columbia 2-speed assembly and a Highland Quickchange. More home-made friction shocks are also used, with inboard Buick Drums and 5-ft-long '35 Ford 'bones. The vintage spoke wheels are 19-inch Gardners all round.

Nothing on this car is off-the-shelf, and that includes the engine. A 1933 Ford C 4-cylinder unit is used. It is totally rebuilt, with many custom fabricated parts, including the intake and the one-off air cleaner atop the two Winfield carbs. A 9-foot chromed sidepipe was custom-fabbed by the owner and is mounted on the left side of the body. A '39 Lincoln Zephyr gearbox sits behind a hand-fabricated bell housing. In the metal work department, a custom die was made especially for this car, in order to punch the cool curved louvers into the narrow hood top. There's also a fully-louvered belly pan beneath the car.

MAKE:	Ford
BODY STYLE:	Phantom Touring
YEAR:	1924
ENGINE:	1933 Ford C 4-cylinder
BUILD STYLE:	Traditional
OWNER:	Richie Willett

'30 Ford Roadster

Some years ago, an article in the hot rod press coined the phrase "New-stalgia", meaning a traditional-looking or influenced car, not ashamed to incorporate the best of modern technology. The term could well apply to this '30 Ford Model A roadster, since what appears to be a very Trad-styled roadster, is actually powered by a 1985 Maserati V6 Bi-turbo – and, yes, that does actually mean one turbocharger for each bank of cylinders! From the original Model A only the body remains and this has had every panel altered in some way, including converting the doors to "suicide" operation and, at the same time, stretching them some two inches. The rear fenders have been stretched the same amount, and the trunk lid was similarly shortened.

In profile, the chassis resembles a modified Deuce, but was completely custom-built for the rod, with wider than normal front frame rails in order to accommodate the Italian thoroughbred engine. The exotic V6 has been detailed throughout with red paint, and chrome features extensively on the overhead cam engine covers, the fuel-injection throttle bodies and the turbos themselves. The engine drives through a BMW ZF transmission and down to a good old Ford 9-inch rear end. This, like the front axle, is suspended on a chromed 4-bar arrangement. It may not rumble like an American V8, but in full song, these high-revving, imported engines howl like the proverbial banshee!

MAKE:	Ford Model A
BODY STYLE:	Roadster
YEAR:	1930
ENGINE:	Maserati V6 Bi-turbo
BUILD STYLE:	Street Rod
OWNER:	David Annacone

▸ Looking very much like an East Coast nostalgic custom rod, the "Masi-Rod" – as it's known – combines old and new technology into a show-winning format.

'32 Plymouth Roadster Pickup

Starting with a Plymouth with too many doors and his own fertile imagination, the builder of this rod succeeded in converting a Mopar more-door into this tasty little 2-door retro Roadster Pickup. Further disguising its origins at the front, is the use of a '33 Chevy grille and a set of big '34 Ford Commercial headlamps. At the back, the truck bed was built entirely at home by the owner and is covered by a custom-made white tarp. Full size rear fenders look like they are the original Plymouth items adapted, the front sports neat cycle type items to stay legal.

There's a Willys front axle under this swap meet special, hung on a set of parallel leaf springs, as per Plymouth's original plan, and the rear axle used is a Ford 8-inch, which takes the power from a Powerglide transmission. This, in turn, is bolted to the Chevy 350 V8 that powers the truck. The fully-detailed engine boasts a brace of Carter 4-barrel carbs and a big Hilborn-style chromed scoop. A set of Block-hugger headers run into the truck's underslung exhaust, which exits just in front of the rear wheel. Chromed reverse wheels are fitted with cool little spinners in the centers. A truly fun truck!

MAKE:	Plymouth
BODY STYLE:	Roadster Pickup
YEAR:	1932
ENGINE:	Chevy 350 V8
BUILD STYLE:	Traditional
OWNER:	Ron Phillips

▶ Anyone can order up a bunch of parts with a phone and a credit card these days, but this guy had more fun searching out the swap meets for cool parts for this handy hauler.

'32 Ford Roadster

This '32 may not have the prettiest paint job in town, but that's more than made up for in its overall look and some very tasty vintage speed equipment. A chopped windshield gives the Deuce plenty of attitude, even before you start examining the parts used. These include a front suspension, comprising a dropped dago'd I-beam on drilled split-wishbones with early friction shocks. Also, just below the trunk floor, we find a Halibrand quick-change rear end. To complete the picture, the front hubs feature a set of Buick brake drums on the Ford spindles.

Instead of vintage flathead or even Chevrolet power, we find a big early Oldsmobile J2 engine between the frame rails. In this case, it's one that dates back to the rock'n'roll year of 1957. Two 2-barrel Rochester carbs feed the big Olds, mounted as they are on an Edmunds manifold. Although the engine features minimal dress-up, a set of Vintage Offenhauser valve covers are used, along with a pair of chromed domed air cleaners. In line with traditional practice, the Lakes pipes are made up from '39 Ford torque tubes in order to add even more "old school cool."

MAKE:	Ford
BODY STYLE:	Highboy Roadster
YEAR:	1932
ENGINE:	Oldsmobile J2 V8
BUILD STYLE:	Hardcore Roadster
OWNER:	Tim Chapman

▶ This Olds-powered Deuce certainly has all the right stuff to make the appropriate nostalgic statement. Well, alright…!

'32 Ford Pickup

We don't know how long this Deuce Pickup served its time as working truck for someone, but it's hard-working days are long since over, now that it sports all the trappings of a high school 1950's hot rod. The fenders and running boards have long gone in favor of the highboy look, as have the hood sides, in order to show off the new heavy duty Chrysler Hemi mill within. The roof of the truck cab has been hammered down to true hot rod dimensions, instead of its previous too-tall look, and the hood top sports four rows of louvers behind the filled grille shell. Wild Raspberry colors the cab and chassis in a bold statement, but contrasts well with the white firewall. This theme is carried forward with the white pinstriping on the upper body.

Plenty of chrome features on the truck, starting with the chromed I-beam and front shocks. Chrome also features on the front brake backplates and split wish-bones at one end, finishing with the custom tail pipes, running from under the frame and up and along the upper bed sides. To further compliment the paint scheme, a white tarp has been added to the bed and – of course – whitewall bias belt tires feature on steelies, with caps and rings. White, rolled trim on the interior of the cab confirms that this is one hauler that's dressed to thrill!

MAKE:	Ford
BODY STYLE:	Closed Cab Pickup
YEAR:	1932
ENGINE:	Chrysler Hemi V8
BUILD STYLE:	Traditional 1950's Hot Rod
OWNER:	Mark Van Acker

◄ This '32 is one Hemi-hammered hauler that wouldn't look out of place at the high school hop.

'40 Ford 2-door Sedan

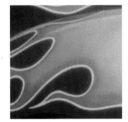

One of the hardest jobs out there in hot rod land is chopping the top on a big car, especially one of which the top and rear quarters don't have a straight line anywhere. It takes a brave man to start cutting metal, knowing that it has to end up with the correct profile, fully-ground welds and positively no distortion. Get it wrong and you'll be hammering forever, or paying out big money to fix it. Fortunately for this hardcore '40 everything turned out fine, making for one streamlined satin Sedan. The chrome and stainless trim that was removed for the bodywork never went back on the car; but plenty of suede black did, this being livened up with a vivid flame job in yellow and red.

This "flaming forty" doesn't just look hot – it is hot! A tuned small block Chevy went in under the hood to make sure. The three pedals make driving more fun, the manual shifter stirring five forward gears, courtesy of a Borg Warner manual transmission. All it needed to complete the picture was the set of Moon discs and whitewall tires to make this hardcore 2-door ready to cruise.

MAKE:	Ford
BODY STYLE:	2-door Sedan
YEAR:	1940
ENGINE:	Chevy 350 V8
BUILD STYLE:	Hardcore Sedan
OWNER:	Chuck Beaulieu

▶ It's not just the early cars that get the totally hardcore treatment, as this flaming forty Ford ably demonstrates.

'34 Chevy 2-door Sedan

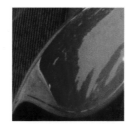

Fords may well have been the first choice of hot rodders since the very start, but who can deny the sophisticated and classy look of this smooth '34 Chevy 2-door Sedan Street Rod? The smooth body features a 3-inch chop that really accentuates the long hood and flowing fenders. The hood sides are smooth, with just two sculpted vents in each side, while the running boards are also smoothed out. The rear view mirrors are painted and minimal in size so as not to interrupt the lines of the slippery sedan. The Brandywine pearl paint is so deep it still looks wet, and not surprisingly, it's a House of Kolors product.

Underneath the skin of this cherry Chevy, the chassis features a fully independent Mustang II front end. A tough Ford 9-inch is installed to handle the smooth power that is provided by the 355 ci stroked small block Chevy. Between the two is a GM 700 R4 4-speed automatic transmission. Fitting snugly under the fenders are a big set of Billet Specialties polished alloy rims, riding on a low profile Good Year Eagle tires. The interior is comfortable and understated, with high-back gray cloth bucket seats and matching trim throughout.

MAKE:	Chevrolet
BODY STYLE:	2-door Sedan
YEAR:	1934
ENGINE:	Chevy 355 V8
BUILD STYLE:	Street Rod
OWNER:	Ron Kistler

◀ Smooth and classy, with deep red House of Kolors paint, this 1930s Chevy Sedan is one comfortable cruiser.

'35 Ford Coupe

While the speed-crazy early hot rodders were tearing up the salt (and the roads) in their stripped-down and hopped-up machines, the early customizers were taking a different route altogether. Working their art with hammer and blowtorch, they started turning the Art-Deco cars of the late 1930s and early 1940s into rolling works of art that influenced many and still look great today. Of that style is this slippery '35 Ford Coupe, so typical of that early "taildragger" style made famous by names such as Harry Westergard and Jack Calori. The emphasis was on improving the lines that were already there, rather than any radical change for change's sake; and although performance wasn't the objective, streamlining for beauty's sake definitely was.

To that end, the art of the roof chop was perfected, with many a tall turret-topped car being hammered down to a lean and mean profile – such as this one. The rear all-enclosing fender skirts are obvious, but the blending into the fenders of the normally pedestal-mounted headlamps is not, with '40 Chevy headlamp pods being the favorite conversion. A lowered stance is a must, with the chassis often being kicked up at the rear or z'ed to raise the mounting point of the axle and thus lowering the car. Whitewalls and Mercury "Dogdish" hub caps provide the only "flash" to this cool but understated ride.

MAKE:	Ford
BODY STYLE:	2-door Coupe
YEAR:	1935
ENGINE:	Ford Flathead V8
BUILD STYLE:	Traditional1940's Custom
OWNER:	Dick Brown

◂ This cool '35 retains its Flathead powered roots, although this it has a full house-tuned engine under the long black hood.

'36 Ford Woodie

▸ If pine is fine, and wood is good, then this cool '36 has all the tricks!

Looking like it just drove straight off a Beach Boys' album cover, this rare but so-cool '36 Woodie almost epitomizes the 1960's Southern California life. All it needs is a couple of long boards strapped to the roof in order to complete the illusion of a West Coast Woodie. Having said that, there was one surfing record about a surfer who was back East with his Woodie all covered in snow! We don't know if this was the very car, but the straight '36 sheet metal on this one – with all its original features, trim and perfect varnished woodwork – belies the hot period, go-faster goodies under the hood.

Those goodies consisting of an early 1960's Chevy 283-ci small block. This is all kitted out with no-name finned aluminum valve covers, a Joe Hunt Magneto and

a Bell air cleaner. There's even a set of race-style fenderwell headers to blow the gases away. Inside the orange crate, the black bench seats are highlighted with orange piping and matching orange Metalflake inserts. A Banjo steering wheel is included in there too. The polished period slot mags are a set of rare Ansens, shod with BR Goodrich raised white letter tires.

Come to think of it, real surfers woodies were never this nice!

MAKE:	Ford
BODY STYLE:	4-door Woody Wagon
YEAR:	1936
ENGINE:	Chevy 283 V8
BUILD STYLE:	Street
OWNER:	Steve Jones

'32 Ford Coupe

 ay up in the North East is a small but enterprising hot rod shop where the only language spoken is "traditional." These guys are known as the Rollin' Bones Hot Rod Shop – and maybe you could be forgiven for not having heard of them. Not many people had, that is, until they not only hit Bonneville with a vengeance, but poured real salt all over the floor at the Grand National roadster show. There, they displayed their primer-finished cars among the glitz and glitter of the famous event, causing quite a stir at the same time. This '32 is typical of their work; a real Deuce, built with real parts and a real flathead!

Made to drive, and then some, the way-cool '32 features a 5-inch roof chop tapering to 4–inch in the rear, more louvers than you could count and all the correct goodies. The 276-inch Flathead engine features Edelbrock finned heads, an Isky cam, plus an Edmunds 2-pot intake with a pair of '94s. Driving through a GM T5 'box, a Halibrand quick-change spins those steelies and bias-plys with alarming regularity. It almost goes without saying that the hot rod Deuce Coupe runs a drilled front axle with drilled, split wishbones and Buick drums; but we don't often see a Shroeder cowl steering set-up on a street car.

MAKE:	Ford
BODY STYLE:	3-window Coupe
YEAR:	1932
ENGINE:	Flathead V8
BUILD STYLE:	Traditional Hot Rod
OWNER:	Ken Schmidt

◄ It looks perfect in primer. So, when a rod gets put together with this combination of vintage parts, who needs shiny paint?

'40 Oldsmobile Convertible

We cannot claim that that there are too many Oldsmobiles in this book. The marque has just never been a popular one for hot rodders to use as their "base material." Nevertheless, a good few overhead valve Rocket V8s have been used to power them, especially in the early days before the Chevy small-block was introduced. Having said that, there's always someone out there looking to build something different. After all, it's all down to your vision and imagination. Even so, it took eight years for the owner of this smooth Olds to realize his dream; then four years to buy it and four more years to build it as a present for his wife.

The radical restyling of the po-faced stock Olds really works. The wings and front panel are blended and molded together for a clean and seamless style that reminds you of the original; but is still very different. The raked Mercedes Benz headlamps really work here too. Keeping it all Oldsmobile, we find a hefty big block 455-ci engine under the nosed, peaked and pancaked hood – although a late model Corvette gave up its independent front and rear suspension for the cause. The rad ride rolls on 17-inch Budnik wheels with low-profile rubber.

MAKE:	Oldsmobile
BODY STYLE:	2-door Convertible
YEAR:	1940
ENGINE	Oldsmobile 455 V8
BUILD STYLE	Show
OWNER	Ginny Baukus

▸ "Dare to be different" someone said once regarding street rods. This custom mix "Apricot Perfect Pearl" 40 Oldsmobile certainly lives up to that adage.

'30 Ford Roadster

A superb recreation of a period Hot Rod by Jim Lowrey's Hot Rods up in New Hampshire, this '30 Model A has it all. The body sits on the pinched '32 rails like it grew there, with the classic Deuce grill all matched together by the Sherwin Williams Mandarin Maroon gloss finish – which, in itself, lends the air of retro-class to the roadster. Traditional red-painted suspension details and steel wheels are set off by the Larry Hook subtle pinstriping. Only the modern radial tires lend a clue to the fact that this is a modern interpretation of a classic hot rod. Well, you can't see the power antennae on the car, can you?

It's all quality hardware under the hood, with many of the vintage speed parts that are available once again for the huge nostalgia market. A '46 Ford Flathead 276-ci V8 is used here wearing a set of Offy heads and Fenton headers. A polished Offy manifold sports a brace of 97s in classic style. These days, it's relatively easy to extract the maximum from the flat engine by using a T5 manual 5-speed 'box, a luxury they would have killed for in the old days; and this '30 has one as well as a super strong Ford 9-inch rear end.

MAKE:	Ford
BODY STYLE:	Roadster
YEAR:	1930
ENGINE:	Ford Flathead 276 V8
BUILD STYLE:	Nostalgic Hot Rod
OWNER:	Gene Scribner

◄ Hardcore traditionalists might baulk at the wide radial whitewalls on this period roadster; but that tells us it was built to drive.

'46 Ford Roadster

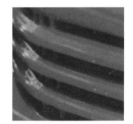

There is no denying that the '42-48 series of Fords are a portly bunch design-wise, and were probably the models that gave rise to the phrase "Fat Fendered" for these roly-poly rods. But look what happens when you put one on a low-cal diet for a while – causing it to shed some of that heavy chrome and stainless and then accentuate its super model looks by chopping the windshield, big difference huh? And, by the way, who doesn't appreciate topless super models? Apart from the dropped top, much smoothing of the body has made this '46 look twice as long as normal, the subtle graphic on the beltline on top of the PPG Pearl orange helping to complete the illusion.

A smooth front-end treatment of the '46 includes subtle Frenched headlamps and full color-coded grille and fender with tiny flush-mounted turn signals. Under the hood is a fully-dressed Chevy LT1 small block, running a tuned-port EFI system that's also been polished to perfection. This is linked up to a 700R4 transmission and a Ford nine-inch rear end for effortless top-down cruising. The 4-wheel JFZ brakes and air-ride suspension feature on the '46 Convertible too, along with 17- and 20-inch 5-spoke rolling stock.

MAKE:	Ford
BODY STYLE:	Convertible
YEAR:	1946
ENGINE:	Chevy LT1 V8
BUILD STYLE:	Traditional Street Rod
OWNER:	Bob Sodano

▼ The smooth body treatment and chopped windshield really accentuate the length of this fab '46.

'30 Ford Coupe

This 5-window Model A is yet another "living history" car that came to light after years of long-term storage. Like a fine wine, its aged patina is something you can't recreate overnight. The rich, dark green lacquer, with its inevitably cracked finish, bears testament to this. Originally built in 1958, it bears all the hallmarks of its day, with a fenderless lowboy look, courtesy of the channeled body and a chopped and peaked Deuce grille shell. As with most rods of the period, the running gear is all early Ford, with a banjo rear end, manual transmission and drum brakes all round.

Obviously built for the street, the early hot rod isn't bestowed with an overabundance of chrome. Instead, some hard-earned 1950's wage packets have been spent at the speed shop or swap meet, in order to coax some more mph out of the Flathead engine. The venerable V8 features a pair of Offy heads – and instead of the almost obligatory Edelbrock, we find an Almquist 2-pot manifold. Strombergs are still the carbs of choice, however, with a pair of 97s bolted right up top. A neat, but unseen, feature is the custom-molded dash with Stewart Warner gauges.

MAKE:	Ford
BODY STYLE:	5-window Coupe
YEAR:	1930
ENGINE:	Flathead V8
BUILD STYLE:	Traditional Hot Rod
OWNER:	Mark Conforth

▶ Straight from the 1950's to the 21st century, this Model A is truly a piece of living history.

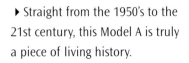

'40 Willys

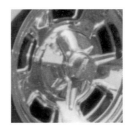

ould this be yet another quarter-mile-hero, Willys Coupe ex-race car, resurrected and given the contemporary Pro-Street treatment ready for a new life on the street? It certainly is a steel car – did any '37-42 Coupes escape the hacksaws and welding torches of the 1960's gasser teams? Just for a change, it's nice to see this product of the Willys Overland Co with all the factory trim intact, including the hood trim and the fenders. Known as "Lime Disease" the Glasurit Daphyne green-themed car – continues the color to the roll-cage inside, the fenders and the mirrors.

Perhaps as a nod of respect to the Chrysler-powered gasser's of the past, this Willys too, has a Mopar V8 engine under the pointed hood. In this case, a 360-cube engine with W2 race heads and a Holley 750. The transmission is a 904 Chrysler product to match the engine along with a much narrowed but stout Mopar 8 rear end. The wheels, much reminiscent of early Halibrand's, are actually fully polished Billet Specialties, rims fitted with American spinners. What else but big Mickey Thompson's fill those huge tubbed rear fenders?

MAKE:	Willys
BODY STYLE:	Coupe
YEAR:	1940
ENGINE:	Chrysler 360 V8
BUILD STYLE:	Pro-Street Rod
OWNER:	Mark Albright

◄ Running all Mopar running gear, this sub-lime Willys Coupe wearing factory brightwork is fooling no-one.

'28 Ford Roadster

It would be easy to assume that just because the owner of a traditional hot rod prefers to build a car with genuine old school parts – scrounged up from 'yards and swap meets for the sake of authenticity – that the car is rarely driven, and that even when it is, it's only to local weekend shows. Well, this is often far from the truth, and just to set the record straight is this well and truly high-mileage '28 Highboy Roadster. This car regularly gets driven right across the country, coast to coast and back again, its owner residing on the East Coast, but belonging to the Outriders hot rod club on the West.

The faded black '28 has all early running gear, with Kelsey Hayes red wires and early Firestone bias-ply tires. Like many stripped-down early hot rods, custom body mods are limited to just the filled '32 Ford grille shell up front. A pair of minimal enginecycle turn signals has been fitted in the name of safety. The trusty flathead that beats in the heart of this roadster is a '41 Military issue unit, fitted with a set of Navarro heads and a Thickston PM7 dual intake, with a pair of 94s. And if that's a good enough set-up to get this car across country on a regular basis, then that's all you need.

MAKE:	Ford
BODY STYLE:	Roadster
YEAR:	1928
ENGINE:	Ford Flathead V8
BUILD STYLE:	Traditional Early Hot Rod
OWNER:	Sketch

◀ Just to prove that automotive reliability is nothing new, witness this coast-to-coast running '28 A roadster!

'48 Chevy Pickup

Always popular with the street rod crowd, these post-World War II pickups always seem to check into pre-49 rod events as 48-49s, don't they? Guess they didn't make many '50-'54s, or else rodders don't build them that much – yeah right! Anyhow, it doesn't much matter if they turn out looking as cool and as mean as this severely whacked example. Many hours and just a few Sawzall blades went into lowering the lid to the max on this classic pickup. Looks like it's had some serious chassis work too, in order to achieve that weed-eating stance.

As well as the major chop job, the straight body has received much attention, including de-chroming and filling, before squirting the pale orange pearl all over, including the color-coded grille, fenders and sports mirrors. There's a neat Frenched aerial on that right hand front wing too. The polished wheels look like a set of Boyd's complete with spinners, shod with BF Goodrich blackwalls. We are a little short on tech-spec on this one but we'll guess at a Chevy small block under the hood. Apologies to owner Barry Franz.

MAKE:	Chevrolet
BODY STYLE:	Pickup
YEAR:	1948
ENGINE:	Chevy 350 V8
BUILD STYLE:	Street Rod
OWNER:	Barry Franz

▶ Just in case he loses the truck in the local shopping mall car park, the license tag will help the owner find it among all the other chopped pickups!

'33 Ford Roadster

Is it brand new, or is it a restoration? Either way, this '33 Lakes Roadster looks like it's moving even when it isn't! The strictly-competition salt flats racer has all the right moves about it and we would guess that the inclusion of headlamps means that it runs in one of the street classes. (They don't run the salt at night, do they?) The windshield has been removed to decrease wind resistance and the driver sits low in the cockpit for the same reason. Note the low height of the chromed rollover hoop, as well as an aluminum grille insert with punched holes for cooling – that replaces the stock grille – and plenty of louvers in the hood side panels also aid cooling on those long burns.

A dropped I-beam on hairpins keeps things nice and traditional up front, albeit with the modern advantage of disc brakes. At the other end of the roadster, a Halibrand Quick Change rear end is hung on a four-bar link. Underneath that aggressive shotgun air scoop on the hood is a blown small-block Chevy full of the good stuff, driving the roadster to three figure top speeds via a TH350 transmission. More tradition is evident in the form of skinny bias ply tires on low calorie steel rims with Moon discs. The Salt warrior is finished off in a cool blue pearl finish with period decals.

MAKE:	Ford
BODY STYLE:	Roadster
YEAR:	1933
ENGINE:	Chevy 350 V8
BUILD STYLE:	Traditional Lakester
OWNER:	Gary Jankowski

◀ This '33 roadster cuts a dash in full salt lakes style with lots of traditional features and a healthy blown engine under the

The Outlaw

The Outlaw is widely regarded as the first true show car built by the famous Ed "Big Daddy" Roth, a larger than life character in every sense of the word – car builder, bike builder, artist, cartoonist and almost the inventor of Kustom Kulture itself. Loosely inspired by the Grabowski T Bucket, Roth wanted to build a car in fiberglass, something few people were using in the early 1960's. Although it looks like a T, it has a unique body designed and molded by Roth himself. It made the cover of *Car Craft* in 1960 and was a regular car show attraction, instantly drawing attention to Roth's pinstriping, painting and T-shirt business.

The crazy rod was built as a functioning car and had a Caddy engine with four carbs – again similar to the Kookie T – not to mention a fully-chromed under carriage. The most unusual feature is probably the molded nose with its wild "eyebrows" over the headlamps. It is made from fiberglass, but the mystery is *how* he made it. Noone has ever seen a mold for it even though the mold for the actual body still exists. After Roth sold it, it was displayed at various auto collections and museums and had several paint jobs over the years. Fully restored, it is now a permanent exhibit at the Petersen museum.

MAKE:	The Outlaw
BODY STYLE:	2-seat Roadster
YEAR:	1960
ENGINE:	Cadillac V8
BUILD STYLE:	Show Rod
BUILDER:	Ed Roth

▸ Molded one-off bodywork, wild paint and much chrome, mean that there are few recognizable parts on the Outlaw apart from the Cadillac engine and the '22 Dodge windshield.

'32 Ford Pickup

 Universally known as "The Grasshopper," this '32 truck was initially built as the shop truck for the Detroit-based Alexander Brothers, creators of some of the finest customs of the 1950s and 1960s. Its status soon grew from humble parts-chaser to being a show circuit favorite itself, and it certainly acted as a rolling billboard for the A-brothers' talents.

In recent years many old rods and customs have been restored, but very few by the same guys that built them in the first place. But this one is an exception, having been bought back after nearly forty years by Mike Alexander, who built the truck originally.

After this amount of time it's understandable that Mike decided to re-furnish the truck with a new repro frame as he wanted it to be a driver, in fact all that remains of the original chassis components is the Bell front axle, the rest being upgraded as necessary.

Most of the steel is the original though, the 2-inch chopped cab, the Model A fenders and even the '37 Dodge truck headlamps are still there. A fully-built '48 Ford Flathead powers the truck once again, just like it did back in 1957 – but this time driving through a C4 Automatic transmission.

MAKE:	Ford
BODY STYLE:	Closed Cab Pickup
YEAR:	1932
ENGINE:	Flathead V8
BUILD STYLE:	Show Truck
OWNER:	Mike Alexander

◀ The restoration of the Alexander Brothers' '32 truck "The Grasshopper" isn't just as good as the original build, it's even better!

'32 Ford Roadster

For over 20 years now, Brizios, as its known, has been *the* hot rod building shop in Northern California. Based in San Francisco and run by Roy Brizio, the shop prides itself on turning out not only top quality hot rods, but also hot rods that are really built to drive as well. Brizios thrives on the family name, as Roy's father Andy has built many cool rods over the years and is also famous for founding the very successful T-shirt company called Andy's T's. A few years ago, the shop built a cool flamed '32 nicknamed the "Rodfather" similar to this one, for Mr. Brizio, Sr. to use, and use it he did, driving it all over the country and clocking up over 100,000 miles in the process.

The '32 shown is its replacement, named Rodfather 2, and is very similar in appearance to its predecessor apart from the colors used. The purple with yellow flames on the old car are replaced on this one with Orange Pearl by Darryl Hollenbeck and multi-hue blue flames by Art Himsl. The body is a new all-steel repro from Rod Bod's in a very traditional style with filled grille shell and a Du Vall screen. In anticipation of further high mileage duty, a new crate engine was installed in the shape of a fully-dressed, 360 hp Ford 351 V8 that is mated to a GM 700R4 transmission and coupled to a Ford 9-inch rear axle. See it at a rod run near you soon!

MAKE:	Ford
BODY STYLE:	Highboy Roadster
YEAR:	1932
ENGINE:	Ford 351 V8
BUILD STYLE:	Street Rod
OWNER:	Andy Brizio

▸ At Brizio's, they like their Ford Hot Rods powered by Ford engines, and Andy Brizio's Rodfather 2 is no exception with its hi-po 351 installed up front.

The Red Baron

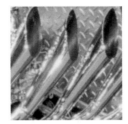

A strange sub-class of hot rodding surfaced in the world of the 1960s indoor car shows, with the advent of the wild show cars. These imaginative creations resembled three-dimensional cartoons and became evermore crazy as the trend continued. Always show-stopping, but rarely drivable, they were the ultimate excesses of rodder's fertile imaginations. Once built, they were very popular with the show-going public, and many were reproduced in both die-cast and plastic model kit form.

Shown here is the "Red Baron" designed by Tom Daniels who was also responsible for many of the way-out hot rod model kits for Monogram. In this case, the model was built first, and then later commissioned as a full size show-rod by show promoter Bob Larivee, Sr. It was built by Chuck Miller in his Styline Customs shop and featured a Pontiac 6-cylinder overhead cam engine and wheels by Keystone, with slicks on all four corners. The car continues to be displayed at shows and still belongs to Chuck Miller.

MAKE:	The Red Baron
BODY STYLE:	Unique
YEAR:	1969
ENGINE:	Pontiac 6-cylinder
BUILD STYLE:	Show Rod
OWNER:	Chuck Miller

◀ With Red Candy paint by Rod Powell, "The Red Baron" is an old show favorite and has been reproduced in many sizes in die-cast and model kits.

'32 Ford Coupe

There are probably more top-class hot rod builders turning out show quality hot rods these days than at any time in the hobby's history. Some even say that – with the quantity of new hot rod's that are built each year, in such a wide range of styles – this is indeed the true "Golden Age of Hot Rodding." Consequently, it is argued that future rodders will be burdened with possible further fuel restrictions or alternatives, plus heavy-handed automotive over-legislation, so will look back at these times with a misty-eyed nostalgia. Perhaps the archetypal twenty-first century, pro-built Deuce Coupe like this one will become tomorrow's much-coveted classic? Hot rods are already beginning to command big money at classic car auctions, so who knows?

If that is the case in the future, then this Brizio-built 5-window is a prime candidate for future speculation. Built using an original '32 steel body, it has all the hallmarks of a Bay Area build, with traditional proportions courtesy of a 3-inch chop and a fenderless highboy profile. The style is right on the money. The Pearl Green by Camilleri's Auto Works is vibrant yet different, and the flames are the unmistakable work of Art Himsl.

But it's not only the paint that's hot, the flaming 5-window packs quite a punch under the hood, with a 514 cube Ford crate engine, stirred with a Richmond 6-speed transmission.

MAKE:	Ford
BODY STYLE:	5-window Coupe
YEAR:	1932
ENGINE:	Ford 514 V8
BUILD STYLE:	Contemporary Street Rod
OWNER:	Keith Grozich

▶ Traditional features like louvers and stainless hairpins are matched to the contemporary look by the big diameter Billet Specialties rims and low profile rubber.

'27 Ford Roadster

The success of the Oakland Roadster Show on the West Coast from 1950 onwards prompted the Michigan Hot Rod Association to inaugurate a similar event – the Detroit Autorama – to showcase the top Eastern-built cars. In order to rival the AMBR trophy (several winners of which are well documented in these pages), the Ridler award was presented at that first show in Detroit; and this is the car that won it. Although California is credited as being the home to many early landmark hot rods – such as the Niekamp and Flint roadsters, Doane Spencer's 32, etc. etc. – this Detroit-built car is every bit as deserving of recognition as those cars. We present here the Frank Mack T.

Like the Niekamp car, it features a track style, hand-formed nose and 3-piece hood, all in aluminum by the original builder, Frank Mack. It also has a full louvered belly pan underneath its channeled body. Additionally, Mack also fabricated the chromed grille and neat nerf bars on the sleek hot rod. Those headlamps could have been made specifically for hot rodders, but, in fact, they are '27 Jordan items and are now fitted with sealed beam headlamps. This is one of the few updates on this original, unrestored early hot rod, which has 15-inch steelies featuring '47 Hudson hubcaps with a brass center spinner.

MAKE:	Ford
BODY STYLE:	Roadster
YEAR:	1927
ENGINE:	Flathead V8
BUILD STYLE:	Traditional Street Roadster
BUILDER:	Frank Mack

◄ Very few early hot rods survive in this condition without major restoration, especially ones with the historical importance of the Frank Mack T.

'40 Ford Sedan

A 1940's Ford sedan with all the right moves to be a real high school hot rod from the late 1950s – although it's doubtful if many of the class of '58 had one quite as cool as this. Nevertheless, all the elements are there. No expensive custom body modifications on this one; just nicely detailed, with flawless Indigo Blue paint and some cool pinstriping by the "one-armed bandit" Charlie Decker. The bumpers have been removed in favor of neat dice-topped nerf bars, and the white running board covers make for a very neat and contrasting effect. Inside, a very cool red and white stitch job is matched by the white steering wheel. The stock '40 dash features Stewart Warner gauges.

The most dramatic change to the 1940's profile is the lack of hood on the car. This highlights the white-painted firewall and (of course) the detailed engine. That engine is a '60 Chevy 283 ci V8, equipped with an Offy intake and a trio of Stromberg 97s. The rest of the running gear is all stock '40 Ford thru to the rear end. Not obvious in the picture is the dropped front axle for that extra hot rod rake; but the '50 Merc steel wheels whitewalls are an unmissable and welcome addition.

MAKE:	Ford
BODY STYLE:	2-door Sedan
YEAR:	1940
ENGINE:	Chevy 350 V8
BUILD STYLE:	Traditional
OWNER:	Mark Conforth

▸ The body of this sedan may well be left as Henry intended; but there's no doubting the period hot rod influences on this super-cool Sedan.

'32 Ford Sedan

Let's face it; all Deuces are cool, no matter what their body style. Although the Sedan body styles make for some great-looking cars, quite often they can also look a bit sedate when left with all the bumpers and running boards intact – neat, but sedate. However, to unleash the real hot rod heart of a sedan, you must ditch the fenders and go the highboy route. Not only do you get to see the graceful curves of the '32 frame, but you can also appreciate all the cool suspension hardware that is normally hidden by the sheet metal. You can do that even better if, like this Baby Blue example, there is a 3-inch chop involved.

All the right front-end parts are clearly on display here. After all, why have a polished I-beam on hairpins, with chrome shocks and Buick brakes, if no one can see them? Come to think of it, leave the hood at home too, and let the folk see the detailed Flathead complete with Offy heads, Vertex Magneto and – best of all – a rare Danekas 6-71 blower topped with a pair of quad carbs. A manually shifted transmission gets the ponies to the pavement via a Ford 9-inch rear end.

MAKE:	Ford
BODY STYLE:	2-door Sedan
YEAR:	1932
ENGINE:	Flathead V8
BUILD STYLE:	Traditional Hot Rod Sedan
OWNER:	Scot Cave

◀ The American Racing 5-spokes with black walls lend a mid to late 1960's feel to this fenderless Deuce Sedan.

'23 Ford Roadster

Sometimes, it seems there are more ways to build a Model T than nearly any other make of hot rod. Lakes style or Fad, Turtledeck roadster or Doctor's coupe, nostalgia or resto – the choice is yours. This one goes for the simple approach; classic T-bucket format with the abbreviated Pickup back end, But it's done in the hardcore black anti-gloss finish that we are so used to seeing on the Model A and Deuce roadsters and coupes in recent years. Conventional Ts are usually the home of chrome as well, so it makes a change to see this one using a good honest dose of gloss black for the suicide front end, hairpins and steering arms. The same goes for the '57 Chevy back axle under there.

With all this anti-shine going on, the few bright bits that have been used draw your attention straight to the awesome engine that sets this T apart from the crowd. No less a lump than a 325-inch Dodge Red Ram Hemi-built .030 pushes along this bodacious bucket. Triple Rochesters on an Offy intake feed the beast, while a set of finned valve covers and Moon angled breathers provide a little dress up. Custom headers are guaranteed to melt your shoes when entering and exiting the hot T. Add red steels and whitewalls and a skull shifter for an instant hardcore classic.

MAKE:	Ford
BODY STYLE:	T Roadster
YEAR:	1923
ENGINE:	Dodge 325 ci Hemi V8
BUILD STYLE:	Hardcore Roadster
OWNER:	Charlie Gish

▼ The normally high windshield is folded down on this hardcore Hemi T-Bucket for a little "wind-in your face" hot rodding.

'29 Ford Roadster

Nothing proves that a car is built to be driven like a fine covering of highway dust. In addition, for those unbelievers who don't think magazine cars ever get driven, may we present this Model A Roadster on '32 rails. This '29 starred in a regular *Street Rodder* Magazine build-up feature in the latter half of the 1990s, culminating in a very popular cover shot and feature. The slick green machine was built from an original design by Chip Foose, dubbed "The California Spyder," and owned by hot rod journalist and photographer Eric Geisert. Once built, the car completed many highway miles and this picture was taken at the El Mirage dry lakes in California at just about the same time that the feature hit the newsstands.

A traditional dropped-tube front was assembled from new aftermarket parts. Power came from a crate engine Ford SVO 302, fully dressed and using a Holley 500 on an Edelbrock Performer manifold. The headers were by Bassani and the transmission was a Ford AOD item. Rear end on the cool, but very dependable, hot rod was a 4.11-geared Currie 8-inch unit on a TCI triangulated 4-link. Budnik wheels featured all round, and the custom Spyder Green paint was a DuPont mix applied by Darryl Hollenbeck. A tan leather interior complemented the green perfectly.

MAKE:	Ford
BODY STYLE:	Roadster 2-door Sedan
YEAR:	1929
ENGINE:	Ford SVO 302 V8
BUILD STYLE:	Street Rod
OWNER:	Eric Geisert

▶ Subject of probably more build-up articles than just about any other hot rod, Eric Geisert's, Foose-designed, roadster expressed a new treatment of the classic '29 on 32 rails.

'34 Ford Pickup

'34 Ford Pickup

The somewhat upright and tall dimensions of Ford's commercial range from the 1930s often lead rodders to take the hacksaw to the top in search of the perfect chop job, Certainly, back in the 1950s, it was fairly common practice to channel them over the frame rails too (and there are a few example of this in these very pages). But this one looks different simply because it has had none of those tricks carried out. What is more, the trad truck looks much more than fine – in fact, just the way Henry intended. It even retains the stock truck grille shell that was always a one-piece painted item, unlike the passenger car range which had the bright finish insert.

Other neat resto touches are the rubber running board covers with step plates, the cowl lights and the opening screen, wound out for a little early air-conditioning. Of course, nothing says hot rod like a fully dressed Flathead. Through the aperture, normally occupied by the hood side panels, we can see the red-painted V8 complete with a dual intake and a brace of carbs. Finishing off the '34 are a set of chrome smoothie wheels shod with some radial wide whites and these are picked out by the subtle period pinstriping on the truck's belt line.

MAKE:	Ford
BODY STYLE:	Closed-cab Pickup
YEAR:	1934
ENGINE:	Flathead V8
BUILD STYLE:	Traditional
OWNER:	Rich Corson

◄ Take on a perfectly restored '34 truck, paint it in an attention-getting color, and add a set of wide whites on chromed rims for some instant cool trucking action.

'31 Ford Coupe

Since many early hot rodders were based in California, a State that was also one of the main homes of the US aircraft industry, it's not at all surprising that many employees brought to rodding the technology, skills and influences they garnered working on and around the aircraft of the day. The traditional "scallop" paint job, which we are so used to seeing on rods and customs, is one such example. In this instance, the bright Red-over-Ivory is very reminiscent of the "Gee Bee" racing aircraft of the 1930s, so it's fitting that this paint treatment should look so hot when applied to a fenderless '31 Model A Coupe like this one.

The chopped and channeled Coupe is loaded with early style, from the equally channeled and filled Deuce grille, to the pinstriped headlamps and custom nerf bar. Boogie Woogie is the name on the cowl – and boogie-woogie this A-Bone certainly does, thanks to the tri-carbs on an Offy intake, on top of the detailed small block Chevy engine. Out of sight here, but not out of mind, are the additional features of a rolled black interior, drilled front axle and a trunk lid punched full of louvers. Boogie woogie indeed!

MAKE:	Ford
BODY STYLE:	Model A Coupe
YEAR:	1931
ENGINE:	Chevy 283 V8
BUILD STYLE:	Traditional Hot Rod
OWNER:	Doug Anderson

◀ This coupe rolls along with bundles of character, thanks to its Gee Bee scalloped paintjob and matching steelies, plus wide whites and Mercury caps.

'37 Ford Coupe

How cool do 3-window '37's look? This is one phantom Ford body style that definitely should have made the production line at Detroit back in the day. Mind you, if it had, they would still have suffered in their numbers at the dirt track, just like their 5-window brethren did. Maybe it is just as well that we have modern fiberglass manufacturers turning out quality raw material for rodders in order that they can start afresh. This very slippery-looking Coupe has been further enhanced with a hard roof chop for a real sneaky profile indeed. The smooth bodywork and v-butted windshield place this hot rod firmly in the contemporary street rod class.

As well as the chop, attention was given to installing custom lights both front and back of the swoopy coupe; and they look like a set of Hagens recessed into the front fenders in place of the stock style teardrop-shape units. The cool two-tone effect is down to some House of Kolor Pearl Blue under the white top, with some dramatic, three-dimensional graphics added by Dales. Beneath the hood we find a 502 ci Chevy Crate engine under one of Street and Performance's injection systems. A 4L60 transmission and a Ford 9-inch complete the '37's heavy-duty drivetrain.

MAKE:	Ford
BODY STYLE:	3-window Coupe
YEAR:	1937
ENGINE:	Chevy 502 V8
BUILD STYLE:	Street Rod
OWNER:	Bob and Karen Mulvihill

▶ A modern high-tech paint scheme needs some matching wheels, a set of 17- and 18-inch Welds do the job on this Phantom '37 Coupe.

'32 Ford Coupe

Don't anyone ask the owner of this hardcore '32 coupe when it's going to get finished, because it looks just about tough enough the way it is. It's all about restraint and knowing when to stop. If you're going to build a car loaded with attitude, pay attention to the stance and the correct parts. Do it right, and the rest will follow. You won't need a fancy paintjob to make any further statement. The gray primer will tell its own tale, as it does here. A stock height Deuce is very cool, even with an unfilled roof, when it's slammed down over the chassis rails like this.

Of course, it helps to have the bite as well as the bark. That is taken care of on this '32 with an early small block Chevy sporting three Rochester carbs – all in a row and dressed with finned no-name valve covers and white-coated headers. Maximizing the fun is a Muncie 4-speed manual transmission and a Chevy rear end. Front end features an unknown origin tube front axle with drum brakes. Bias-ply whitewalls look fine on black painted steelies. Who needs hubcaps? We guess that they'd only get stolen!

MAKE:	Ford
BODY STYLE:	5-window Coupe
YEAR:	1932
ENGINE:	Chevy 327 V8
BUILD STYLE:	Hardcore Coupe
OWNER:	Lee Osborne

▶ When a little says a lot, all you need is a stock-steel body, the right stance and a loud engine to go get yourself some hardcore fun.

'32 Ford Roadster

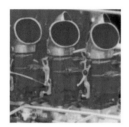

This fully-loaded, dripping with nostalgia '32 Roadster has definitely got the best of both worlds. It's "arrest me" red paint and attention to detail is going to attract admiring glances, and from not only from every passing Street Rodder who happens to like old-timey stuff. It's also running enough period and vintage hardware to draw a crowd from the younger hardcore guys, too. Only the perfectly straight body and gloss finish separate the two camps. In fact, the car would look just as good in primer as it does in paint.

The tan top sits low over a chopped roadster windshield, but it's the engine, which really shouts for your attention – how could you miss those huge chrome valve covers that are the hallmark of a vintage Chrysler Hemi? Top that off with six deuces on a log-style manifold and you are on to a winner already – and we haven't even begun to appreciate the louvered trunk lid, the Lakes pipes or the cool rolling stock yet. How about those whitewall slicks on early Halibrands? They were cool enough before the spinners were added, let alone the Buick drums.

MAKE:	Ford
BODY STYLE:	Roadster
YEAR:	1932
ENGINE:	Chrysler Hemi V8
BUILD STYLE:	Nostalgia Hot Rod
OWNER:	Walt and Cathy Cartwright

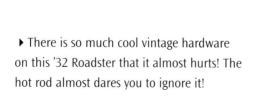

▶ There is so much cool vintage hardware on this '32 Roadster that it almost hurts! The hot rod almost dares you to ignore it!

'32 Ford Roadster

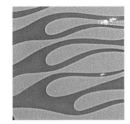

There are many ways to approach the build of a '32 Ford hot rod, and this contemporary treatment of a Deuce is just one of them. The fenderless highboy look is a classic among hot rodders anyway – plus the polished and raked windscreen and the chrome hairpins on the front suspension are further classic touches. But the 20-inch billet aluminum wheels, the super-low profile tires and the smooth hood sides are all examples of the modern clean-and-uncluttered build style made popular in recent years.

Although built to show quality throughout, this car was made to be driven – and driven it is, despite having neither fenders nor provision for any kind of top at all. A reproduction '32 Ford frame was used as a basis for the mostly home-built project and all the parts used were brand new items for reliability, including the 350 Chevy crate engine. A cool touch is the fact that those candy blue flames licking around the front are also painted on the inside of the hood. Note too that the color of the hot licks match nicely with the blue leather interior trim. It is attention to details like this that set apart the really great hot rods, both in the eyes of judges at shows and the public at large.

MAKE:	Ford
BODY STYLE:	Highboy Roadster
YEAR:	1932
ENGINE:	350 Chevrolet V8
BUILD STYLE:	Contemporary Street Rod
BUILDER:	Keith Atkinson

◀ The bright orange paint on this '32 has become somewhat of a trademark color for the builder of this car, Keith Atkinson.

'39 Chevy Coupe

Have you ever noticed how much bigger these late-1930s Chevys look compared to the equivalent Fords of the same period? That is especially when they're painted in a solid, dark color, like this big black heavy Chevy Coupe. It must be the down to the length of the hood. Back then, Chevrolet were still fitting the big 6-pot engine, (as they would until 1954) that was much longer physically than Ford's compact Flathead V8 engine. Hence the longer front end. Nowadays, these big 2-doors just look plain classy – and, of course, these art-deco period rides make great street rods.

A well-designed car needs nothing more than a good straight paint job and a set of cool wheels to make the scene in the mixed-make company of a rod run. The owner of this fine '39 obviously agrees, and keeps it real subtle. There is a deep black paint finish, highlighted by the finest of pinstripes along the waistline. Also, a v-butted windshield is a contemporary touch, as is the big-inch Colorado Custom wheels. Keeping the running gear as a simple plot, there's an Edelbrock-equipped 327 in there, with a GM350 gearbox and an 8-inch rear end.

MAKE:	Chevrolet
BODY STYLE:	2-door Coupe
YEAR:	1939
ENGINE:	Chevy 327 V8
BUILD STYLE:	Street Rod
OWNER:	Jack Evans

▾ From its molded tan interior to its super straight black paint, this big '39 Chevy Coupe just oozes class from every angle.

'32 Ford Roadster

Some professional hot rod shops have names that seem to have been around forever; or so it seems. Maybe it's just good marketing but more likely, it's because of the accolades that their finished products receive in both print and at shows. As a result of this, sooner or later, a shop will become known for a certain style of car. If you want a rod built a certain way, then go to the specialist. For example, if you're on the East Coast and you want the old school look, you could easily end up at Jim Lowrey's in Tilton, NH. If you need convincing, check out this "new" old timey roadster that he built for Bob Covino.

Using a brand-new steel Brookville body, they created this maroon marauder with a tan Haartz top that any petrol-headed post World War II GI wouldn't have thought twice about deserting his unit for! The desirable Deuce runs a Ted Wingate full-race Flat engine with Edelbrock heads and same-make intake, twin carbs and Fenton headers. Naturally this is linked to a faithful '39 trans and a '40 Ford rear axle. A '40 Ford steering wheel is a right-on interior detail, along with the gorgeous brown leather seat. Wide whitewall bias plies on red steelies were the only choice on this jalopy. The fine pinstriping is by Larry Hook.

MAKE:	Ford
BODY STYLE:	Roadster
YEAR:	1932
ENGINE:	Flathead V8
BUILD STYLE:	Traditional 1940's Hot Rod
OWNER:	Robert Covino

▶ Try and find one part that doesn't fit or is out of place on this Deuce and I'll eat my canvas tool roll!

'36 Ford Cabriolet

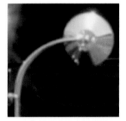

When setting out to create that perfect "old school" ride, some hot rodders get out the history books, then hit the swap meets looking for all those hard-to-find but desirable vintage pieces. For them, that's half the fun. For others, the cool comes from having the righteous retro look but knowing the rod is built with the best driving, riding and handling package of hardware available today. This sweet-as-candy '36 Cabrio is built with such a mandate. The Henry Ford black paint bears testimony to the straightness of the body, which has received a little cleaning up, with the removal of the handles and front fender horn covers. The original hinge mirrors and rubber running boards add authenticity.

Underneath that nostalgic layer of automotive veneer, the whole plot is mounted on a repro TCI chassis, complete with a fully-independent front suspension setup, giving the sneaky black 'rod a sweet'n'low stance. The rear of the frame features a 4-bar link set up to attach the Ford 9-inch rear axle. Chevy engines are not unusual in trad style hot rods, but this cute cabrio turns up the heat with not just any bowtie small-block, but a ZZ4 unit complete with a Street and Performance TPI system and a GM700 R4 transmission.

MAKE:	Ford
BODY STYLE:	Cabriolet
YEAR:	1936
ENGINE:	Chevy 350 V8
BUILD STYLE:	Traditional Street Rod
OWNER:	Dave Gazaway

◂ Things aren't always what they seem: a ZZ4 with a TPI setup features heavily in the build specification of this otherwise nostalgic '36 Soft Top.

▲ Not only a star of the early 1960s show circuit, this deuce was a star of movies and TV, appearing in the "Asphalt Jungle", "Bus Stop" and on the Ozzie and Harriet show.

'32 Ford Roadster

This superb example of a 1950's-style '32 Ford hot rod could have fitted into several of our categories in this book. Built by L.A. Roadsters member Tony La Masa back in the mid-1950s, Tony wanted the car to be a "real" alternative to all the imported sports cars popular at the time. Performance-wise, he accomplished this using the stock V8 from the then newly-introduced Chevy Corvette. Tony regularly drove it on lots of the club's long road trips at the time, as well as winning many a trophy on the indoor show circuit.

The '32 roadster body has been channeled down over the frame to achieve that low, ground-hugging look and the attention to detail on the car is second-to-none for the period. Note the hood bulge to clear the carbs, the shaped cycle fenders on all four corners, the drilled nerf bars and the beautiful metallic green paint. The white upholstery is set off by the white grille insert, the pinstriping and the whitewall tires. What you can't see in the picture is the neat '40 Ford dashboard fitted to the car. Not only did this rod make the cover of *Hot Rod* magazine in 1960, it also made numerous TV and movie appearances.

MAKE:	Ford
BODY STYLE:	Roadster
YEAR:	1932
ENGINE:	265 Chevrolet
BUILD STYLE:	1950's Show Car
BUILDER:	Tony La Masa

'48 Ford Pickup

In the late 1940s, with the war effort over and Detroit once again geared up to civilian production, new designs for cars and trucks started appearing to satisfy the ever-expanding market, many of them featuring more and more chrome and brightwork trim, a trend that would spiral to ever-greater excess as the next decade progressed. This included, of course, Ford's light truck series, now re-designed and featuring full-width grilles with integral headlamps. After years of farm abuse, many of these old trucks are once again looking showroom-new and sporting all their original trim, thanks to restorers, and of course hot rodders.

Of course, hot rodders like to put their own spin on to a ground-upwards rebuild, so it's no surprise to see this classic Ford F1 sitting on top of a full custom frame for the unmistakable Pro-Street look. While the rear of the chassis is radically narrowed to allow those big Mickey Thompsons (separated by a narrowed 9-inch rear end) to stay inside the rear fenders, the front of the frame has been adapted to take an independent front end for a super-low stance. The Resto-Pro look is backed up with a 460-inch, big-block Ford V8 fed by an Edelbrock Performer and Holley intake combo.

MAKE:	Ford F1
BODY STYLE:	Pickup
YEAR:	1948
ENGINE:	Ford 460 V8
BUILD STYLE:	Pro-Street
OWNER:	Bruce Vaal

▸ Unusual nerf bar treatment sets this '48 Ford F1 apart from the classic resto trucks – that and the tough Pro-Street treatment, of course!

'32 Ford Chassis

There's much reference in this book to the frames and the custom underpinnings of the various rods that are featured. Of course, on fenderless roadsters and especially on '32s, the frame is clearly visible in profile; and on cars that run without a hood, it's easy to appreciate the detailing on the engine too. But just to illustrate further the work involved, here is a full turn-key chassis and engine, all assembled and ready to go. So, before the body is bolted in place, you can at least get some idea of the craftsmanship and superb detailing that is usually hidden from view on a quality-built hot rod.

This is a Pro-Street Deuce chassis. However, with the headers in place, you can't see the swage line stamped into stock 1932 Ford frames that make them so neat to look at. What you can see, however, is where the chassis is notched in – that's in front of the rear tires to keep those wide rubbers from taking over two lanes of highway! Nestling down between those narrow rails is a polished Halibrand Champ 500 rear end. The killer engine towering above the grille shell is a 502-inch big-block Chevy, wearing Brodix ally heads and a mighty BDS 8-71 blower, with a pair of Holley quads and a Hilborn style scoop.

MAKE:	Ford
BODY STYLE:	Roadster to be!
YEAR:	1932
ENGINE:	Chevy 502 V8
BUILD STYLE:	Pro-street
OWNER:	Jack McDevitt

▲ A fully-detailed hot rod chassis is a thing of beauty to behold, and sometimes it's almost a shame to hide it by mounting the body on top!

'37 Ford Coupe

File this under "Some guys get all the luck!" This incredibly clean coupe is a genuine 6,000 mile car that was advertised in *Hemmings Motor News* as just a low-mileage '37 Ford. When the current owner saw the ad run again a few months later, he called up the seller and found out that not only was it a low mileage coupe, but that it had a zero-mileage 283 Chevy installed that had never been run. The car had been purchased back in 1962 from the original owner, and although the Chevy was in and running with an adapter to the transmission, with Hurst engine mounts and a partial hydraulic braking system installed, the Coupe had never been finished. Some find, huh?

A deal was done and the '37 was soon sorted for the street, with a new dropped front axle and a new set of steelies and wide whites. It also had a new exhaust installed and was re-wired to 12 volt. The rear transverse spring was reversed as well; and that was about it. One more surprise was to come, though, in the form of a brand new Tri-carb intake with three new Strombergs complete with air cleaners that had never made it as far as the engine compartment. Like we said at the top, some guys do indeed seem to have all the luck.

MAKE:	Ford
BODY STYLE:	5-window Coupe
YEAR:	1937
ENGINE:	Chevy 283 V8
BUILD STYLE:	Period Hot Rod
OWNER:	Dave Simard

◀ The sweet nerf bars on the front of this low-mileage '37 match the profile of the lower grille exactly.

'40 Ford Coupe

Who let that very tidy, but staid, stocker in here? This is supposed to be a book of hot rods! You know, big wheels, dropped suspension, fancy paint and all that stuff; so what's with the Resto '40 coupe, nice as it is. Is it a stocker – or maybe a Resto? On the outside maybe, but beauty is only supposed to be skin deep. Here, you need to see under the hood to ascertain the true character of this swing-era Coupe. This is an example of what is sometimes referred to as a "sleeper," a mild-looking antique auto that might just surprise you when it's time to "git up and go."

There may well be faster cars around these days, but there was a time when a '40 coupe like this with a blown flattie would have been a pretty hot ticket. The flat-out Forty uses a '47 Mercury block, displacing 250 ci with rare "block letter" Edelbrock finned aluminum heads and an Isky race cam; plus, there's still plenty of room under the stock hood for a Weiand supercharger fed by a pair of 97-series Strombergs. Although the '40 running gear is still man enough for this setup and remains stock, a Columbia 2-speed axle is installed for better top-end cruising. So the lesson here has to be not to judge a book by its cover.

MAKE:	Ford
BODY STYLE:	2-door Coupe
YEAR:	1940
ENGINE:	Flathead 250 ci V8
BUILD STYLE:	Traditional
OWNER:	Jim Lowrey Sr.

▶ Just a hint of red striping on the flawless Lyons Blue hints at the devilish flat engine hidden within this fine '40.

'23 Ford T Roadster

Every now and then, someone builds a hot rod to their own agenda without necessarily following the crowd, or even the current trends of the day. These are the cars that usually split the vote, with some folk scratching their heads and saying "why?" and others just saying: "Well, I don't care why, it's just cool." We suspect that may have been the case in the early 1960s when this unusual 4-banger T was put together. The steel T body was narrowed by 4 inches at the rear and 3 inches at the cowl, with same taken from the windshield frame. The doors have been welded shut for additional rigidity and the big 1917 Studebaker headlamps give the little jalopy a bug-eyed look, either side of the cut-down '34 International grille. Meantime, the Chrysler front axle seems to add a chromed smile to the frontal aspect, giving the car real personality.

You could probably tell from the size of that megaphone exhaust that there was a story waiting to be told in the engine department. The builder, Joe Gemsa, was an accomplished Sprint Car racer who specialized in 4-cylinder engines and was known as the "King of the Four Bangers." Using a Model B block, the 220-ci engine features Gemsa's own head and overhead cam design giving a massive compression ratio. A dual ignition system is used from a 1920 Stutz Bearcat and the dual Stromberg 97s rest on a Gemsa intake. A '39 transmission is mated to the Model B lump via an adaptor that was made by – you guessed right – Joe Gemsa. The car is a true one-off, and very skillfully engineered too.

MAKE:	Ford
BODY STYLE:	T Roadster
YEAR:	1923
ENGINE:	Ford/Gemsa 220 ci 4-cylinder
BUILD STYLE:	Vintage Roadster
OWNER:	Joe Gemsa

▶ After a successful career on the dirt tracks of the 1940's and 1950's, Joe Gemsa put together this neat 4-banger T for the street.

'40 Ford Convertible

A '40 Ford convertible is handsome looking car from which ever side of the old car hobby fence you may stand, even more so when you appreciate its particular historical rodding significance. This accessorized drop-top, with its fender end guards, wide whites and fender skirts, was once the pride and joy – not to mention high school daily drive – of one Jim Lowrey Sr. Through hotting-up this old classic all those years ago, he cultivated a love of all things rodding that he was able to pass on to son Jim Jr. in later years. Young Jim grew up to own and operate Lowrey's Hot Rods and there are several examples of his skilled handiwork in this book.

As for the '40, it was sold by Jim Sr. years ago, but was amazingly relocated and bought back into the family. There it has received a complete restoration back to its maroon red former glory. The car is no stocker though. It runs an AB Flathead V8 with Offy heads, a 2-pot intake with a pair of 97s and a full race cam. That is all fired off with a Harman Collins ignition. To make the most of this increase in vintage ponies, a Columbia 2-speed overdrive is installed on the '40's rear end. These days, it is now the car that the young Jim wanted it to be way back in those blissful high school days.

MAKE:	Ford
BODY STYLE:	2-door Convertible
YEAR:	1940
ENGINE:	Flathead V8
BUILD STYLE:	Period Resto Rod
OWNER:	Jim Lowrey Sr.

▶ For the Lowrey family, what goes around, comes around. That's certainly true of this returned-to-the-fold family heirloom '40 Convertible.

'32 Ford Roadster

If you've glanced at the picture on this page and thought that this old Lakes Roadster might have some history, you'd be right. It has lots. Long-time salt fans will recognize this as "The High Grade Plating Special" owned and driven at Bonneville by Jim Lattin, who campaigned it from 1965 to 1976. In fact, its history at the dry lakes goes even further back with its previous owner, a Mr Miller, who bought it in 1938.

The car often ran in multiple classes, Jim changing from the HAL double overhead cam 4-banger to a maxed-out injected Flathead at will, while already at the event. The Flathead engine is a 325 ci thumper, with a 4-inch crank, Potvin Eliminator cam and Sharp heads, as well as having the Hilborn injection system.

The car was bought from Jim Lattin with both engines, the four and the eight both intact, and the big engine has been fitted back into the car by its now current owner, Dave Simard. The old racer still has all its old period features such as the '39 transmission and home-brewed, quick-change rear axle, which is mounted on the original wishbone. The front axle is a Deuce dago'd item and is mounted on an un-split chromed wishbone with Hartford shocks. The car also has an original Bell steering wheel, a genuine early Moon tank and those early, spindle-mount "kidney bean" front wheels. Since Dave bought the car, it has run at Bonneville again, just for fun. It remains, though, an un-restored and original gem.

MAKE:	Ford
BODY STYLE:	Roadster
YEAR:	1932
ENGINE:	Flathead V8
BUILD STYLE:	Traditional Lakes Roadster
OWNER:	Dave Simard

◀ There's a ton of salty history attached to this dry lakes '32. Its best speed ever was at El Mirage, where it topped 165+ mph with an Ardun-equipped Flathead installed.

'48 Belly Tank

The thought of actually being propelled at over 200 mph across the flat, but rutted surface of a dry salt lake, only inches from the ground, in the searing heat, with an un-silenced and unseen V8 at full revs just behind your head, is to a hot rodder both a terrifying yet exciting prospect indeed. But that's what you got if you signed up to drive a belly tank racer. Safety equipment? Well, there's a small roll hoop, and crew mate Chuck has a small extinguisher in the pickup, but that's about half-a-mile away back down at the start line! Apart from that, it's just you, the tank and the distant horizon. Were these guys heroes or just a little crazy? It's one thing seeing old pictures of these things tearing up the salt, but look at one in the cold light of day, as here, and you begin to wonder.

This belly tank lakester is the real deal all right, a Lockheed P-38 Lightning tank fitted with a mid-mounted AB Flathead and Edelbrock heads, a Harman Collins magneto and four Strombergs on a custom intake. Known as the "Salty Shaker." it was built by Bill Burke in 1948 and run by Eddie Meyer engine-builder Ray Brown until 1961. Then it was sold to Ted Frye who upgraded it to a blown 301 ci Chrysler Hemi (I told you these guys were crazy). The front end, mounted to the custom tube frame inside the tank, uses '37 Ford parts with a transverse spring, and the rear end, which is a Halibrand Quick Change, is solidly mounted directly behind the transmission. Scary stuff indeed!

MAKE:	P-38 Belly Tank
BODY STYLE:	Lakester
YEAR:	1948
ENGINE:	Flathead 325 ci
BUILD STYLE:	Unrestored Original
BUILDER:	Bill Burke
OWNER:	Dave Simard

▸ This P-38 belly tank is a rare and unrestored original from 1948 and in its day has run both a Chrysler Hemi as well as an early Flathead V8.

'34 Ford Roadster

Originally built to race in the 1960's by Charles Scott, this '34 soon became known as the "Scotty's Muffler Roadster" from San Bernadino, California. (Incidentally, Scotty's is still in business, est. 1946.) It was originally a 3-window Coupe, but had the top removed to turn it into this low-slung Lakes Roadster. It spent many seasons racing at both Bonneville and El Mirage, and at the former at least, regularly achieved speeds of over 250 mph. Most of these incredible speeds were achieved with a mighty Chrysler Hemi under the hood. The next time this roadster hits the salt (and knowing owner Dave Simard, it will), it is planned to have a 256-inch supercharged Ardun V8, the same one that was featured in the *Rodders Journal* #25 and was previously owned and raced by the late Tom Senter.

The much-modified topless Coupe body has been altered to be as aerodynamic as possible, with an aluminum cover over the grille opening and solid hood side panels in place of the original louvered items. The opening in the hood is obviously there as clearance for the large competition-style "bug catcher" installed on the engine, but a covering panel has been constructed to surround the centrally positioned driver's seat and roll hoop. The driver sits lower than normal in a Lakester, again for added streamlining.

▼ Now part of the Simard Collection, this '34 roadster will live to run again, this time with blown Ardun V8 power.

MAKE:	Ford
BODY STYLE:	Roadster
YEAR:	1934
ENGINE:	Ardun Flathead V8
BUILD STYLE:	Traditional Lakester
OWNER:	Dave Simard

'32 Ford Coupe

Just tell us if there is a brand new car on the market anywhere in the world that even comes close to looking as sweet as the timeless good looks of a chopped '32 3-window like this. With its lid lowered to perfection, its laid back screen posts, rake, stance and paintwork as black as your father's hat, it's not just cool, it's ice cold, baby! This car was originally rodded back in 1950, and even back then it was considered sharp enough to make a feature in the April '54 issue of *Rod and Custom Magazine*. Of course, in those days, it was always Flathead powered, and stayed that way until the early 1960s, when the then owner decided to upgrade it to Chevy power.

A '56 Chevy 265 ci V8 was duly fitted, complete with 4-barrel carb and finned Corvette covers, mated to the already installed '39 transmission and fully chromed '39 rear end. There was plenty of chrome on show under the front too, with a dropped front axle that had also been dipped in the plater's vat. The car stayed pretty much unchanged, apart from a fresh coat of black lacquer, although going through a couple more owners; and even made its second magazine appearance in *Street Rodder* magazine in the early 1970s. Always a West coast car throughout its life, ironically it is now living on the East Coast in the Dave Simard Collection.

MAKE:	Ford
BODY STYLE:	3-window Coupe
YEAR:	1932
ENGINE:	Chevy 265 V8
BUILD STYLE:	Traditional Hot Rod
OWNER:	Dave Simard

▶ As the main text here clearly illustrates, sometimes, if a car is done right first time, you can't improve on Deuce perfection even fifty years later.

'36 Ford Pickup

Y ou'd better skip this page if you are in any way offended by hardcore Pickup trucks, as this one is just plain nasty! To give you a clue, the owner refers to it himself as "Scrap Iron II" and it all goes down hill from there on. Once upon a time, it was a '36 Ford that roamed the wide open spaces of South Dakota, but that was before it had 6 inches removed from its profile and had the body taper-channeled 4-6 inches front to back. This was over a C'd '34 Ford frame with custom cross members for a real, so-low stance. The sinister spider web grille was not a stock item on '36 Fords, none that we've seen anyway! It was owner-built, and it was he who also added the cross and the Model A headlamps.

True to its name, the V8 power house in the red oxide rod was indeed a junk yard find, a '56 Chrysler Hemi lump that had lain unloved for 30 years since retiring from its orchard crop spraying duties! In the truck, it is now back in business, but these days it wears its swap-meet-find Firepower valve covers and Moon breathers with pride. A Holley 600 fuels the born-again engine, which breathes out via home-made Lakes headers. A Muncie 4-speed with three pedals keeps the ride entertaining, and a Mexican blanket inside the hammered cab is as close to luxury as it gets. You want air? Roll down the window!

MAKE:	Ford
BODY STYLE:	Fenderless Pickup
YEAR:	1936
ENGINE:	Chrysler 331 ci Hemi V8
BUILD STYLE:	Hardcore
OWNER:	Jim Derzius

▼ A revived Chrysler hemi, once consigned to the junk yard provides all the bite for this hardcore '36 Ford Scrap Iron II.

'32 Roadster

If you want to talk the real deal on nostalgic roadsters, and 32 Highboy's in particular, check out this East Coast beauty that will equal any California-built car, or one from anywhere else, for that matter. In fact, you may well recognize it from the *Rodders Journal* #11, if you have that publication. Although the rod sits level, it hasn't been channeled as have so many other right Coast cars. It achieves its stealthy stance by way of a "Z" to the original '32 frame, which also features traditional goodies all the way, including a dropped and chromed I-beam with '40 spindles, homemade hairpins and an early Ford transverse spring. A Halibrand quick-change center section is suspended from a Model A spring, with lengthened '36 radius rods and '50 Chrysler chromed tube shocks.

Once you've got past the dazzling combo of Ford blue paint and Radir 5-spokes shod with bias-ply tires, Goodrich on the front and Commander on the back, there's that truly awesome Flathead mill to consider. Looking twice the size of any normal '48 block Flathead, it is dominated by the sheer bulk of the super rare Ardun overhead valve conversion cylinder heads, as well as the S.C.o.T. polished blower, with twin carbs. The maxed-out 258 ci engine's power is even further maximized by a later Ford 4-speed top loader transmission. But this exercise in unashamed Flathead tradition is no show queen and has been used regularly by its owner, both on the street and (at one time) on the strip too.

MAKE:	Ford
BODY STYLE:	Highboy Roadster
YEAR:	1932
ENGINE:	Ardun Flathead V8
BUILD STYLE:	Period Hot Rod
OWNER:	Ron San Giovanni

◄ Only a true dyed-in-the-wool Flathead guy could produce a Deuce as perfect as this. Well the owner is that guy, and he did it.

'32 Ford Coupe

Elsewhere in these pages you'll find the '32 roadster of Ron San Giovanni, almost a period-perfect East Coast roadster as it's possible to build. This is the other hot rod in the family, and it's likely to be Mrs San Giovanni behind the wheel, as this Coupe is her car. Also sharing a feature in *Rodder's Journal,* this steel 5-window is the perfect compliment to the Ardun-powered roadster. As you'd expect from a die hard Flathead family, this maroon and white Deuce is powered by one of Ford's finest – in this case, a ported and relieved '50 Ford block wearing Navarro heads, a S.C.o.T. blower, Fenton headers and a pair of 2-pot carbs. A trick addition is the adaption of a C-4 automatic transmission via a custom-built torque converter.

The 2-inch chopped top on the Coupe sports a neat white roof insert to match the white pleated interior trim. In fact, everywhere you look on this '32, there are cool features to check out – like the chromed reverse early Ford wheels, the bobbed steel rear fenders, and the Pierce Arrow dash insert with Stewart Warner gauges. The chassis is set up much like husband Ron's roadster, with the highlights being the Halibrand quick-change center section, the '36 radius rods at the rear, the chromed early Ford I beam with '48 Ford chrome split wishbones, and '40 Ford juice brakes. Believe us, all the proper early parts are present and correct.

MAKE:	Ford
BODY STYLE:	5-window Coupe
YEAR:	1932
ENGINE:	Flathead V8
BUILD STYLE:	Street Coupe
OWNER:	Laura San Giovanni

▲ Only the modern early radial whitewalls stop this car from appearing as if straight from the hot rod pages of days gone bye.

'34 Chevy Coupe

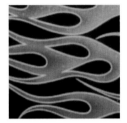

Some years ago, it was rare to even find a 1930's-era Bowtie coupe at a rod event. Nowadays, not only are they accepted as righteous hot rod material, but you can even buy fiberglass versions of Chevrolet's 3-window, as this flaming Pro-streeter testifies. The 3-inch chopped body is as it came from the molds at Outlaw Performance, the body and chassis combination from Outlaw's being one of the most comprehensively available on the market. The frame features a fully independent Heidts front end setup and a triangulated 4-bar mounted, 9-inch rear axle. These sophisticated packages, that are readily available, take a lot of the guesswork out of contemporary rod building, resulting in safer rods and quicker build times.

In this case, the rear axle is a narrowed item, allowing those big Weld wheels sufficient room to nestle in under the rear fenders. The smooth body is finished in PPG Blackberry paint-work and those busy flames, licking rearward from the silver grille shell and splash apron, are painted in PPG Prismatique and fade from silver, through blue to magenta. Under the flame-heated hood is a B&M blown Chevy small block measuring 355 ci. It's topped with twin Holley 600's and is detailed to the max. Inside the Chevy, a magenta tweed trim and Dakota Digital dash make it a cool place to be.

MAKE:	Chevrolet
BODY STYLE:	3-window Coupe
YEAR:	1934
ENGINE:	Chevy 355 V8
BUILD STYLE:	Street Rod
OWNER:	Steve Van Blarcom

▸ Excellent 'glass body and chassis packages mean that non-Ford lovers can also build cool hot rods while still maintaining Bowtie brand loyalty.

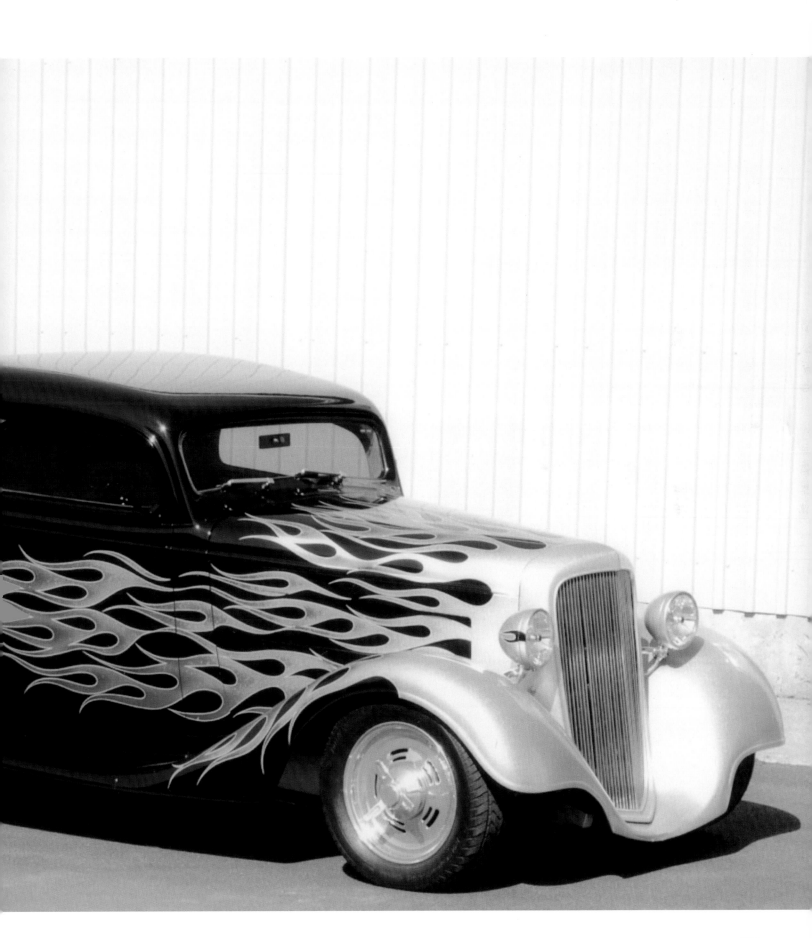

'33 Dodge Sedan

Long before Chrysler came up with the concept for the Voyager, Dodge were carrying whole families around in style in big'n'classy cars like this big '33 Sedan. Not always the first choice of hot rodders, this Mopar more-door has no trouble in carrying off the act, with its super low stance, tasteful chop and with eight pillars and four suicide doors. It's unlikely that the builder of this rod could have finished with the welder in just one weekend! Having, literally, brought the house down by 2 inches, work then started on installing the Volvo electric Moon roof. We might as well mention the interior luxury as well, which boasts bucket seats in the front and a split rear seat, all covered in acres of pale cream leather.

The big Dodge chassis has been boxed throughout and now benefits from the smooth ride of a Mustang II front end and a 4-bar and coil over suspended 8-inch rear axle. Keeping it all Mopar muscle-motivated is a strong '70 340-inch detailed engine with X heads and a Mopar purple cam. An Edelbrock 600 is entrusted with feeding in the gas, and headers by Sanderson dispense the exhaust once the power has been extracted from said gasoline. That power is then sent down to the 8-inch via a 727 Torqueflite transmission; but it's the big Budniks and low profile rubber wrappers that put it to the pavement.

MAKE:	Dodge
BODY STYLE:	4-door Sedan
YEAR:	1933
ENGINE:	Mopar 340 V8
BUILD STYLE:	Street Rod
OWNER:	Ray Long

◀ It may have more doors than yours, but no one is going to mistake this '33 Dodge for any old big yellow taxi.

'33 Ford Coupe

You often hear the phrase "Bad to the Bone." No, not that George Thorogood album, but in connection with tough-looking cars and trucks of all sorts. So, whilst we hate to repeat an over-used phrase, that's exactly the words that spring to mind when you first look at this downright "nasty dawg" of a '33 Coupe. Straight black paint and a 4-inch chopped Ram Rods 'glass body are only half the story, the Coupe maintaining a stealthy low-level stance via a channel job over the frame. As with most fenderless '33s, the stock chromed grille appears to float between the frame rails – this one flanked by a pair of Harley-Davidson V-Rod headlamps mounted in custom buckets.

Just in case anyone should doubt this bad boy '33's performance threat, it's got 496 ci of big block Chevy engine available to prove its point. Further, the killer motor is loaded for bear with a BDS 8-71 supercharger and dual quad carbs underneath a polished shotgun scoop. That scoop carries the legend "700 HP" – and who are we to argue? The whole shooting match is detailed and polished to die for, including the tough, 4-into-1-sprint style pipes. Frame and suspension details include independent front end; and between those big Hoosier rear tires, is a 4-bar mounted 9-inch rear end. Wheels are a contemporary 5-spoke design from American Racing.

MAKE:	Ford
BODY STYLE:	3-window Coupe
YEAR:	1933
ENGINE:	Chevy 496 V8
BUILD STYLE:	Performance Hot Rod
OWNER:	Shane Rancourt

▸ The killer stance, big block Chevy motor, plus Shotgun scooped BDS Blower, make this Coupe a real heavyweight contender. File it under "Triple Threat."

'35 Chevy Coupe

All of a sudden it seems like Chevrolet, for so long the favorite modified car of the drag racing and street machine set, are making serious inroads into the Ford-dominated pre-1949 rod scene. If it's heavy Chevys like this blown pre-World War II Coupe that are ringing the changes, then bring it on! After all, what could be more natural than a Chevy in a Chevy, no matter what the year? This stovebolt Coupe makes a dramatic Pro-street statement, while wearing a coat of '69 AMC bright orange, and certainly looks good doing so.

Riding on a narrowed rear-frame, Pro-street chassis, the tubbed and full-fendered body features a 4-inch chop, shaved handles and mirrors. There are also smooth running boards and only the subtle graphics draw your eye from the polished engine up front. The firewall has been recessed just enough to squeeze in the bulky, big block 427 Chevy lump, with its polished Brodix aluminum heads – both combining with the equally hi-shine BDS blower, twin Holleys and the B.D.S. scoop for the onlookers' attention. More of the same metallic razzle-dazzle is provided by the polished Billet Specialties rims.

MAKE:	Chevrolet
BODY STYLE:	3-window Coupe
YEAR:	1935
ENGINE:	Chevy 427 V8
BUILD STYLE:	Street Rod
OWNER:	Larry Mullen

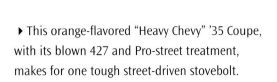

▶ This orange-flavored "Heavy Chevy" '35 Coupe, with its blown 427 and Pro-street treatment, makes for one tough street-driven stovebolt.

'34 Pickup

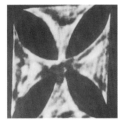

The name Jimmy Shine is almost a household name these days – well, it is in houses where the language of hot rodding is spoken. Even since taking up the hammer and torch at So-Cal Speed shop, and having serious input on several top notch cars from that establishment – not to mention a few TV appearances – still-young Jimmy is already well-known in the hot rod fraternity. A lot of it has to do with this truck, a masterwork of handcrafted steel and vintage parts brought together in a total hardcore style. It really does celebrate workmanship in bare metal without the need for paint of any kind.

Starting with a rough '34 cab and frame, Shine got busy with the old school metalwork skills and soon had a kicked-up rear and a suicide front installed for a super-low ride. That was before a 5-inch chop of the cab channeling the truck by six. The short bed was made by Shine and features a B-52 bomber's hydraulic tank to carry the fuel. The truck just had to be Flathead-powered from the start. It has a '49 8BA engine featuring a Potvin cam, Edelbrock heads and twin Edelbrock '97s on an intake. Hand-made details abound on this radical truck, most of them made by Shine, and most of them bare metal.

MAKE:	Ford
BODY STYLE:	Closed-cab Pickup
YEAR:	1934
ENGINE:	Flathead V8
BUILD STYLE:	Street
BUILDER:	Jimmy Shine

◄ A detailed flathead and bias ply tires aren't even half the story on this hardcore truck that lets the metalwork speak for itself.

'41 Willys Coupe

Anew and fresh-out car, this Willys was completed just in time to get in front of our photographer's lens and sneak into these pages before the deadline – and we're glad it did. There's only two ways to go with the stance of a tough '41 Coupe stance – either go up for the Gasser style or go down for the contemporary Pro-street look. This one takes the latter option. With contemporary and cool flame-and-flag graphics heating up the hood grille and fender area, it's the right choice. The fine and intricate airbrush work that's gone into creating the Willy's hot licks take the traditional flame job in a new direction – and just when you think the theme is all flamed out.

Providing an ample amount of heat under the hood, is a fire-breathing 502-ci big block Chevy engine, running a 1050 Dominator carb on an Edelbrock intake. It's fully dressed, of course, including highly-polished finned valve covers and all the goodies. A TH 400 handles shifting duties and the narrowed rear end is highlighted by the presence of the polished Winters Quick change running 4.10:1 gears. Those big rear meats are Hoosiers and are wrapped around a super-wide set of Weld Racing polished rims, with a similar but suitably skinnier set up front. After all, this car is street-driven and will need to negotiate the odd curve or two!

MAKE:	Willys
BODY STYLE:	2-door Coupe
YEAR:	1941
ENGINE:	Chevy 502 V8
BUILD STYLE:	Performance
OWNER:	Ron Lowrey

▶ Willys Coupes on the street always get the looks, but this one guarantees attention by neat use of contemporary airbrushed flame work.

'34 Oldsmobile Sedan

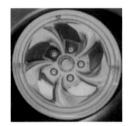

The General Motors brand of Oldsmobile doesn't figure too much when it comes to a hot rodder's choice of ride. However, look what happens when someone decides to step outside the norm and push the envelope with some vision, flair and a lot of talent. Although the rear roof and trunk area are kind of square in design, the heavy roof chop and superb stance, combined with the flowing fender line, gives this Sedan a real classy look that really works. If those big bullet headlamp buckets aren't aircraft inspired, I don't know what is.

The super-low stance that lends everything to the big Old's appeal is courtesy of Fat Man Fabrication chassis parts, combined with a full set of 'bags from Air Ride Technologies. The big-inch directional billet wheels from Colorado Custom add extra bite to the otherwise monochrome shaved body of the titanic two-door The Prowler Orange Pearl then adds the right finishing touch to the slick sedan. Meanwhile, under that long, low hood, a GM ZZ4 engine is coupled to a 350 transmission, working with an '88 T-bird rear end, to give motion and life to the innovative and unusual Super-Olds.

MAKE:	Oldsmobile
BODY STYLE:	2-door Sedan
YEAR:	1934
ENGINE:	Chevy ZZ4 V8
BUILD STYLE:	Street Rod
OWNER:	Denny Bianco

▾ Only in profile can you really appreciate the long low lines of this heavily-chopped super-sized Oldsmobile Sedan Street Rod.

'40 Ford Coupe

A cool and totally smooth '40 Standard Coupe that is awash with PPG Ocean Blue Pearl from stem to stern. The body is nosed, decked and totally de-chromed (apart from the grille), with all trim holes filled, handles shaved and the Hagen headlamps frenched into the front fenders. Minimal custom mirrors feature on the doors and the running boards have been smoothed; plus, who could miss the business-like hood scoop? Weld wheels with spinners complete the tough look and contrast with the otherwise monochromatic finish.

So what engine would you expect to find under the hood of a killer Coupe like this? Chevy, probably? Big block, maybe? You'd be wrong though. How about a '53 Mercury 8BA with a 4-inch crank, Jahns pistons, Crower full-race cam, Edelbrock heads and a B&M 4-71 blower with a chrome 650 Holley? Yep; and what's more, it was all prepped by Motor City Flathead, before being hooked up to the C4 automatic transmission and 8-inch Ford rear end. Even in hot rodding, looks can sometimes be deceiving. Here is your proof.

MAKE:	Ford
BODY STYLE:	2-door Coupe
YEAR:	1940
ENGINE:	Flathead Mercury V8
BUILD STYLE:	Street Rod
OWNER:	Stoney Stonesifer

▸ A flat-engine-powered high tech, monochrome painted '40 Coupe? Why not? There are no rules in hot rodding.

'30 Model A Sedan

What's the point of spending hard-earned dollars on a fine repro chassis by TCI, then spending hours in the garage painting and detailing it, just to hide it under your early Sedan with a typical East Coast channel job? This rodder decided to leave all that fine workmanship on show and just strip the fenders to create a classic "jalopy highboy" look.

Plenty of period Solid Maroon gloss covers the chassis and suspension components, as well as the hood top and the stock original body – classic post-World War II hot rod Tudor appeal. A matching vinyl top is a nice touch, as is the stock grille, looking great in original chrome and set off with the Model A flying bird accessory rad cap.

Meanwhile, back to that chassis, and a painted 4-inch dropped tube features Pete'n'Jake shocks and color-coded 4-bar up front, with another 4-bar locating the Ford 9-inch out back. The gap in between the two axles is filled with a new GM 350 ci crate engine, with the designation of the TH transmission bolted to it. The engine features interesting big-block-style finned valve covers, though the manufacturer of them is unknown. Between these covers is a 650 Holley on a GM intake, with neat polished Lakes pipes adding extra brightwork.

MAKE:	Ford
BODY STYLE:	2-door Sedan
YEAR:	1930
ENGINE:	Chevy 350 V8
BUILD STYLE:	Period Hot Rod
OWNER:	Eliot Bensel

◀ This neat '30 Model A Tudor displays excellent use of a period solid color to tie-in the early theme of this Highboy Sedan style.

'31 Model A Coupe

Forget the jaw-dropping, mega-buck checkbook show queens for a moment. Also, move up a few notches from the hardcore so-called "rat rods," with their devil-may-care, rusty-and-loving-it attitude. Then, you'll find way cool rides like this one. We are talking very trad cars, with very cool parts, but built by guys who are not awash with dollars, yet still want to present a relatively finished and complete look to their rides. The thing is, most everybody digs them. The old guys like 'em 'cos they remind them of days gone by; and the young 'uns can appreciate them 'cos they'll probably build the same when they've got a few more bucks together. So everybody's happy!

This little fun '31 sit on its stock rails, fenderless and Highboy style, though a 3-inch chop prevents it from staring over the neighbor's fence and scaring the kids. The Deuce grille and big commercial headlamps give it plenty of presence, and the choice of Pale Lemon yellow and green detailing is nothing short of inspired. We just don't see enough Nailhead-powered hot rods around. Yet this coupe has one; a 425 ci, class of '64, and what's more it's running a Weiand Dragstar log-styled intake complete with six '97s and plenty of finned aluminum dress up.

MAKE:	Ford Model A
BODY STYLE:	5-window Coupe
YEAR:	1931
ENGINE:	Buick 425 Nailhead V8
BUILD STYLE:	Traditional Hot Rod
OWNER:	Robert Fischbein

▶ Some rods just have it, and this one certainly does. Just check out the picture and you'll know exactly what we mean.

★ ★ ★ ★ ★ ★ ★ ★ ★ ★ ★ ★ ★ ★ ★ ★

'32 Ford 5-window

'32 Ford 5-window

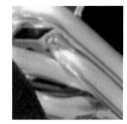

Here's a cool 5-window Coupe that doesn't conform to any specific build style, apart from "simply" being a hot rod. A 3-inch chopped Downs body sits fenderless on a Pete'n'Jake frame, features bobbed front frame horns – a popular modification back in the minimal obsessed 1980's. Other body modifications include a filled roof and a smooth-filled grille shell, which also features a Downs aftermarket grille insert; note the lack of a crank hole. The Deuce is finished in Midnight Blue Metallic Pearl with spooky airbrushed "specter" graphics that make a change from "ghost" flames!

A Super Bell chromed and dropped I-beam is the major feature up front. All other front end items are also finished in the shiny stuff, including the shocks and hairpins. A 4.11:1 geared 9-inch is the major rear end component. The Chevy motor is a neat item, being a rare '69 Chevy DZ 302, with ported and polished heads that's been bored to 308 ci. A Lunati cam bumps the valve gear and a vintage Edelbrock Tunnel Ram dominates the motor. Equipped as it is with a pair of 450 Holleys, the potent small block is mated to a 350 transmission to complete the running gear assembly.

MAKE:	Ford
BODY STYLE:	5-window Coupe
YEAR:	1932
ENGINE:	Chevy 302 V8
BUILD STYLE:	Street Rod
OWNER:	Craig Yeske

◄ Wheels Vintique Billet Cruizer rims add to the eclectic mix of parts used on this demon-graphiced Deuce 5-window.

'40 Ford Coupe

If you want to know the definition of dedication and perseverance, it could well be wrapped up in the completion of this fat '40 that is finished in '69 Chevy Hugger Orange. The car was on the street soon after a 9-year build, when it was almost totaled by a major rear end crunch that also took out the front on the car in front. Of course, you wouldn't know it now, thanks to the determination of its owner to get it back on the street, where it belongs. While not a unique tale, it's one worth telling, and totally to his credit. The car wears its original stainless bright trim with only the lack of a front fender, one-piece side windows and smooth black painted running boards deviating from stock.

The '40 sits low, thanks to a Mustang II front end a Plymouth 3.7:1 rear. The Ford theme is continued under the hood with the engine, which is a Ford 5.0 wearing an Offenhauser lo-rise inlet and a pair of Edelbrock quads. A late-model Lincoln gave up its transmission for the car, the included overdrive making for a stress-free highway drive. Polished Weld wheels are finished off with a set of center spinners in order to add extra flair to the cool rolling stock.

MAKE:	Ford
BODY STYLE:	2-door Coupe
YEAR:	1940
ENGINE:	Ford 5.0 V8
BUILD STYLE:	Street Rod
OWNER:	John Holder

▶ It's a tough enough deal to get a car like this '40 on to the street in the first place. This rod got wrecked after first completion and so was effectively built twice.

'23 T-bucket

Another one for fans of killer T-buckets, this '23 keeps the paintwork subtle, relying on the awesome blown engine and Pro-street stance to attract admiring attention. Any T–bucket ought to be the easiest car on which to get a quality paint job done, there is scarcely any bodywork to start with, let alone any door and trunk shuts and other fiddly but important bits to deal with. This T uses a Total Performance '23 body, with the shortened pickup bed popular on Ts. The purple pearl paint is a Sikkens color and has been matched in shade by the upholstery trim that's been two-toned with cream for the interior stitching.

Of course, with such minimal bodywork, the centerpiece of any Fad T has to be the engine. This one certainly looks the part, with a detailed and fully polished, stroked-out 355-ci small block Chevy. That familiar supercharged whine from the V8 is provided by the Simonek Performance prepped BDS 6-71 huffer. In turn, that is fed by twin Holleys

▶ This T runs massive Convo-Pro rear rims wrapped in Pro-Street Hoosier rubber, in stark contrast to the skinny wires and motorcycle derived front runners.

topped with a businesslike BDS polished scoop. Someone got busy with a pipe-bending machine to produce those neat zoomie headers too. Transmission is a TH350, which is connected via a very short propshaft to a '64 Chevy 10-bolt rear end. The front end is all chromed drop tube hardware, an absolute must on any show quality T-bucket.

MAKE:	Ford
BODY STYLE:	T Roadster
YEAR:	1923
ENGINE:	Chevy 355 V8
BUILD STYLE:	Pro-street Fad T
OWNER:	Dave and Sandy Phillips

'30 Ford Roadster

 t's a fact that the phrase "old school," as used to describe the traditional way of doing things or building cars and bikes, is already in danger of being over used. But what else can you say about this rockin' roadster? There's so much nostalgic eye candy here, so where do you look first? Burnt Orange shorty scallops stand out against the Yellow-cream body, while the white top sits low over the chopped windshield frame. A Deuce shell, Moon discs, Cheater rear whitewalls, chromed split wishbones and an Eelco front mounted fuel tank – it's all here and it's all cool.

This rod is already scoring high in the nostalgia stakes and would be just as cool with a small block or a Flathead V8. But, no – this one takes it that extra mile with a full-on De-Soto Fireflite Hemi (check the valve covers), plus a polished 6-71 Blower, dual quads and a Hilborn style scoop. Just in case that's still not enough, this baby's got three pedals on the floor, a stick shift 4-speed and a quick-change rear end, just for good measure. Did we mention the whole shebang was mounted on a Deuce frame too? It just goes to prove that you can't have too much of a good thing.

MAKE:	Ford
BODY STYLE:	Model A Roadster
YEAR:	1930
ENGINE:	De Soto Hemi V8
BUILD STYLE:	Traditional
OWNER:	James Wagner

◄ This '30 roadster is almost an exercise in nostalgia hot rod building, incorporating a host of cool vintage features.

'36 Ford Coupe

Sometimes, you get used to certain body styles being created in the same way, so much so that when someone takes a particular look and adds it to an otherwise familiar car, it can be a real eye opener. Such is the case with this '36 Ford 5-window coupe. For years, '36s have either been customized and rodded so as to straddle that fine line between rod and custom, or been given the Resto look due to their relative rarity. This one takes Ford's first real fat-fendered Coupe and takes it to the track, style-wise. The hood and side panels have been left back in the home garage to make way for the full Pro-street treatment that resulted in the stock headlamp buckets being replaced here by smaller chrome numbers.

The '36 isn't bluffing either, with 427 ci of blown Rat motor between its portly fenders. The big-block Chevy is fully detailed to the max with a Littlefield blower, plus vintage Hilborn injection under the chromed same-make scoop. It takes both feet and a handful of Borg Warner's best T10 4-speed gears to handle this brute, even if there is a 4.56:1 equipped and narrowed 9-inch between the big Hoosier rear tires. American 5-spokes, polished to match the motor's shine, roll this rod on down to the local quarter-mile strip. By the way, the front end is an independent Fat Man Fabrications setup.

MAKE:	Ford
BODY STYLE:	5-window Coupe
YEAR:	1936
ENGINE:	Chevy 427 V8
BUILD STYLE:	Performance
OWNER:	Tim and Joyce Pearl

▶ With a blown 427 up front and super sized Hoosiers out back, this is one '36 that's not afraid of taking care of business.

'32 Ford Roadster

It doesn't matter how many times that you see a classic '32 Highboy at a show, with the traditional paint treatment of black basecoat with flames, you just have to step over and take a closer look – even if it's just to check out what makes the version you're looking at different from the rest. But it will be different, as they all are, and the more you know about hot rods, the easier it will be to spot the unique features that the builder has incorporated so as to make the car his own. Take this one, for example. Three rows of nearly identical flames stretching back to the rear quarters are a simple enough design, but they get the message across effectively. In addition, the flames' starting point is the lower firewall, which integrates the paint into the car, rather than just laying on top of the exterior.

The choice of whitewalls on red wires rather indicates the fact that the builder opted for radials over bias ply, showing that he intended to put some miles under the steel Brookville body. The same goes for the "vintage" induction on top of the 350 engine. It's actually an electronic fuel injection developed by Moon, though cleverly engineered to resemble an early 6-pot carb system. Once again, this is an example of hot rodding finding a way to blend the classic with the practical. Chromed I-beam, hairpins, big commercial '32 headlamps and a chopped windshield complete the picture.

MAKE:	Ford
BODY STYLE:	Fenderless Roadster
YEAR:	1932
ENGINE:	Chevy 350 V8
BUILD STYLE:	Traditional Highboy
OWNER:	Steve Ramsey

◀ Try telling the uninitiated bystander that this is virtually a brand new car. With a Brookville steel body, a Moon EFI and radial tires, it's probably newer than your neighbor's Honda!

'40 Mercury

With a custom heritage that stretches back to when these were virtually brand new cars, the 40-41 Mercury has a history of being one of the most desirable custom cars to own and trick out. Indeed, the car that first put George and Sam Barris on the on the map was Nick Matranga's '40 hardtop, while other notable customizers of the period, such as the Ayala Bros, Jimmy Summers and Tommy the Greek, all turned out fine early Merc Customs. This fine '40 follows faithfully in that tradition, with its chopped Carson top, filled seams and frenched lights front and rear. Like any true custom, the hood and trunk have been nosed and decked, the door handles shaved and the hood has been punched full of louvers.

To get that essential tail draggin', led-sled look, the rear end has been swapped for a Mustang axle and leaf springs. The springs having had the eyes reversed, been de-arched and then fitted with 2-inch lowering blocks. The front end, meanwhile, retains the stock '40 axle, but has been fitted with AMC 3-inch dropped spindles. GM power steering has been added for more driving pleasure. The Merc may be a cool custom, but under the hood, it's pure hot rod – with a 350 Chevy engine that sports an Edelbrock intake and the traditional touch of three copper-plated Stromberg 97s.

MAKE:	Mercury
BODY STYLE:	2-door Convertible
YEAR:	1940
ENGINE:	Chevy 350 V8
BUILD STYLE:	Traditional Custom
OWNER:	Bob Johnson

▶ Deep Burgundy Wine paint with Candy scallops from House of Kolors feature on this outstanding '40 Mercury Convertible custom.

'41 Chevy C.O.E

A phenomenon of recent years on the street rod scene has been the trend towards rodding early trucks. That is, not your average half-ton pickup, but proper trucks! These 1940's cab-over-engine designs may have been ungainly beasts when stock, but look what happens when a rodder gets his hands on one. This particular, well-traveled '41 Chevy cab once saw duty as a fire truck in Colorado, before being rescued derelict from a farm in North Dakota many years later. It now sits on an '81 Chevy bread truck frame that's been narrowed at the front to enable the air-bagged Mustang II suspension to fit under the cab's narrow cab and fenders.

The truck's rear flatbed has been constructed from aluminum and then lined with cypress wood. This is where the truck's new V8 engine is now located, under that wood packing case. The 502-ci Chevy engine gives new meaning to the term "crate engine!" The area under the cab where the original 6-pot would have lived is now home only to the big alloy radiator and the twin, 8-feet foot cooling pipes leading back to the engine. A 700R4 transmission transfers the power down to the 10-inch GM rear axle. Ironically, the toughest job involved in building this heavy hauler was restoration of the cab and all its original chrome trim.

MAKE:	Chevrolet
BODY STYLE:	C.O.E. Flatbed
YEAR:	1941
ENGINE:	Chevy 502 V8
BUILD STYLE:	Street Rod Truck
OWNER:	Greg Saunders

◀ A hot rod truck with a difference! This '41 Chevy C.O.E. is hot rodding on an altogether grander scale.

631

'23 T-bucket

You could easily be forgiven for thinking that this is another resurrected old T roadster, lovingly restored after lying neglected since the 1950s. An East Coast car maybe, with that radical channeled stance? You'd be wrong on both counts. This T was hand-built for the first time way back in the 1970s no less. At that time, Flatheads really were yesterday's news, the upright Fad T and Resto Rods being the norm. In fact, way out in the farmlands of the Mid-West, it was pretty tricky to even buy a fiberglass T body, So, the owner of this one fabricated it himself – and everything else on the car, too, including the chassis.

Using all-Ford running gear, a vintage-forged '32 front axle and spring was used, with '40 Ford juice brakes on '40 spindles and split 'bones – all of which have been liberally covered in chrome. The rear end features a Halibrand quick-change on a Model A spring, again with '40 juice brakes. Shocks all round are tractor seat items. The Flathead engine used is a 258-ci V8, with an Isky cam and Jahns pistons. The heads are Offy and so is the four-in-a-row intake with quad Ford 94s. This drives through a Weber clutch to a '39 tranny. Finally, as with so much of this cool T, the headers and exhaust are also owner-made.

MAKE:	Ford
BODY STYLE:	T Roadster
YEAR:	1923
ENGINE:	Flathead V8
BUILD STYLE:	Street Rod
OWNER:	Dan Holck

◂ The super-low stance and built Flathead mill make this 1970's-built T real hot stuff – some 30 plus years after first being made.

'27 T Lakester

31 Barney Navarro's name is synonymous with the early lakes racing scene. Barney was also a manufacturer of early speed equipment, such as intakes and Flathead cylinder heads, and was also credited with being the first to fit a GMC blower to a Flathead V8. This is the car on which he did it, using it as a test bed for developing his speed parts and regularly racing the car at El Mirage from 1947 to 1953. The '27 T roadster had all-early-Ford running gear, including a V8 engine that was de-stroked down to 179 ci and fitted with his own intake and heads – plus the aforementioned GMC 3-71 blower fed by four Stromberg 48s. Running through a '39 gearbox to a 4.11:1 geared rear end, this resulted in the little '27 running a top speed of 146.8mph in the early 1950's.

Navarro sold the car in 1953 to a Californian racer in the Fresno area, the car being bought by its present owner via an ad in *Hemmings* in 1991. A full restoration has since been carried out, with the lower three inches of the body having been replaced because of corrosion. Another major job was locating a replacement Art Ingles nose for the car, the correct part being pictured in a magazine article on a Colorado swap meet. After six months of searching, the vendor was located and the nose acquired for the project. The restored car is now on loan to the NHRA Motorsport Museum in Pomona.

MAKE:	Ford
BODY STYLE:	T Roadster
YEAR:	1927
ENGINE:	179 ci Flathead V8
BUILD STYLE:	Traditional Lakes Roadster
OWNER:	Scott Perrott

▶ A true classic of the vintage lakes racing scene, Barney Navarro's '27 was the first car to run a GMC blower on a Flathead V8.

'38 Oldsmobile Coupe

A rare enough Coupe in stock form, this big, hot rod Olds is an even rarer sight in wild street/strip guise, let alone with a multi-color competition style paint job to match. This is actually the second incarnation of the Olds, since it was involved in a front and rear fender bender while on a showground some years back. A custom vertical bar grille replaces the original chromed horizontal bar item that these cars have as stock. The rest of the bodywork is largely stock, apart from the fiberglass hood that now incorporates the big snorkel air scoop. That huge rear wing is also a 'glass item and is supported on steel struts, though it's mainly for show. But having said that, the car has posted a 13-second quarter-mile time at half-throttle. Not bad for such a heavy car.

Keeping the car all Oldsmobile in body and soul is a big 468-ci Olds mill under the hood, being mostly stock apart from a Crane cam and a 750-cfm Holley. There's some neat aluminum ductwork under there too, drawing the air from the scoop down into the single carb. Behind the 468, is a GM Turbo 400, linked to the 9-inch rear end, which is equipped with Strange shafts. It runs 4.11:1 gearing and is 4-bar, mounted with coil overs. A similar arrangement attaches the drop tube front axle. In the brake department it runs big Jaguar ventilated rotors and 15-inch Center Line wheels complete the competition look with the Mickey T big rear tires.

MAKE:	Oldsmobile
BODY STYLE:	2-door Coupe
YEAR:	1938
ENGINE:	Oldsmobile 468 V8
BUILD STYLE:	Performance
OWNER:	Tony Melcer

◀ Plenty fast enough for the street, this big '38 Olds is not quite the racecar that it looks to be – but big fun!

'32 Ford Roadster

There's no mistaking that classic profile with just the right amount of rake provided by the big and little white-wall tires. It all defines a true hot rodding classic, a '32 Highboy running a Flathead Ford. This is no old-timey salt survivor though; rather it's a well-detailed and faithful recreation of earlier hot rodding. From the Guide headlamps to the drilled split wishbones, this Deuce Roadster has got the look down pat and – and this is enhanced with the use of a genuine Duvall raked windshield. The deep Maroon paint and contrasting cream wheels are echoed in the maroon and vinyl candy stripe interior trim that is, sadly, out of sight in this shot.

The repro body and chassis package is suspended on a Flatlander's chromed I-beam, with '40 juice brakes and Buick drums. Suspension is provided by So-Cal shocks and a Posies front spring at the front; and at the rear, an early Ford rear also rides on So-Cal shocks and an early Ford spring. As mentioned above, drilled split wishbones feature on both sets of axles. During the build-up, however, the biggest stroke of luck was finding the engine. A race-prepped flat engine was located languishing in the body of a 1950's Alfa Romeo racecar awaiting restoration. It came complete with vintage speed equipment already installed. On inspection, it was found that the Edelbrock -and-Harman-&-Collins-equipped engine had barely covered 500 miles since its last rebuild.

MAKE:	Ford
BODY STYLE:	Highboy Roadster
YEAR:	1932
ENGINE:	Flathead V8
BUILD STYLE:	Traditional Period Hot Rod
OWNER:	Jim Turnbull

▸ For this cool Deuce, finding an already race-prepped Flathead mill was the icing on the cake for this vintage slice of period hot rodding .

'32 Ford 5-window Coupe

 lthough any chopped and fenderless 5-window will put you in mind of the *American Graffiti* (despite the fact that the movie car had bobbed fenders), this Deuce has its build style aimed squarely at a few years later, the mid-1960s. The clue lies in the polished Appliance 5-spokes on the back and matching AREs on the front, especially as those rear rims were found with an early Ford stud pattern, matching the pattern on the '40 Ford rear brakes. The white tires are narrow band as well, which helps create the overall image. The rod uses a mostly fiberglass body with a filled roof; but an original steel firewall has been incorporated and the '32 is built on an original frame for added authenticity. The '57 Chevy Sierra bronze metallic on both body and frame helps add the correct feel to the copper Coupe.

Keeping everything looking traditional under the frame is an aluminum I-beam from Super Bell, with owner-made batwings and radius rods. Between the rear wheels, a Winters quick-change rear end on a narrowed '40 axle, again using home-built radius rods. Power comes from a little Chevy 283 engine, rebuilt with forged pistons and a Comp Cams bumpstick. Apart from this, the engine is stock, save for the Holley 500 on a Weiand intake – with the adequate power getting stirred through a Toyota 5-speed manual transmission, just for a change.

MAKE:	Ford
BODY STYLE:	5-window Coupe
YEAR:	1932
ENGINE:	Chevy 283 V8
BUILD STYLE:	Traditional 1960s Hot Rod
OWNER:	Merv Barnett

◀ Narrow white band bias-ply tires on polished 5-spokes lend a mid 1960's feel to this fab 5-window.

'37 Ford Cabriolet

The beauty of these late-1930's bodied Cabrios over the earlier roadsters is two-fold. Firstly, they can be built as 4-seaters, ideal for family oriented rodders who still want to enjoy some top down driving. Secondly, their full-fendered style means that late model suspension setups can be successfully used without any visual detriment to the car. The builder of this lemon-flavored '37 had both these factors in mind when setting out to build this cool Cabrio. He was indeed a family man and he wanted to build a comfortable car with excellent handling car too. Ordering the '37 body was the easy bit, but the second requirement only became reality with the purchase of a wrecked Jaguar sedan, which was raided for all of its suspension components.

With the geometry all figured out, these parts were adapted to the TCI chassis, although the width factor meant that narrower early arms had to be installed on the independent rear axle. A small block '68 Chevy 327 engine was installed up front and then fitted with Fuelie heads, a Competition Cams camshaft and a Holley 650 on a Performer manifold. The result was a car that drove and handled exactly as planned. A set of Weld Drag star wheels provide shiny contrast to the Pineapple yellow paint, with Violet Pearl scallops, that completes the well-thought-out '37.

MAKE:	Ford
BODY STYLE:	Cabriolet
YEAR:	1937
ENGINE:	Chevy 327 V8
BUILD STYLE:	Street Rod
OWNER:	Tracy Ward

▶ A folding top from a late-model import was adapted to provide a factory-like fit to the practical and comfortable custom Cabriolet.

'47 Chevy Coupe

After the major interruption to production of World War II, it took most American car manufacturer's a couple of years to re-tool and re-design for the new models that the public were hungry for. In the meantime, most designs were the pre-War '42 models with updated cosmetics. For stopgap models, the '47 Chevy Coupes were a good-looking car with their full-width, chromed grille. They still make great looking hot rods, although many seem to have been favored by the Low Rider crowd. This one remains totally stock, body-wise, but has the neat detail of a Chevy bowtie-shaped fuel filler flap set into the right rear fender. The stunning paint color is a custom mix of Yellow Mica pearl and it positively glows on the Fat '47.

A Mustang II front end with power steering gets the forward end a little closer to the pavement than stock, and the rake is accentuated by the adjustable air shocks mounted on the Chevy 10-bolt rear axle hanging on a set of RB parallel leaves. A 350 Chevy with a 600 carb and a Performer intake helps the engine breath in, while a set of Ramshorn headers leading to a 2-inch full system help it breath out. The engine is fully polished and detailed and Center Line Modular wheels wear a set of Cooper white band tires in order to add that extra touch of Fleetmaster class.

MAKE:	Chevrolet
BODY STYLE:	Fleetmaster Coupe
YEAR:	1947
ENGINE:	Chevy 350 V8
BUILD STYLE:	Street Rod
OWNER:	Shaun Grant

▾ The bodywork and trim may be stock, but there's no mistaking that classic hot rod stance on this fat '47 Fleetmaster Coupe.

'34 Ford Roadster

While not as common as '32s or '29s on Deuce rails, '33-34 roadsters still look hot as a fenderless Highboy style. Straight black will do and it always looks good as a gloss backdrop to plenty of polished alloy and chrome; even better if it has a Duvall-style screen like the moody looking example pictured here. Using an original frame picked up at a swap meet and then boxed, this '34 fiberglass-bodied roadster has all the moves in a nostalgic but understated style. Those particular moves include a Super Bell dropped I-beam on Pete'n'Jake hairpins, with chromed shocks, So-Cal hubs with Buick finned rotor covers, and a multi-leaf spring. Getting serious out back, a complete Currie Enterprises 9-inch Ford is mounted on coil overs, with homemade hairpins and Panhard rod.

The 283-ci Chevy 'vette engine small-block punches out 325 hp, courtesy of a set of bench-flowed cylinder heads, a Crane Cam, Manley stainless steel valves and Mallory ignition. What's more, the power gets to the 9-inch via a Muncie 4-speed with a Hayes clutch. With the power from this package readily available, the car often sees strip time; hence the slicks in the picture mounted on the polished ARE rims. Other neat details are the big repro '34 headlamps and the machine-turned dash panel that is reminiscent of vintage racecars.

MAKE:	Ford
BODY STYLE:	Highboy Roadster
YEAR:	1934
ENGINE:	Chevy 283 V8
BUILD STYLE:	Street Rod
OWNER:	Dan Williams

▶ Both the '34 grille and the Duvall-style screen were handmade for this car, both adding bags of character to the mean, black Model 40.

'30 Sedan Delivery

There's a strong, no-nonsense performance theme running through this neat fiberglass Model A sedan Delivery, hence the un-fussy straight Blue Pearl paint job on the little truck. Inside, there's no room for hauling anything, the interior being filled with a pair of bucket seats, a full cage and a pair of NOS bottles – although it is trimmed and carpeted in there too. The repro A chassis features independent front suspension, based on Ford components and fitted with rack and pinion steering. The rear end is a Mustang unit hung on a stainless 4-bar with AVO coil over shocks. If the truck looks a little low, that's because it is – it's been channeled over the frame.

To maintain the A's street credibility and performance image, a Goodwrench 350 Chevy crate engine was installed and then fitted with plenty of polished dress-up and a Holley 600 and Edelbrock Performer package. This is maximized by the addition of an Art Carr performance 350 transmission. The Hooker headers on the engine lead virtually straight into the fender-well-mounted Super Trapp mufflers. That's just as well, since the car rides a little low for a full system to be installed. Sharing the fenderwells are the Champ 500 wheels, further adding to the racecar theme.

MAKE:	Ford
BODY STYLE:	Sedan Delivery
YEAR:	1930
ENGINE:	Chevy 350 V8
BUILD STYLE:	Street Rod
OWNER:	Paul Gartside

◀ Just straight Blue Pearl is all that's needed to finish off this hot little Model A hauler, the Sedan Delivery finished in an understated, no-nonsense Hi-Po style.

'29 Ford Roadster

esearch any history on the early days of dry lakes racing, and one thing becomes apparent: in those days, if you wanted to race your street roadster on the salt, you had to first drive it there. Once on the lake, you then had to set about removing the street trim, such as fenders, lights and windshield, in order to lighten the load in the search for top speed. It was in the spirit of these early racers that this car was conceived, first by "Kiwi" Steve Davies – who originally built it – and then by the joint team of So-Cal Speed Shop employees – Tony Thacker and Jimmy Shine – who made it a running reality.

The goal was to build a roadster that would drive the 800 miles from their base in Los Angeles, up to Bonneville, and with just a few changes, then top 200 mph in a street-driven car when competing in the C/blown Street Roadster class. It took a while and several ever-improving trips to the salt. Then, in August 2004, with Jimmy Shine at the wheel, the suede black '29 Roadster on original '32 rails (boxed of course) topped the double century at 201.821 mph. That major feat was accomplished using a 750-horsepower, 355-ci Chevy engine, featuring a Lunati bottom end, Arias pistons, Pro Action/Pro Topline heads and an 8-71 Littlefield blower fed by twin Holley 750s. The engine was put together by John Beck's Pro-machine shop in Placentia, California.

MAKE:	Ford
BODY STYLE:	Highboy Roadster
YEAR:	1929
ENGINE:	Chevy 355 V8
BUILD STYLE:	Performance
OWNER:	Thacker and Shine

◀ Just about managing to stay road legal, with working lights and removable pipes, this unassuming '29 on '32 rails nevertheless drove to the salt, did 200+ mph – and then drove home.

'34 Dodge Pickup

The '34 Dodge is by no means a common choice for a hot rod truck project. Yet, this can only be down to the rarity of the beast, as it certainly cannot be on the basis of its looks; the mo-haul Mopar is good-looking little wagon, for sure. This is probably down to the fact that it shares common sheet metal with its passenger car cousins. In addition, it's got a proper stainless grille whilst many trucks make do with painted pressed steel. The suicide doors on the cab are unusual on a truck too. So, here's one rodder who saw the Dodge's potential and decided to keep it all firmly in Mopar country as well.

The bright yellow hauler was built entirely at home, with only the paint, trim and some engine work being farmed out to local companies. If you think that that alone makes this truck special, you haven't looked under the hood. Keeping it within the Dodge family is a 270 ci Dodge Red Ram Hemi from 1955, also fully detailed in yellow and wearing an Offy intake with three Holley '94s just for good measure. The engine drives through a 4-speed manual transmission (also Dodge, but from a 1970's model) and down to the very non-Dodge, 9-inch rear end, being the only Ford part on the whole truck. The wide whites on chrome steels look dazzling against the all-yellow bodywork.

MAKE:	Dodge
BODY STYLE:	Pickup
YEAR:	1934
ENGINE:	270 ci Dodge Hemi V8
BUILD STYLE:	Traditional Rod
OWNER:	Jack Buete

◀ Dazzlingly yellow paint and a 1950's Hemi motor set the scene for this cool period Pickup, originally built by Dodge.

'39 Ascot Dirt Tracker

We make no apology for including a couple of circuit racing dirt racers in the book, recognizing that they too are part of the fine history of American hot rodding. By that, we mean cars screwed together using spare parts, ingenuity and old-fashioned grass roots know-how – and all done in order to produce more speed and performance than the next guy. This superb single-seater is an old Ascot racer from 1939, made from a partially-built set of parts and restored to former glory by Paul Kosma of Kosma Design and Fabrication. The aluminum body is the original, as is the steel track nose. The hood was re-made in aluminum by Paul.

Based on a pair of Essex chassis rails, the Ascot uses the axle from a '34 Chrysler with a Model A transverse spring and Franklin steering. The rear axle is a narrowed Model A Ford unit. Ford also produced the 4-cylinder engine in the racer, it being a '32 Model B item with a Cragar crossflow head. This drives through a Model A gearbox, via a Mustang clutch, and provides more than enough vintage power for the narrow Dayton Dentabite spoke wheels to cope with. The only braking system on the car is a hand-operated '40 Ford master cylinder. There are no stop pedals!

MAKE:	Ascot
BODY STYLE:	Single-seat Race Car
YEAR:	1939
ENGINE:	Model B/Cragar 4-cylinder
BUILD STYLE:	Traditional Dirt Track Restoration
OWNER:	Jimmy Dodds

◄ Many of these old dirt trackers are used regularly, this one placed No.9 out of a field of 32 on its first time out after its restoration.

'32 Ford Coupe

This red 3-window represents the consummate rendition of a classic Deuce Coupe built with all the correct old but "new" parts, put together professionally with no expense spared to create the perfect period hot rod. The Highboy Coupe was built in the late 1990s by Pete Chapouris' PC3G shop in California for car collector Bruce Meyer. It featured in *Street Rodder Magazine* under the name "Ruby Red." The steel body has been sliced 3 inches and features a 2-piece louvered hood and a filled grille shell. It was all then sprayed red, although the actual color is Porsche India Red.

All early-style parts have been used, including a raised front cross member, split bones and '40 Ford brakes at the front. The rear is pretty much stock wishbone but with a Columbia 2-speed axle and the same '40 juice brakes. You would expect to find a Flathead in a nostalgic Deuce like this, and whilst it has one, it's not just any Flathead. This one boasts a set of original Ardun heads, as well as a S.C.o.T. blower with dual Strombergs and with ignition is by Mallory. A '39 transmission shifts the gears for some period West coast cruising in this truly classic Coupe.

MAKE:	Ford
BODY STYLE:	3-window Coupe
YEAR:	1932
ENGINE:	268 ci Ford Flathead V8
BUILD STYLE:	Period Hot Rod
OWNER:	Bruce Meyer

◀ 3-window Deuces always look cool, especially so when they have the unmistakable Ardun cylinder heads visible on an early flat engine.

'32 Ford Roadster

Why is it that so few hot rods are painted white? Is it just that black is a traditional Ford color, or maybe it just looks meaner and more purposeful? Red has to be the next most popular color, even though it's often nick-named "Arrest Me Red" – for it has been proven in surveys that law enforcement officers stop and issue tickets to more red cars than those of any other color. You might want to think about that next time you reach for the painter's color chart on your next project. Just for a change then, here's a classic trad '32 Highboy that's been built the "white" way.

The first thing you notice is how well the red detailing stands out against the ivory Gibbon fiberglass reproduction Deuce body, with the engine, chassis components and upholstery all contrasting in a very, well, 1950's nostalgia style on this '32. Those red components include a dropped Super Bell axle on hairpins at the front and an 8-inch with a buggy spring at the rear. The engine is a Chevy small-block displacing 305 ci and fuelled by three 2-barrel carbs. A dash of chrome is provided by the detailed engine and the baby Moon hubcaps, in equal measure.

MAKE:	Ford
BODY STYLE:	Highboy Roadster
YEAR:	1932
ENGINE:	Chevy 305 V8
BUILD STYLE:	Traditional
OWNER:	Gary Gerberdine

◀ There are plenty of black '32's in these pages, but look how substituting white makes this Deuce stand out among other roadsters.

'32 Ford Coupe

This '32 can truly be described as a Highboy Coup. Not only does it have the classic fenderless stance so often found on same year roadsters, but also its profile stands tall with an unchopped, 5-window roofline. It's not only the roof that is stock height, so is every other aspect of the Coupe's bodywork – bearing in mind that it is a fenderless and hoodless car. The rest is all modern, but remains classic hot rod stuff, In this case, it's an original Ford chassis supported by a Magnum dropped axle. There is a Posies Superslide front spring and a four-bar at the front, with a 10-inch Ford axle hung from a '36 Ford buggy spring at the rear. Brakes are discs up front and stock Ford drums at the back.

A few years ago, Flathead V8s were somewhat of a rarity at rod shows, having been heaved out of early hot rods in favor of Chevy small blocks. But with the big resurgence of nostalgia cars in recent times, many cars now run them. This Coupe has a 239 ci '46 Flat engine up front, fully detailed and fitted with 3 Strombergs on an Offy intake. As usual, the hot setup for a Flathead engine transmission-wise is a '39 'box, and this Coupe has one of those too.

MAKE:	Ford
BODY STYLE:	5-window Coupe
YEAR:	1932
ENGINE:	Flathead V8
BUILD STYLE:	Traditional
OWNER:	Jack Miller

◀ Traditional black with red steelies, this Highboy '32 Coupe runs Flathead power and a stock height roof for a tall, but cool, profile.

'37 Ford "Phantom" Pickup

In hot-rodding parlance, a phantom rod is a body style that was never produced by the factory – and believe us, Ford never made a '37 passenger-based pickup for the US market (though there was a "ute" built in Australia). So, this '37 is very definitely a phantom. It uses an all fiberglass pickup body from the Wild Rod Factory mounted on a California Dreamin' Hot Rods chassis. The front suspension is an aftermarket Scotts I.F.S with Air Ride Technologies air bag system to get that ground scraping stance. Colorado Custom supplied the big diameter 18-inch and 20-inch five-spoke wheels and Falken Tires are responsible for the super low profile rubber bands.

Produced with all the best components money can buy, this project was put together by New York's Tucci Engineering, with parts donated by many companies, to be the 2004 "Give Away" car for the Right Coast Association, sponsors of many East Coast shows and events. The 302 Ford crate engine was stroked out to 347 cubes before being fully detailed and installed in the frame. While this futuristic style is not to every body's taste, there's no denying this is a true 21st century hot rod.

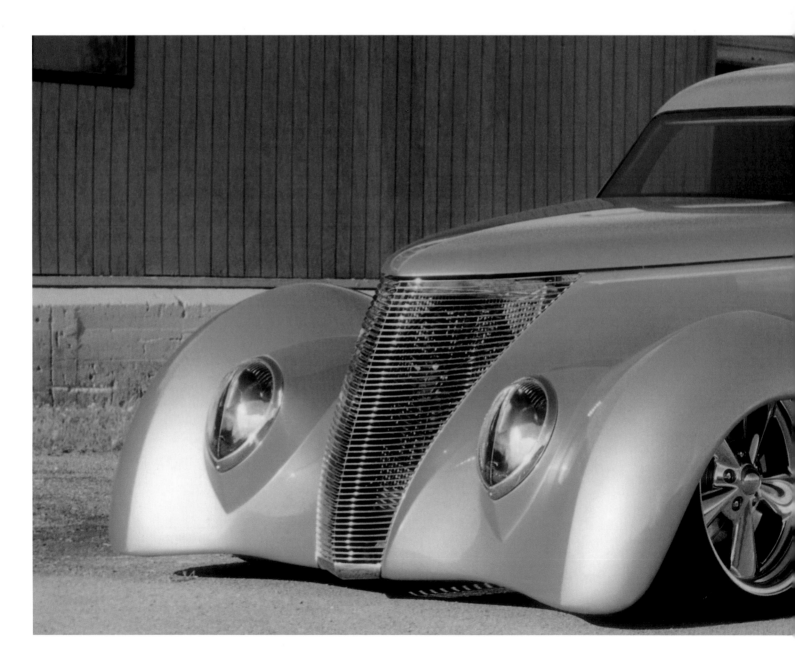

MAKE:	Ford
BODY STYLE:	Phantom Pickup
YEAR:	1937
ENGINE:	302 Ford V8
BUILD STYLE:	21st Century Street
BUILDER:	Dave Tucci

▼ It may look green to you in print, but this unusual color is known as Citrus Yellow Pearl – and it continues inside across the custom dash panel.

'32 Ford Phaeton

So you want a roadster but need more space for family? Why not go for a Phaeton instead? These 4-door soft tops are not common street rods, but they do look the part. This particular one was built back in the 80s but still looks fresh in the twenty-first century. Its smooth looks and Porsche Guards red paint remind you of a Coddington-built car – that is, until you notice the stock, chromed front fender and Zenith fine-wire wheels. Billet screen posts and hidden hinges combine with shaved handles for that unfussy 1980s appeal.

Under the 3-piece aluminum hood is a Chevy 350 with Z28 heads. Also in the mix is a Competition Cams camshaft and a Carter carb on an Edelbrock manifold. This flows the gas out via a fully polished, stainless steel exhaust system. Shifting is taken care of by a B&M 350 transmission. The frame is a repro with tubular cross members. The car runs a 4-inch tube front axle on a stainless 4-bar at the front with a Detroit locked 9-inch at the back, which has been converted to rear disc brakes. It may be a full hood-down hot rod touring car. but it still has the comforts of air-conditioning and a full Connolly leather trim job.

MAKE:	Ford
BODY STYLE:	4-door Phaeton
YEAR:	1932
ENGINE:	Chevy 350 V8
BUILD STYLE:	Street Rod
OWNER:	S. Foster Yancey Jr.

◄ A 4-door Phaeton makes a lot of sense for sociable types who still like to shoot the breeze!

'27 Ford Track T

Just about as close as you can get to driving a vintage, single-seat racecar on the street, has to be building and driving an early-style T Track Roadster. These cars use the same basic T-bucket body as regular Fad Ts, but are then narrowed. This one has been slimmed by a total of eight inches in order to give it that skinny racecar feel, ideal for those who prefer to fly solo. As with most of these track-style cars, they depend heavily on one-off custom engineering, usually by the owner. In this case it was the owner who also built the complete frame and carried out all the body modifications – including painting it. Built with many early Ford components, it nevertheless features '31 Chevy headlamps and Ross steering from a '42 Jeep.

The narrow chassis configurations mean that these little track roadsters are built almost exclusively with inline 4-bangers, just as their predecessors would have had back on the day. For reliability, this one sports a 120 ci Toyota with a stock 4-speed tranny, just to be different. The Japanese engines rev and go well from stock, and so engine work was limited to a ported head and a Weber carb conversion. A homemade stainless exhaust exits on the left-hand side and so is unseen in our picture. Suspension is all early Ford stuff, a 3-inch dropped axle carries '48 Ford hubs and brakes, and a '39 Ford with A Halibrand does the work out back.

MAKE:	Ford
BODY STYLE:	T Roadster
YEAR:	1927
ENGINE:	Toyota 120 ci 4
BUILD STYLE:	Traditional Track Roadster
OWNER:	Jim Vermeire

▶ Skinny 16-inch Ford spoke wheels are always the order of the day on dirt track inspired roadsters like this one.

'30 Ford Sport Phaeton

One of the few Phaetons in this book, as they are pretty rare hot rods when one considers the number of true roadsters around. However, no less fun is this Model A 2-door Sport Phaeton on '32 rails. As with all As on Deuce rails, the frame has been narrowed or "pinched" at the cowl to maintain the correct body-to-frame relationship. The body is stock, but the red and white scalloped paint is both striking and effective. A tan tonneau cover is buttoned down over the cockpit, and its tan velour Porsche 944 bucket seats, when the car is unattended.

A Magnum 5-inch dropped axle gets the tub down in the weeds with early Ford spindles and a set of Buick brake drums. At the back, a 10-bolt Chevy axle with 3.57 gears is installed on a stainless 4-bar. Power for the red and white Rodney comes from a stock but B&M blown Ford 302 with a Crane cam and a 600 Holley, which should make it scoot along. The transmission is a Ford C4 'box with a Transgo shift kit and the wheels are Super slots with B.F. Goodrich rubber.

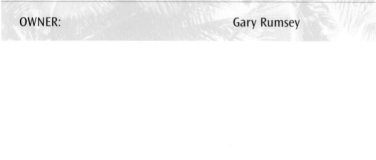

MAKE:	Ford
BODY STYLE:	2-door Phaeton
YEAR:	1930
ENGINE:	Ford 302 V8
BUILD STYLE:	Street Rod
OWNER:	Gary Rumsey

▶ The striking red and white scalloped paint on this low tub really accentuates the rake on the car, courtesy of the 5-inch dropped axle.

'23 Ford Roadster

One of the rarer, but definitely wilder variations on the T-bucket roadster theme is the so-called "Street Digger." It is an almost cartoon-inspired creation that combines as many drag racing cues as possible for a truly neck snappin', double-take first impression. Often using an extended wheelbase to accentuate the street-altered look, the frame is usually hand-built in chromed moly tubing, as per real strip machines. As with all true rail dragsters, the front wheels are the skinniest available. This one uses 18-inch Hallcraft wires, while at the rear, it's simply the bigger the better. A rare set of E.T. Funny car wheels on this car are one of only four pairs made and they wear 18 x 36 Goodyear Eagle racing slicks.

But you can't build a rod in this style unless you have a killer engine to go in it. How about a '70 Plymouth Hemi, displacing 492 ci with Keith Black fuel heads, triple valve springs, a Crower cam, KB pistons, aluminum rods and a Vertex Magneto? Then there's the 23% over-driven Weiand blower and totally mad zoomie headers. The transmission behind this monster engine is a 747 Torqueflite that's manually shifted via a RM Kendrick 4800 rpm converter. Rear is a Mopar 8-inch with a fully reinforced quick-change. Heavy metal indeed! The fuel consumption is measured in city blocks rather than in miles!

MAKE:	Ford
BODY STYLE:	T Roadster
YEAR:	1923
ENGINE:	Chrysler 492 ci Hemi V8
BUILD STYLE:	Show Rod
OWNER:	Eddie Anderson

▶ A handsome, brass T grille shell adds a touch of antique class to this wild "Street Digger" T. The top of the engine is the highest point on the car!

'33 Ford Roadster

In the early 1980s, two similar rods stood out as landmark cars heralding a new direction for hot rod styling. Both were Thom Taylor designed and Boyd Coddington built. Vern Luce's 33 Coupe was one; the other was this '33 that went on to be America's "Most Beautiful Roadster" at the 1982 Oakland Roadster Show. We are now used to seeing this sleek and uncluttered look, with its emphasis on high-tech milling and aluminum-made parts; but this was the car that spawned a thousand copies and influenced nearly two decades of rod building. It was also the first car to wear a set of Boyd aluminum billet wheels.

Although an original steel car, no area was left untouched in the search for smooth lines and perfect panel fit. The credit list for the build process is a veritable "who's who" of top craftsmen in the industry. Powered by a 355 ci Chevy small block built by Art Chrisman, the engine's most striking feature was its quad Weber carbs, along with custom aluminum dress-up features and bracketry. Suspension on the show-winning roadster is a mix of Coddington-built components, with a Corvette rear center section and a John Buttera front end, featuring billet Aldan prototype coil overs. The gearbox is a Doug Nash 6-speed.

MAKE:	Ford
BODY STYLE:	Roadster
YEAR:	1933
ENGINE:	Chevy 355 V8
BUILD STYLE:	Hi-Tech Street Rod
OWNER:	Jamie Musselman

◀ Although the Vern Luce Coupe debuted first, the Jamie Musselman '33 was topless – so as a roadster, it was eligible for the AMBR award that year. Needless to say, it won.

'30 Model A Sedan

▲ More vintage cool is provided to this dirty '30 by the early set of Halibrand slot mags front and rear.

This isn't just a 70+ year-old Model A sedan, it's a sedan with a 70+ year-old paint job as well. The original body on this Tudor is a solid as a rock, however, and just nicely aged with a tinge of vintage ferrous oxide for good measure. Sitting on a Model A repro chassis, the rodded A-bone was built into a hot rod back in 1989. But it was then put away and left in a lock-up garage for some 10 years before being bought and put back on the street by the current owner – and needing nothing more than some fuel and a new battery to bring it back to life. But it's under that aged sheet metal that the story really gets interesting.

Squeezed under that 4-piece faded hood, is a fully detailed 350 Chevy engine with 4-bolt mains and wearing a humungous B&M Megablower with dual Edelbrock 500s. The engine has been fitted with a special blower cam and a set of low compression pistons, but apart from that, it is mostly stock. Even so, the car is capable of, and has run, 12.6 in the quarter-mile. Transmission is a TH400 and this drives down to a genuine Frankland Quick-change rear end with 9-inch Ford shafts and a set of late model Corvette rotors.

The front end is kept off the blacktop with a Vintage Chassis Works drop tube that is mounted on a stainless 4-bar. Custom alloy hubs feature Jaguar discs and JFZ Rotors.

MAKE:	Ford
BODY STYLE:	Tudor Sedan
YEAR:	1930
ENGINE:	Chevy 350 V8
BUILD STYLE:	Traditional
OWNER:	Pete Angell

'37 Ford Sedan

Fat-fendered Ford Sedans make great family-sized hot rods – even when built in the Pro-Street style with big 22-inch Mickey Thompson tires tucked underneath the stock rear fenders and custom-built wheel tubs intruding into the trunk area. This smooth and graphically painted '37 has all that and more. It still manages to get driven almost daily as a family car besides. Dubbed "Purple Dayz," it was completely home-built by its owner, who always intended for it to get plenty of regular use, rather than just for high days and holidays. A gray leather hide trim job on the inside keeps it practical and comfortable for the family.

A tried and trusted combo, a detailed Chevy 350 with an Edelbrock carb and manifold and a TH350 transmission, pushes the sedan along via a narrowed Ford 9-inch on a four-bar with coil overs. At the front, an independent setup features Jaguar components and brakes on a custom cross-member grafted to the front of the boxed '37 frame. Although the owner has replaced the original rubber running boards with smooth painted ones, the car retains other original external features – the original door handles and steel hood sides as well as the original split windshield glass. All in all, a neat example of old meets new style.

MAKE:	Ford
BODY STYLE:	2-door Sedan
YEAR:	1937
ENGINE:	Chevy 350 V8
BUILD STYLE:	Pro-Street Rod
OWNER:	Stuart Flitton

▲ Deep Purple pearl paintwork is saved from a too-subtle statement
by the Tangerine "ripped and torn" graphics along the belt line.

'33 Ford Coupe

Instantly recognizable as the car that introduced hot rodding to the MTV generation, it was a stroke of genius to introduce ZZ Top front man Billy Gibbons' own hot rod into the story line of their music videos – and just as the genre took off. It also featured on their album cover art and both that recording and the car were dubbed "Eliminator." Suddenly, everyone wanted a 33-34 Coupe – and a red one, and preferably with copycat graphics too! Couldn't quite stretch to a hot rod? No matter, just paint the ZZ graphics on anything you've got. Sadly, that's what many did. The cool '33 was so popular in the meantime, that a second fiberglass clone was built, just to go on tour and attend shows. Not many noticed the difference!

The "Eliminator" itself was built by Don Thelan at his Buffalo Motor Cars rod shop back in 1983. For such an influential car, it boasts nothing more than fairly standard street rod components under the sheet metal, or indeed, the 'glass. Power comes from a stock 350 Chevy, with a Z 28 Hydro cam and a 500 AFB Carter carb – though it's worth mentioning the neat valve covers that have the Kenny Youngblood-designed ZZ graphics milled into each one. The front axle is a dropped Super Bell item and a Ford 9-inch handles the power out back. Have Mercy!

MAKE:	Ford
BODY STYLE:	2-door Coupe
YEAR:	1933
ENGINE:	Chevy 350 V8
BUILD STYLE:	Street Rod
OWNER:	Billy F. Gibbons

◀ There's no doubt that the ZZ '33 was the real star of the Texas blues-rock bands music videos, albeit filled with long-legged models!

'40 Ford Coupe

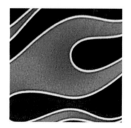

J ust what is it about black'n'flamed hot rods that make them so cool? Many rodders paint with flame designs in many colors, and sometimes you just know by looking that it was an after-though; something to liven up a paint job that just looked a bit too staid. But a black car with red and yellow flames done well will always stop a true hot rodder dead in his tracks. This is one such car, a flaming '40 built by the So Cal Speed shop that had been in the mind of its owner since he graduated from high school back in the 1960s. Its visual impact is undeniable, but look further and you'll see that it's a hot rod through and through.

If you were wondering where the hood is, there isn't one – or, rather, there's an abbreviated hood front section fitted to cover the radiator above the '39 Deluxe grille. This means the onlooker is free to cast their gaze on the mighty Chrysler 426 Hemi contained therein. The car is fitted with a classic Hilborn injection setup, so reminiscent of 1960's drag racing machinery, and has been converted to electronic operation for modern reliability. Cool period touches abound, such as the one-off nerf bars and the 5-spoke Halibrands front and rear. Incidentally, those front ones are genuine spindle mounts.

MAKE:	Ford
BODY STYLE:	2-door Coupe
YEAR:	1940
ENGINE	Chrysler 426 Hemi V8
BUILD STYLE	Traditional 1960's Hot Rod
OWNER	Chuck de Heras

▼ "An injected Hemi in a flamed '40 Ford." These words alone are almost the holy grail of hot rodding!

'28 Ford Roadster

Anyone who regularly bought *Street Rodder* in the 1980s is bound to recognize this traditional A roadster as Ol' Blue, the regular driver of the late Bill Burnham, the man who regularly "told it like it is" in his monthly column for the magazine. A hot rod traditionalist to the end, his tales of life on the road at the wheel of this cool A became a firm favorite for the readers. Bill drove the roadster regularly to rod runs all over, including his annual pilgrimage to Bonneville.

Trends may have come and gone over the years, but Ol' Blue stayed true to Bill's earlier hot rod origins. The classic '28 A on a '32 chassis is a tried and tested recipe, but this one is slightly different in having a 4-inch stretch in the Deuce frame, this done to accommodate the big, 390 ci Ford big block V8 in the car. A filled Deuce grille shell is matched to the '28 cowl with a steel three-piece hood, which also features a "bubble" on each side panel to further clear the wide V8 engine. Suspension on the roadster was strictly old school, with I-beam and unsplit wishbones at front and rear.

MAKE:	Model A
BODY STYLE:	Highboy Roadster
YEAR:	1928
ENGINE:	Ford 390 V8
BUILD STYLE;	Traditional Hot Rod
OWNER:	Bill Burnham

◀ Seen here displayed at an indoor show after the passing of its owner, Bill Burnham's roadster stands as a celebration – and real tribute to his hot rodding lifestyle.

'29 Ford Roadster

What do you do if your hot rod was already a magazine cover car in 1971 and 1973, and you'd had over twenty years of fun driving since then? Sell it? Or perhaps, like the owner of this '29 Highboy, you'd completely rebuild it and win the top trophy for "America's Most Beautiful Roadster." That's the impressive pedigree of this slick little red hot rod, with its much re-shaped steel panels, from front to back. There are many subtle modifications going on here, but they all blend together seamlessly for a smooth overall effect. The rod is mounted on custom '32 frame rails that were constructed to fit the new contours of the reworked body.

With all this metalwork going on up top, something special was reserved for the engine compartment – in the form of a fully polished, all-aluminum, Indy Hawk 406-inch small block with Dart heads and a B&M blower. The engine is filled with all the best speed goodies and is backed up by a Doug Nash 5-speed manual transmission. Both the dropped front axle (with hidden shocks) and the Halibrand Champ quick-change are suspended by torsion bars hidden in the frame rails. This car is simply full of neat features like this.

▶ Having won one of the most prestigious trophies in the hot rod world; the owner of this '29 roadster celebrated by driving it clear across the country and back.

MAKE:	Ford
BODY STYLE:	Highboy Roadster
YEAR:	1929
ENGINE:	Indy Hawk 406 ci V8
BUILD STYLE:	Show
OWNER:	Dennis Varni

'25 Ford Roadster

Having already won the coveted "America's Most Beautiful Roadster" (AMBR) award at the Oakland Roadster show, albeit with a different car, the year before, you would think the owner of this incredible T Roadster would be content. Instead, he decided to "do the double" and come back the following year with an even wilder offering. Obviously, the construction of such an effort had started prior to his first success, but there was no denying the incredible effort that went into creating this "The Golden Star," which took the trophy for his second AMBR award. The twist to the story is that the car was rebuilt once more and won the award yet again in 1991 with the version shown here!

The track-nosed T roadster was the first car in history to win the AMBR award twice and it's not hard to see why. One of the most striking features is the very rare choice of engine, a 1965 Double overhead cam Ford "Indy" engine featuring four Weber 48 IDA carbs with 24-carat gold plating. The cylinder heads of the exotic race car engine were actually switched from side to side to get the exhausts to exit down each side of the roadster. Many hot rod craftsmen had a hand in the project; but credit for the overall build goes to Don Thelan's Buffalo Cars.

MAKE:	Ford
BODY STYLE:	Track Roadster
YEAR:	1925
ENGINE:	Indy DOHC V8
BUILD STYLE:	Show Rod
OWNER:	Ernie Immerso

◀ In the show car world, there is no such thing as too much. This roadster features 24-carat gold plating on many of its components, including many small items, such as all the fasteners.

'26 Ford T Roadster

Built in the late 1940s, this little T hot rod has done it all; cruised the Californian streets through the 1950s, street raced, been wrecked, been rebuilt and taken some top trophies too. In the early 1950s, it was entered into several West coast indoor shows including the Oakland Roadster show where it first was given its nickname, "Shish Kabob Special." It was so called because during the course of the show, the owner (with some help) regularly tipped the car up on its side in order for folk to appreciate the fully-chromed undercarriage beneath the roadster. In 1955, it tied for first place for the AMBR award.

Its original claim to fame was for being the first "uni-body" hot rod, as the cowl and the body was leaded to the chassis. The car features a heavy channel too, as well as a Deuce grille shell, sprint-style nerf bars; and, of course, it's always been run with a built Flathead and was a very quick car in its day. Its owner went on to become quite a collector of hot rods and the car lay neglected in a chicken coop for many years – that is, before undergoing a complete restoration ready to enter into the 50th Grand National Roadster show, which that year celebrated and showcased past winners of the show.

MAKE:	Ford
BODY STYLE:	Roadster
YEAR:	1926
ENGINE:	Flathead V8
BUILD STYLE:	Show Rod
OWNER:	Blackie Gejeian

▸ A very stripped-down, minimalist look was the hallmark of this show winning hot rod T. But what was there was generally chrome plated – if it wasn't painted.

'32 Ford Roadster

For some hot rodders, the top accolade is entering and winning one of the long-standing big indoor shows that are held around the USA. To this end, builders experiment and innovate, trying to push the standards of design and finish to ever-further fields. These cutting-edge cars often contain ideas and practices that are then swiftly taken up by other rodders, as well as by the aftermarket rodding industry looking for new products. However, in 1988, at the Grand National Roadster show at Oakland, something different happened. This full-fendered '32 took the trophy, employing accepted practices and retro style to do it.

Obviously the fit, finish and workmanship on the "Orange Twist" was second to none – and it needed to be in such elite company. Nevertheless, the car definitely bucked nearly all of the trends that were popular at the time. The flamed roadster featured a fully detailed Flathead V8, equipped with Ardun over-head valve heads and three carbs, just like in the old days. The Halibrand wheels featured 3-spoke spinners with "Ardun" milled into the centers, cool nerf bars and hairpin radius rods to complete the nostalgic theme. What's more, the owner of the "Orange Twist" returned the following year with another car – and won the trophy again!

MAKE:	Ford
BODY STYLE:	Full Fendered Roadster
YEAR:	1932
ENGINE:	Ardun Flathead V8
BUILD STYLE:	Traditional Rod
OWNER:	Ernie Immerso

▲ With its polished Halibrands, hairpins and Ardun equipped Flathead, the "Orange Twist" '32 introduced a strong statement of tradition back into the Oakland Show in 1988.

'29 Ford Roadster

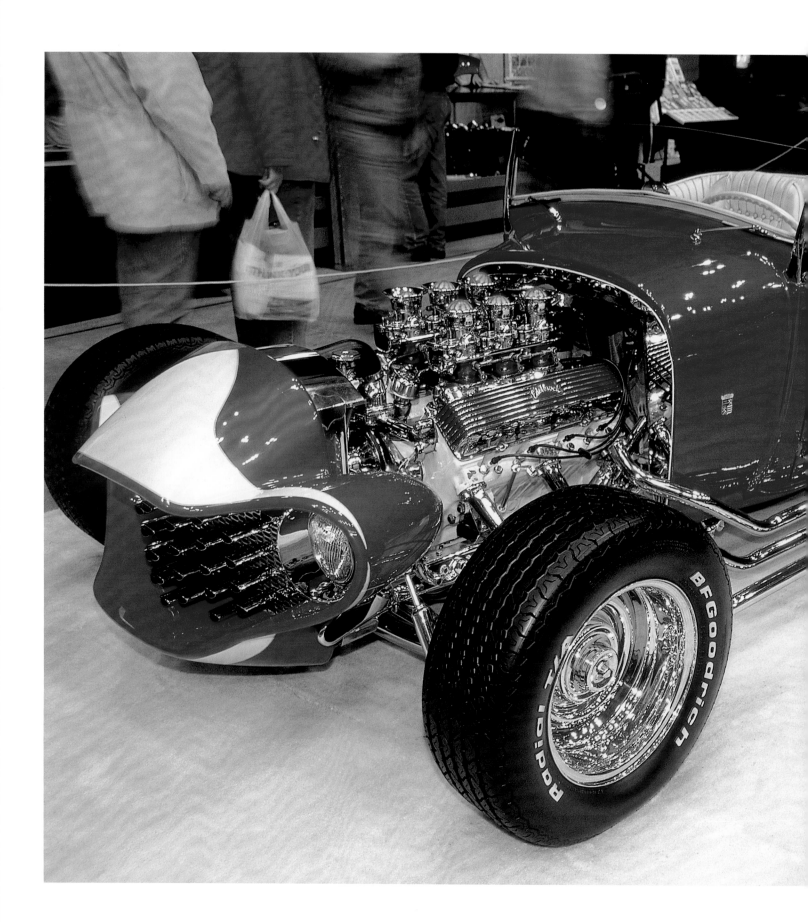

Back in 1959, this '29 Roadster was originally purchased by its then-teenage owner, Kirk "Chuck" Krikorian, as a car in which to go drag racing. Two of his friends persuaded him otherwise, convincing him to make a show car out of it instead. With help from them, one of whom now owns the car, and one George Barris, they not only turned it into a stunning show car, but also scooped the "America's Most Beautiful Roadster Award" in 1960. Having said that it was a show car, which it was, it was also regularly used. Indeed, it once set a strip record for the Street Roadster class at Kingdom Drag strip with a 106-mph pass – though it blew the engine up in the process!

The most memorable feature of the car is the custom nose created by George Barris, though the owner added the oval tube inserts later. These custom grilles were a notable feature of Custom Rods in the early 1960s, often featuring wild molding and extra headlamps. The rear pan of the car features custom rear lights and molded bodywork too. The fully detailed and chromed engine is a '57 Cadillac mill, dressed with 6 twos and a set of Edelbrock valve covers. Gears are shifted via a La Salle Manual transmission. White Naugahyde graced the rolled and plated bucket seat interior.

MAKE:	Ford
BODY STYLE:	Roadster
YEAR:	1929
ENGINE:	Cadillac V8
BUILD STYLE:	Show Rod
OWNER:	Blackie Gejeian

◄ The "Emperor" was preserved for many years by its builder, and remains in unrestored original condition to this day.

'37 Chevy Sedan

This '37 Chevy Sedan is a truly superb restoration job. Only its low stance on Tru-Spoke chrome wire wheels and the two-tone bronze metallic paint belie the fact that, under the skin, it's actually a Street Rod. This bowtie Resto-rod is typical of the types that were built in the late 1970s and early 1980s, prior to the billet explosion that suddenly opened up the boundaries and changed the look of hot rods forever. While they were always neat to look at and had loads of cool features, you couldn't call this style "exciting" in the way hot rods should be. Yet, with hindsight, it's easy now to be too critical.

With an Edelbrock-equipped 350 Chevy under the hood and a 350 transmission behind it, there's no doubt that this '37 was well equipped for highway mileage. A Mustang II front end smooths its passage down the black top, while a 67 Chevy Nova brings up the rear end. All the creature comforts are here; power steering, power seats, cruise control and (unique to this car) twin air conditioning units for front and rear passengers. The paintwork colors are Kandy Root Beer over a Cadillac gold base coat supplemented with House of Kolors lacquer.

MODEL:	Ford
BODY STYLE:	2-door Sedan
YEAR:	1937
ENGINE:	Chevy 350 V8
BUILD STYLE:	Street Rod
OWNER:	Bob Hogsdon

▶ A typical Resto-rod, this '37 Chevy sedan is equipped with many modern features for long-distance luxury cruising.

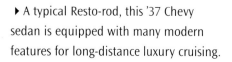

'37 Ford Flatback Sedan

Once the smooth look was well and truly established as a defined style, and every possible model of early Ford and beyond had been painted red, people started to experiment with the use of color much more, So, two-tone solid paint colors became popular, often with the contrasting shades separated by a wild graphic design. This '37 sedan shows an eye-catching split color scheme, with Butter Cream White over a pastel '57 Chevy Teal Green lower half. This treatment extends to the wheels, which have been color coded rather than having been just chromed or polished.

Of course, this Sedan is more than just a paintjob. It has a subtle 1-inch chop, smoothed drip rails and a one-piece front with a split hood arrangement. The doors have also been re-designed to open "suicide" style by mounting the hidden hinges in the B pillars. Note also that the sides have been changed to one-piece windows via the removal of the vent post in the doors. Power is provided by the rodders' favorite engine – the 350 Chevy coupled to a TH 400 transmission and Chevy S10 rear axle.

MAKE:	Ford
BODY STYLE:	2-door Sedan
YEAR:	1937
ENGINE:	Chevy 350 V8
BUILD STYLE:	Street Rod
OWNER:	Tony Tocco

▶ The two-tone pastel paint with graphics on a smooth body style give this away as a 1980's rendition of a '37 Ford street rod.

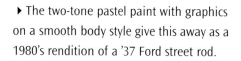

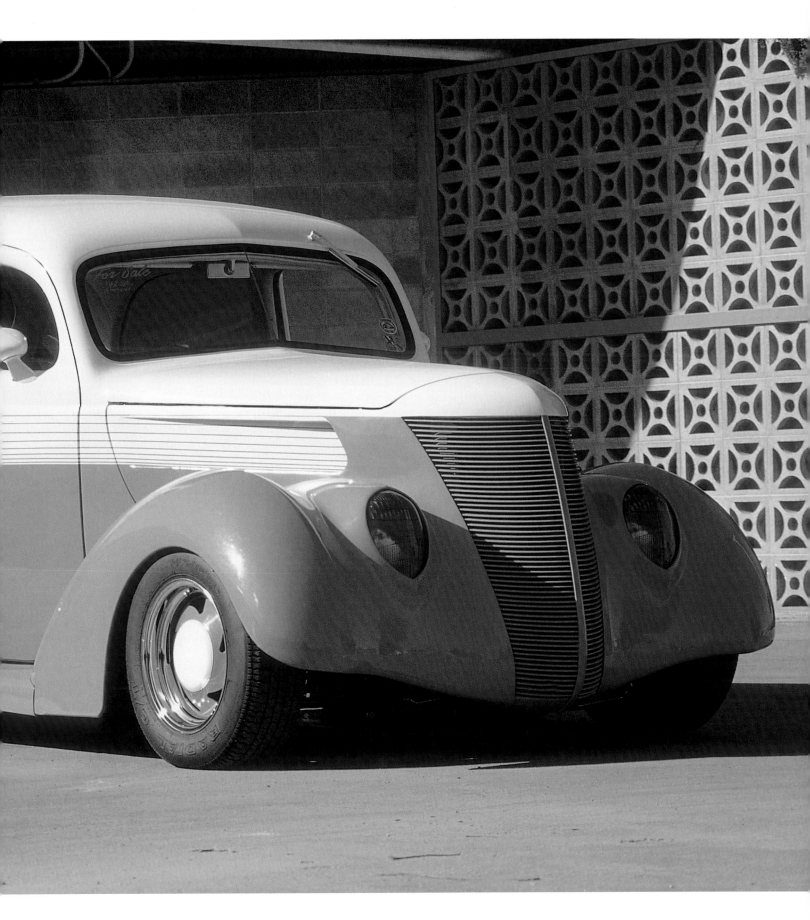

'30 Model A Coupe

The tall, un-chopped profile of this Model A Coupe, with its rich and dark Candy Green paint and chromed Tru-spoke wire wheels, immediately tells you that this a steel Resto-rod. The actual body remains totally stock and unmodified, although fiberglass fenders by Poli-Form have been used at the rear. There is a custom '32-style gas tank installed between the stock boxed frame rails that have also received a K-member installation for additional stiffness. To achieve the healthy rake on the car, a 4-inch dropped tube front axle is installed on a Pete'n'Jake 4-bar, with a Mustang steering box. At the rear, another 4-bar from TCI attaches a '71 Maverick rear axle with a set of coil over shocks.

A stock 350 Chevy engine powers this Model A, which runs a stock 4-barrel carb and a set of dual exhausts with Turbo mufflers – although this is more than enough to power along the little Coupe – and a TH 350 transmission handles the shifting duties. Model A Coupes are known for being somewhat small on the inside, so this one has the added comforts of tinted glass, a tilt-adjustable column for the Vega GT wheel and a handmade walnut dash. Silver gray velour makes it a comfortable place to be, but also dates the car to the late 1970s, when the Resto scene was still a big part of the hobby.

▲ Plenty of chromed trim, and chromed wire wheels against rich Candy Green identify this immediately as a 1970's Resto-rod Model A Coupe.

MAKE:	Ford
BODY STYLE:	2-door Coupe
YEAR:	1930
ENGINE:	Chevy 350 V8
BUILD STYLE:	Street Rod
OWNER:	Rick Nau

'33 Ford Coupe

This profiles shot shows off the swoopy lines of the Ford Model 40 Coupe that rodders everywhere love so much. The fender design just flows from back to front and is enhanced here by the 4-inch chopped top. With the hood removed, however, the eye is immediately drawn to the chromed and polished engine lurking between the cowl and the radiator. The engine in question is a fully loaded Chevy 350, complete with ported and polished Fuelie heads, a Crane cam, Venolia pistons and solid lifters. The block itself has been bored, balanced and blueprinted. With the BDS supercharger, this all puts out an estimated 500 hp, with a little help from the twin 750 Carter carbs. A modified TH400 transmission is required to transfer the power to the '57 T-bird 9-inch rear end.

A Progressive frame has been boxed and put under the rod. This was bolted to the 4-inch dropped front axle, hung on a Pete'n' Jake 4-bar and a Posies Super slide front spring. It was P & J who also supplied the front shocks, and also the 4-bar that attaches the rear axle. Other front end hardware includes '68 Mustang steering, '48 Ford spindles and Z28 Camaro front brakes. A set of Appliance fine-wire chrome spokes add a touch of Resto-class to the otherwise high-performance-flavored, 3-window coupe.

MAKE:	Ford
BODY STYLE:	2-door Coupe
YEAR:	1934
ENGINE:	Chevy 350 V8
BUILD STYLE:	Street Rod
OWNER:	Joe Martin

▾ A full-on small block Chevy, with a blower to go, provides the excitement for this all-steel '34 Coupe, the rod having an estimated 500 hp on tap.

'34 Ford Roadster

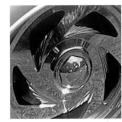

The Model 40 series '33-34 Roadsters really lend themselves to the swoopy, high-tech treatment and are probably the favorite of all the Fords from the early 1930s for this build style. In fact, there are now a great many stretched and stylized fiberglass bodies out there that are derived from these '33-34 models. Yet, despite its slick look, this isn't one of them! Granted, it is a fiberglass body, but it came out of the mold as stock and so all the modifications are owner-made. These includes the neat lift-off hard top, which was molded from a steel buck. That, in turn, was made from a steel boot lid panel. This is but one example of this car's neat features, Another is the owner-fabricated windshield posts and the windshield itself. Would you believe that it is from a British Austin Mini Cooper? It's the original one, of course.

The chassis is a modified but original '34, with an air-bag-equipped independent front end and a fully detailed Jaguar independent rear. That rear has also been bagged for the "flat on the floor" look. The 350 Chevy is mostly stock, except for the Holley 600 and Performer manifold. Hooker headers lead to Hooker mufflers, via an owner-made system. The transmission is a stock GM 350. Outside, the exterior is awash with a pleasing shade of custom-mixed Pearlescent Blue, set off by the highly polished Billet Specialties 15-inch rims. Not visible is the tan leather interior with matching Billet Specialties steering wheel and custom digital dash.

MAKE:	Ford
BODY STYLE:	Roadster
YEAR:	1934
ENGINE:	Chevy 350 V8
BUILD STYLE:	Street Rod
OWNER:	Frank Gautier

◄ The owner-fabricated hard top and custom curved windshield to really give this '34 Roadster a custom look all of its own.

'40 Ford Sedan

There will always be room for another '40 Ford, especially one as pleasing as this Sedan. Built in a clean Resto style, the body is as stock as they come, and still retains all of its original brightwork and trim. The color is a deep, rich Pearlescent Green that's usually found only on imported Audi cars – but it suits the big Sedan admirably. Polished American Racing Torq Thrusts add class to the car; and not being huge diameters hoopsters, they won't go out of fashion when the next fad comes along.

The stock chassis is still in place under this '40. That is, albeit with new cross members and some suspension mounting kits from Chassis Engineering for the parallel leaves, rear shock kit and a C.E. 4-inch dropped I-beam and split wishbones. The steering is a mix of an Ididit column and a Flamin' River steering box, The 350 Chevy crate engine is fully dressed with goodies from Billet Specialties, though it remains stock internally – apart from an Edelbrock Performer Cam and the almost obligatory 600 cfm Holley plus intake. The engine is backed up by a GM 350 transmission.

MAKE:	Ford
BODY STYLE:	2-door Sedan
YEAR:	1940
ENGINE:	Chevy 350 V8
BUILD STYLE:	Street Rod
OWNER:	John Hall

▼ Some body styles are best left well alone. When you see a '40 Ford as clean and classy as this , it's easy to understand why.

'27 T Modified

It's amazing what a seasoned and talented hot rodder can build with a bunch of scrounged parts. In fact, some of the coolest and most innovative, not to mention traditional, cars are built this way. A good example is this Lakes Modified style T. Built only a few years ago, the only significant part bought brand new was the fiberglass body, the rest being owner-built or "swap meet" finds. The frame was the first part built at home – and on the garage floor! This was soon fitted with the '37 Ford front axle and batwings mounted on semi-elliptical leaves, these being made from a stock rear spring from a '48 English Anglia, but cut in half.

The other Anglia spring from the pair was mounted across the 1960's Volvo Amazon rear axle. This was chosen because the stud pattern is the same as in the Chrysler Imperial wire wheels, as painted and mounted on the back. As was common with Lakes Modified cars, a 4-banger engine lives under the hand-rolled hood. However, this one is a stock Pinto 2-liter engine. With 4-speed manual transmission, it provides plenty of power for the lightweight car and rasps nicely through the home-brewed, twin-pipe side exhaust. This T is maximum fun for minimum outlay!

MAKE:	Ford
BODY STYLE:	T Roadster
YEAR:	1927
ENGINE:	Ford Pinto 2.0 4 cylinder
BUILD STYLE:	Traditional Lakes Modified
OWNER:	Nick Harrison

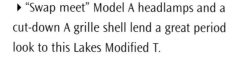

▶ "Swap meet" Model A headlamps and a cut-down A grille shell lend a great period look to this Lakes Modified T.

'27 T Coupe

Looking just about as close to an Ed Roth cartoon image as it can get, a tall T Coupe body channeled hard down over a Model A frame makes for a wild and wacky hot rod. Indeed, the only reason this hardcore ride doesn't have any rustoleum on display is that it's been built with a fiberglass body instead of steel. The frame rails were home built to Model A dimensions, but include a 6-inch kick up in order to keep the whole plot low.

A Vintage chassis works dropped tube is mounted up front but suicide style, with a single-leaf, 36 Ford split wishbones and a set of Pete'n'Jake chromed shocks. The rear axle is a Tri-Chevy item mounted on homemade hairpins with a set of Gaz coil overs and a Panhard rod for stability.

That mighty engine sitting high in the front frame rails is a '65 Wildcat Buick Nailhead, 425 cubic inches of big block Buford, with a pair of Holley 750's and some neat dress-up stuff. The four pipes each side dump the gas fumes on to the blacktop via some homemade baffles. Ahead of the engine is a chromed A grille shell, and some big chromed headlamps from a "swap meet." No one knows what they're originally from, but they sure look the part. Chromed reverse rims with whitewalls finish off the purple suede exterior. The white padded top is also a neat period addition.

MAKE:	Ford
BODY STYLE:	2-door Coupe
YEAR:	1927
ENGINE:	425 ci Buick V8
BUILD STYLE:	Hardcore
OWNER:	Nick Harrison

▶ This is the only way to build a T Coupe; cartoon styling, a big inch engine, and a Buick Nailhead fitting the bill perfectly.

'23 Center-door T

If you think of a 1923 Model, it probably won't be this particular body style that springs to mind. Instead, you will most likely think that, because the Center-door Sedan is such a rare model, that it is not even from the era. Not so: the 1923 was actually the peak year of production for Model Ts and a goodly number were Center-door Sedans that year. This one was first rodded back in the 1970s and originally ran a Pinto lump. The current owner bought it at the '78 NSRA Street Rod Nats and has owned it ever since – but through several rebuilds. This latest incarnation sees it sitting lower than ever, thanks to a 4-inch dropped tube front axle, Pete'n'Jake shocks and a single monoleaf spring. At the rear is a fully-plated Jaguar independent rear axle mounted on the reproduction home-built T chassis.

The body, which is now more than 80-years-old, has survived well and still retains many original features – such as the fuel tank, original seats, lights, fenders and even the steering wheel. It must be good for it to be painted in the high-gloss black paint it now wears. Replacing the Pinto engine that came with the car, a Ford 302 has been squeezed under the narrow cowl and steel hood, the engine staying mainly stock, save for the 600 Holley on an Edelbrock intake and some dress-up items,. The transmission is a stock C4. Polished ARE Torq Thrusts that contrast with the black paint to provide some early "razzle dazzle" to the very early Ford sedan.

MAKE:	Ford
BODY STYLE:	Center-door T
YEAR:	1923
ENGINE:	Ford 302 V8
BUILD STYLE:	Street Rod
OWNER:	Alan Spittle

◄ The Center door T is a 2-door, 4-seat sedan body. As its name suggests, it has two doors fitted amidships and so agile folk climb over the seats to sit up front.

'34 Coupe

When setting out to build a '34 Coupe in the Hi-tech style these days, most rodders opt for the flowing lines of a fully-fendered car and then start the smoothing process from there. Having said that, this whole style was initiated by the Coddington-built Vern Luce fenderless '33. So, I guess we shouldn't be surprised if this silver bullet (or should we say billet?) takes some of those cues and re-works them for the twenty-first century. The fiberglass Coupe is obviously chopped; but did you notice the stretched front with hand-made aluminum hood and side panels? The front grille and lower apron panel are also custom one-off and have been fitted with special attention to the panel gaps and fit.

Under the custom hood, the finish is just as good, with a specially-fabricated engine cover over the injected LT1 engine. The latter has been totally color-coded to match the exterior paintwork. It runs a Street & Performance serpentine pulley and belt system. The repro '34 chassis is also fully detailed in silver and is C'd at the rear in order to drop the body low over the 4-bar suspended Ford 9-inch rear end. At the front, an independent setup was custom made for the '34 and features tubular A-arms, inboard shocks and (clever) longitudinally-mounted leaf springs that act as torsion bars. The spindles and rotors are Jaguar.

MAKE:	Ford
BODY STYLE:	Fenderless Coupe
YEAR:	1934
ENGINE:	Chevy 350 LT1 V8
BUILD STYLE:	Street Rod
OWNER:	Ian Burton

▶ This '34 takes High-tech styling cues and goes the extra mile, with a host of neat and unique features all of its own.

'32 Ford Pickup

You only have to look at the dimensions of a stock Deuce truck in order to realize that, to any hot rodder's eyes, they came from the factory just "too darned tall," giving them a slightly top heavy appearance. So thank goodness someone invented the chopped top! It doesn't need a lot taken out of the lid to get the proportions spot on. Indeed, if you need proof, check out this yellow hauler. Is this not the way it should have been from the outset? If you look at the back of the cab, you will notice that the back cab window remains stock size, furthering the illusion of a stock-height truck. But there's a lot more to this flawless '32 Pickup than just the roof chop.

The stance of this truck is perfect, thanks to the aluminum dropped I-beam and matching hardware up front and the 9-inch rear axle under the bed. The wheels also have a lot to do with the overall appeal of this hot rod truck, with ET rims used all round, ETVs on the back and 4 x 15 10 spokes on the front for a real rod flavor. The theme is most definitely carried on in the engine department, too. That's a 522-hp 350 Chevy in there, fully detailed and featuring Eagle bottom-end parts, plus Edelbrock RPM heads and a pair of Holley 600s on a polished Weiand blower. With that amount of power on tap, it's no surprise to find a 350 reverse pattern transmission built by Coan Racing behind the engine.

MODEL:	Ford
BODY STYLE:	Closed-cab Pickup
YEAR:	1932
ENGINE:	Chevy 350 V8
BUILD STYLE:	Street Rod
OWNER:	J. Steve Bird

▶ Just straight eyeball-searing yellow covers the sheet metal on this hot rod '32 truck. The cab is original but the fenders and bed are steel repro items.

'36 Ford Coupe

The great thing about showing Resto-style rods, with what is still essentially stock bodywork and exterior trim, is that they serve as a benchmark, or point of reference, when looking at detail on other more modified rods. Only by comparing the two can you appreciate the work that goes into building either. This is one such car that illustrates the beauty of a '36 Ford 5-window Coupe. The subtle hot rod cues are there though, the red powder-coated steel wheels, the Denman wide whites and the Briz ribbed fenders, to name but a few. The top has also been filled and '39 taillights have been frenched into the rear fenders, with a Hagan recessed fuel filler in the left rear fender too.

The '36 frame runs a Mustang II front end and a Ford 8-inch rear. Between the two are just about all the parts that TCI engineering make for a '36 chassis, including a parallel leaf kit, engine mounts, brake items, pedals, shocks and anti-roll bars, etc. All parts have been powder coated and have been assembled with stainless steel fasteners, all polished to perfection. The same goes for the engine, which is a Ford 302. This time, it's the Edelbrock company who get the credit for the aftermarket components that were used – including a 600 carb, intake, cam and dress-up items – all crowned with a Bitchin' Products Caddy style air cleaner.

MAKE:	Ford
BODY STYLE:	5-window Coupe
YEAR:	1936
ENGINE:	Chevy 350 V8
BUILD STYLE:	Street Rod
OWNER:	Pete Whiteside

▸ It takes a keen eye to spot the hot rod details on this superb Resto/Traditional Blue '36 Coupe.

'29 Ford Roadster

First put together entirely by its owner in 1951, this classic '29 Model A on '32 rails was entered into the Oakland Roadster show ten years later, where it took first place. Unfortunately its owner, Rich Guasco, was not present to collect the award in person as he was away serving his country at the time. Known as "The Imperial" back then, it differed from this picture in having a Magenta lacquer finish called "Wild Champagne Orchid" and a '57 Chevy 301ci V8 with a Clay Smith cam and three twos. It was usually displayed minus hood so as to show off the chromed-out engine.

The later restoration of this cool '29 was carried out so the car could be shown at the 50th anniversary Oakland Roadster Show, which had started back in 1950. This included a few updates, necessary as the car still gets used as a regular drive. Most obvious is the change to the Deep Purple color – and the fact that the car now runs a louvered 3-piece hood, with cut outs for the Lakes pipes. Chromed reverse wheels with '50 Merc hubcaps have always featured on the car, though modern radial tires are now fitted. The classic hot rod still runs a Chevy engine, but the three twos have long gone in favor of a single 4-barrel. The gear change is a stick shift that still makes the driving fun, even after over some fifty years of ownership.

MAKE:	Ford
BODY STYLE:	Roadster
YEAR:	1929
ENGINE:	Chevy 350 V8
BUILD STYLE:	Traditional Hot Rod
OWNER:	Rich Guasco

◀ The full-height windshield and bobbed fenders are classic, early 1950's touches that are thankfully preserved on the real fine '29.

'41 Willys Woodie

There's a long story as to how this one-off '41 phantom Woodie came to exist. It really is too long to recount here, but suffice to say it involves two racecars and a change of plan. One of the racecars involved was an Austin Devon ex-gasser, which ended up donating its tubular pro-street chassis as a basis for the one-off project. The other was a Willys Coupe that, although providing the inspiration for the rod, didn't actually donate any parts. In fact, the Willys front end, i.e. the hood cowl and fenders, were salvaged from a fiberglass body that had a damaged rear half. From these humble beginnings came this purple Woodster hot rod.

The rear wooden body was entirely hand-fabricated from ash, a slow and time-consuming task. Nevertheless, one has to say that it was definitely worth it – and the inside is as good as the outside. The body was fitted to the length-ened race-style chassis, which was installed with a Jensen Healey (British sports car) front suspension assembly. The English theme continues with Jaguar parts incorporated into the trick rear suspension. A 350 Chevy blueprinted engine

▲ The purple pearlescent paint really contrasts well with the varnished American Ash woodwork that is a highlight of this phantom '41 Willys.

powers the phantom '41. It runs a Holley 650 on a Torker II intake, and there also some chromed fenderwell headers under there too. Big Convo Pros lend an air of the rod's racecar heritage, as does the Pro Street stance.

MAKE:	Willys
BODY STYLE:	2-door Woodie
YEAR:	1941
ENGINE:	Chevy 350 V8
BUILD STYLE:	Street Rod
OWNER:	Doug Fouracre

'32 Ford 3-window Coupe

Looking for all the world like a typical East Coast show car of the early 1960s, this slam-dunked period 3-window was actually built in the mid-1990s with many repro early parts and a firm eye on the past. The mildly-chopped fiberglass body has been channeled hard over the frame rails for a totally right coast stance. A 46-inch TCI I-beam and hairpins, with Pete 'n' Jake shocks and a monoleaf front spring keep the front riding right. At the back, much notching of the frame has taken place in order to ensure clearance and travel for the big Halibrand quick-change, which has had wider shafts and casings made for the super-wide rear track

The whole car is detailed to perfection – from the polished Moon tank mounted on the polished spreader bar ahead of the channeled grille shell, to the custom cast exhaust bezels that surround the tailpipe tips. The small block Chevy dressed for the period look is actually a ZZ4 aluminum-headed, crate engine, with a tri-carb setup on an Edelbrock intake. The stainless headers with cut outs are one-off pieces made especially for the car and leading to a full stainless system that exits through the rolled rear pan. A white rolled interior complements the custom-mixed Lavender Pearl paint, along with white detailing for the finishing touch to an outstanding hot rod.

MAKE:	Ford
BODY STYLE:	3-window Coupe
YEAR:	1932
ENGINE:	Chevy ZZ4 V8
BUILD STYLE:	1960's Show Car
BUILDER:	John Golding

◄ Big, stock Model B headlamps and chromed reverse rims with whitewalls are the hallmarks of this slammed 1960's throwback with its killer, low stance.

'23 Ford Roadster

Although we often think of the 1960s as the era of the Fad T, it was this car – built in 1955 – that kicked off the style. Norm Grabowski's T-bucket was featured on the cover of *Hot Rod Magazine* in October 1955, sporting black paint, and a 3-71 blower on top of its Cadillac engine. Two years, later Norm and his T also made the cover of *Life* magazine when a photographer snapped them hanging out at an L.A. drive-in for a feature on cruising. By then, the rod was known as the "Lightening Bug" and had been painted blue with flames; and the blower had gone in favor of four Strombergs. It's this version of the car most people are familiar with, thanks to its regular appearances on TV in the vintage show *77 Sunset Strip*.

The exposure of the little hot rod on the small windshield, driven by Ed "Kookie" Burns, meant that the car was evermore known as the "Kookie T." Norm actually built the car from a cut-down touring car body, mounting it on a Model A frame, the high rake coming from a high A spring mounted under the cut-down pickup bed. Other neat details included the tall '22 Dodge windshield that was raked backwards, the cut-down Deuce grille shell and the wild, chromed headers that kicked up beside the rear body. The original car spawned several copies around the country.

MAKE:	Ford
BODY STYLE:	Fad T Roadster
YEAR:	1923
ENGINE:	Cadillac 354 ci V8
BUILD STYLE:	Traditional Street Roadster
OWNER:	Norm Grabowski

▶ As well as the car's famous TV appearances as the "Kookie T," Norm Grabowski, its builder and owner, went on to feature in many Hollywood motion pictures.

'34 Ford 5-window

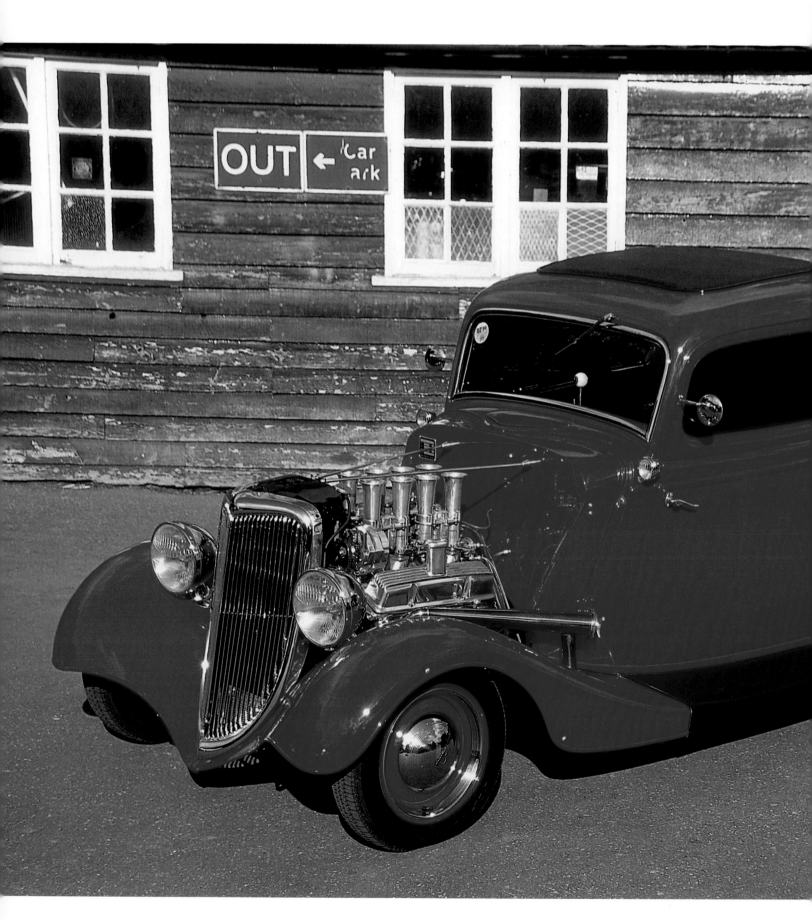

O nce built as a Show Car sometime in its distant past, this 5-window was in serious need of some TLC when it was brought into a rod shop. Initially, this was just for some rear fender work, but it was soon clear that it would need a lot more doing; so work commenced straight away on the old hot rod. This included a new repro frame, a complete new front axle and hardware in the form of a 46-inch Magnum dropped I-beam, a new spring and new shocks. A replacement Ford 8-inch was also hung on a rear 4-bar to complete the refreshed underpinnings.

The bodywork needed sorting too, including remounting the body and repairing many of the panels. The car now has a definite nostalgic flavor, with red paintwork and red steels with blackwall tires. It has the unfilled top and the louvered trunk lid, and this look is helped by the neat Lakes-style pipes that exit the engine and pass down through the fenders to the system below. The 355 ci small block is a built engine and features chromed Fuelie heads and that so-cool quad Weber 48IDA setup on an Inglese intake.

MAKE:	Ford
BODY STYLE:	5-window Coupe
YEAR:	1934
ENGINE:	Chevy 355 V8
BUILD STYLE:	Show Hot Rod
BUILDER:	Jon Golding

◀ These days, so many fiberglass hot rods come straight "out the box" with chopped tops, that as soon as you see this stock height Model 40, you just know it's a steel car.

Volvo T6 Roadster

There will be no prizes for guessing which is the most controversial car in these pages – after all, it's not even American! This single car has probably sparked off more "is it a hot rod or not" discussions than any other, before or since. Well, if it's good enough for *Hot Rod Magazine* to recognize it as their 2005 "Hot Rod of the Year," then that's good enough for us in this book. Although it looks like it was constructed in a corporate design studio somewhere, it was actually built at home, in a garage, and by just one guy. It's fast, it has no fenders, it's a roadster; and that sure sounds like a hot rod.

Built in Sweden, the aluminum body was formed over a wooden buck from full-size drawings after working out the dimensions required to house the all-modern running gear. The running gear is a rear-mounted Volvo 2.9 twin turbo 6-cylinder engine. It still sits in its factory steel sub-frame, but has been re-worked to produce more power – to the tune of 330 hp. The suspension system is a work of art but incorporates lots of stock Volvo parts. There are inboard gas shocks, cantilevered arms and all sorts of trick stuff which we do not have space to even begin describing here. The car also runs ABS and O.E.M. data systems. It is environmentally friendly, with catalytic converters on board. The question is: is this the shape of things to come?

MAKE:	Volvo T6
BODY STYLE:	Roadster
YEAR:	2002
ENGINE:	Volvo 2.9 6 cylinder
BUILD STYLE:	Concept Rod
OWNER:	Leif Tufvesson

▶ Although pictured here with its acrylic double bubble roof, this is fully removable to turn the Volvo lowboy rapidly into a futuristic, fenderless roadster.

'30 Model A Sedan

When it became time for the owner of this eye-zapping Model A sedan to freshen up his ride, he was unashamedly influenced by the Billet Specialties '32 coupe with the similar paint scheme. So, all the way down to the 3-dimensional effect shaded flames along the sides, he transformed what was previously a classy, but understated, Tudor into the show-winning Sedan that you see here. A smooth, color-coded grille shell and sculpted hood sides set the tone, although the car is not a total smoothster. It still uses stock door handles, a stainless windshield surround, chromed peep mirrors and chromed headlamps on a stock bar. A neat touch is the gas filler that is hidden behind a flip-out door in the rear panel.

The body is a fiberglass repro sitting on a repro Model A frame, though that's a Rootleib 3-piece hood covering the engine. To save weight, the engine is an aluminum Buick 215 ci unit with a Borg Warner 65 transmission. This little but light engine is fully dressed, with Moon chromed finned goodies and a Holley 390 cfm carb on an Edelbrock inlet and with Mallory ignition. A custom tubular independent front end keeps those neat nerf bars from digging into the pavement. The big billet wheels that were the other big transformation from this A's previous look are Budnik 20-inch rims on the back and cool 17-inch on the front.

MAKE:	Ford
BODY STYLE:	2-door Sedan
YEAR:	1930
ENGINE:	Buick 215 V8
BUILD STYLE:	Street Rod
OWNER:	Mark Grant

◀ It's amazing what a fresh paintjob and a set of wheels can do to complete a stunning makeover on an already well-built hot rod like this Model A.

'29 Model A Roadster

One of the big drawbacks in building a steel car from scratch can be the amount of time needed to fully restore the ageing steel, which more than likely has a lifetime of knocks and dings to straighten before the fun stuff can start. This is part of the reason why fiberglass bodies are so popular, that and the fact that there are not enough steel cars around these days. Gratitude all round then for the steel repro bodies that are becoming more and more common. There's no doubt that using a Brookville body, as this '29 does, speeds up the building process and gets the car out on the street – right where it belongs. With a strong 1950's theme, the red and white on this roadster really stands out – and you really should see the candy stripe leather tuck-and-roll interior.

The body is mounted on an early TCI frame and uses a chrome I-beam with a stainless Pete'n'Jake 4-link, Panhard rod and P'n'J shocks. The rear features a Ford 8-inch with chromed '56 brake drums. Under the steel, 4-piece Rootlieb hood is a healthy ZZ4 350 and a 700R4 transmission for easy cruising. To keep the area under the hood within the period look, however, the 350 has been fitted with an Offy manifold and half a dozen 94s – although the center two are blocked off to avoid over-fueling the Chevy engine, which is polished and detailed with a red block.

MAKE:	Ford
BODY STYLE:	Roadster
YEAR:	1929
ENGINE:	Chevy 350 V8
BUILD STYLE:	Street Rod
OWNER:	Sam McCormack

◀ Those red steelies in each corner sport a set of Mercury hubcaps inside the wide white tires, which look great on this '29 with its matching white top.

'27 T Roadster

While many hot rods are built ground up from start to finish, many others seem to evolve over a period of time as updates are made. Sometimes, this happens because the rod has changed hands; other times because the long-standing owner has gradually improved the car over the years. This T roadster is one of the latter. Originally, the project was to be a Chrysler-powered A, but Flathead fever caught hold. There was also the owner's desire to own a split V windshield, and so it ended up on the street as a fiberglass T Roadster. The body was then upgraded to a steel original, which was painted the same color. The end result is the car you see here.

The little roadster still runs an original, but boxed, Model A chassis, fitted with all stock '32 front-end hardware. It has a '37 Ford rear axle on a Model A spring, although '40 Ford juice brakes are now fitted all round. The wheels are 16-inch Ford wires, with a mix of Avon bias-plys on the front and Goodrich's out back. Since the car enters quite a few Flathead race events, something special was required up front. This was achieved in the shape of a 286 ci bored 8BA flathead block filled with all the good stuff on the inside. It has modified Offy heads, with a hi-rise Tattersfield intake and a pair of '94s. There are even more hidden tricks that included enabling the T to better 14.00-second runs, when the gloves are off!

MAKE:	Ford
BODY STYLE:	Turtle deck Roadster
YEAR:	1927
ENGINE:	Flathead V8
BUILD STYLE:	Traditional
OWNER:	Tony Cardy

◄ Those Lakes pipes mean business, so much so that the doors can't be used when in street trim; the pipes can be removed for racing.

'34 Coupe

"It ain't easy being green!" said the frog, but this Pro-street style Highboy Coupe seems to manage very well. The Kermit-colored car sports plenty of Applejack green over the body, chassis, engine and running gear. The owner-built '34 also features plenty of one-off billet parts for extra detailing, including a polished "quartic" – (that's square, to you squares who don't know!) steering wheel. The 3-inch chopped Coupe body has been slightly tabbed at the rear, although it's not especially noticeable, but it also features a hood top molded to the painted grille shell for a smooth blended look at the front. The blacked-out grille is a cool and contrasting touch too.

A repro '34 frame supports the 'glass Coupe body and supporting the frame is a narrowed and braced 9-inch. It is hung on a stainless four bar and AVO coil over shocks at the back and a 4-bar suspended dropped tube at the front. Powering the mean green machine is a healthy Chevy small block, bored out to 355 ci, and equipped with a Crane cam and lifters, a Holley 600 and a Torker II manifold with ignition by Mallory. With so many billet details on the Coupe, the wheel choice needed to match the theme of the '34, so a set of Budnik Famosas were chosen to add some extra gleam to the green.

MAKE:	Ford
BODY STYLE:	2-door Coupe
YEAR:	1934
ENGINE:	Chevy 355 V8
BUILD STYLE:	Performance
OWNER:	Steve Bradley

▶ The tasteful color-coding and attention to detail on this '34 Pro-street Coupe is enough to make you green with envy!

'34 Ford Coupe

A cool and traditional '34 Coupe unearthed from a barn somewhere, dusted off and put back on the street, maybe? Wrong; this is an all-fiberglass car on a repro chassis that was bought by a normally contemporary-style-biased rodder who needed something at short notice to drive for the summer! It was found as a loosely assembled rolling project, but five months of thrashing in the garage brought it back to the street in double quick time.

The truth is, it was only painted in satin anti-gloss to save time, although the beltline and trunk lid have been pinstriped for added interest.

Despite its traditional theme, it uses all the regular Street Rod build tricks. There is an independent front end made up of sub-compact Ford parts with coilover shocks, while at the back, a Jaguar center section diff is used with aftermarket hub carriers and arms. A touch of tradition here is the cast dummy quick-change cover. A 327 Chevy was rebuilt with forged pistons, a double roller timing chain and a 600 Holley on a Performer intake. It was then liberally coated with an electro-platers special sauce. The nostalgia illusion is completed by a set of polished Torq thrusts and wide whites.

MAKE:	Ford
BODY STYLE:	Coupe
YEAR:	1934
ENGINE:	Chevy 327 V8
BUILD STYLE:	Street Rod
OWNER:	Keith Atkinson

▼ Easily classed under the "Newstalgia" banner, this suede '34 combines the traditional look with some distinctly non-trad chassis hardware under a 'glass body.

'32 Ford 3-window Coupe

It doesn't seem like so long since every-body in hot rodding was 1950s crazy. Of course, some still are and so there are some very fine early Elvis era cars in these very pages. Yet, it also seemed like the clock had stopped at around the period of "American Graffiti" for nostalgia cars, the alternative being the Resto cars of the 1970s and the billet smoothies of the 1980's. For a while there, the 1960s seemed to be forgotten. However, we are glad to say they are back with a bang – and here is another '32 built that way to prove it. One glance tells you 1960s straight away; and that's down to the Moon tank and American Racing spindle-mount 12-spokes on the drilled I-beam. Wow…12-spokes!

However, this gorgeous gold coupe was put together some thirty years after the swingin' decade and is an all-fiberglass car on a very well-put-together repro and home-fabricated chassis. The frame rails are tied together with plenty of 15/8 inch tubing and that front end is a Vintage Chassis Works item on home-brewed hairpins, with '40 Ford spindles and a TCI spring. The rear end is a Ford 8-inch hung on more homemade hairpins and the frame was also C'd at the back for extra clearance. A rebuilt 350 resides under the 4-piece Rootleib hood, complete with Edelbrock Performer heads and a trio of Rochesters on a Tri-power intake.

MODEL:	Ford
BODY STYLE:	3-window Coupe
YEAR:	1932
ENGINE:	Chevy 350 V8
BUILD STYLE:	Traditional 1960's Style Hot Rod
OWNER:	Bob Jeffries

◄ This 1960's-flavored '32 3-window is built in true "golden oldie" style with its 12-spokes and drilled I-beam as its hot rod hallmarks.

'32 Ford 3-window Coupe

If you've already made a classic hot rod, such as Deuce 3-window, you can't go wrong by painting it black. There are not that many cars on which it doesn't look cool, whether its hi-shine gloss or even a suede satin finish. Often, though, it may be necessary to just add a little more to give the car a unique identity, flames are a classic favorite, but there are plenty of those too. So how about scallops, they're cool, even more so when checkered out like on this hammered '32 coupe? The checker theme also is carried through to the firewall, so it looks twice as cool with the Rootleib hood removed as well.

A perfect hot rod stance is achieved with a Vintage Chassis Works dropped tube axle, a homemade stainless 4-bar and a Magnum transverse spring, all hung on the repro '32 chassis. At the back, a 9-inch Ford converted to disc brakes is hung from another home brewed four bar with AVO coil over shocks. No surprise to find a small block Chevy powering this boss 3-window. In this case, it's a lightened and balanced 383 ci with forged pistons, a crane cam and Edelbrock Performer package (including aluminum heads and intake), with a Holley 600 to feed the juice.

MAKE:	Ford
BODY STYLE:	3-window Coupe
YEAR:	1932
ENGINE:	Chevy 383 V8
BUILD STYLE:	Street Rod
OWNER:	Steve Lang

▶ The checkered scallops on this '32 give it real hot rod personality. The fenderless stance and Moon tank don't hurt either.

'49 Nash Airflite

Although the hot rod mandate of this book has remained pretty faithful to the generally-accepted pre-1949 rule for earlier style cars, perhaps the purists will allow us to put our toes over the line in respect of this wild 1949 Nash Airflite. After all, what's the least-likely American car to receive the full Pro-Street treatment and a blown 427 than a bathtub Nash? So, if someone did build such a beast, check out the result right here. It's bad, its blown and (what's more) it's got the biggest back-side in hot rodding!

A full custom chassis was constructed for awesome Airflite, and a much narrowed 9-inch Ford is located by ladder bars and AVO coil over shocks. Owner-built independent suspension features tubular arms; and it's also bagged with Air Ride Technologies hardware providing 5-6 inches of suspension comfort. The 427 big rat is fitted with LS6 heads, forged pistons and a Crane cam; and is crowned with a twin-carb-equipped Weiand 6/71 blower. It is all polished, detailed and finished off with stainless steel headers and Corvette mufflers. Somewhere under all that bodywork lies a set of Indy Champ 500 wheels, though few people have ever seen them.

MAKE:	Nash
BODY STYLE:	2-door Sedan
YEAR:	1949
ENGINE:	Chevy 427 V8
BUILD STYLE:	Performance
OWNER:	Tracy Chantry

▶ As if the whole concept of this nasty Nash wasn't awesome enough, it had to get painted in Aquamarine Cromaflair paint that changes hue depending on the light. Subtle it ain't!

'32 Ford Roadster

We consider that the well-known Californian hot rodder Pete Chapouris has a lot to answer for. Not content with helping to put hot rodding back among the restos in the 1970s, with the much-copied "California Kid" featured elsewhere in these pages, he wowed the troops again with his hot "Limefire" '32 roadster some years later. This Deuce roadster obviously draws inspiration from Pete's car, but also retains its own identity and is no way a "clone" car. The basic formula of a '32 highboy is a classic in its own right and this car follows that winning look with a dropped Vintage Chassis Works axle on hairpins, 40 Ford brakes and Buick drums at the front and a Ford 9-inch on ladder bars and coil overs on the back.

Right from the start, however, this car was destined to be Mopar big-block powered, and a Chrysler 440 is the engine of choice, though not being quite big-block enough, it's been bored to 446ci and been fitted with a steel crank, forged pistons, TRW con rods and a Lunati cam. A 750 double pumper feeds the brute through a Holley intake and the transmission is a reworked Torqueflite 727. One cool feature of "Limefire" was the hood exiting side exhausts, and these are often referred to as "Limefire" headers. Needless to say, this roadster has them as well as a Duval screen, Moon tank and lots of louvers, could it be any cooler?

MAKE:	Ford
BODY STYLE:	Roadster
YEAR:	1932
ENGINE:	Chrysler 446 ci V8
BUILD STYLE:	Traditional Hot Rod
OWNER:	Carl Frith

◀ Orange flames over wild metallic lime paint plus big stock '32 headlamps and a Moon tank means this is a Highboy that with one look begs closer inspection.

'29 Ford Pickup

Just about everybody likes these early examples of a hot rod pickup. While not as rebellious as a fenderless roadster, or as mean and moody as a heavily-chopped Coupe, they just have a certain "olde worlde" charm about them that's hard to define. I guess this is true whether trucks are stock or rodded; but they're especially cool when they display the classic hot rod stance and a cool set of wheels. This closed-cab '29 is perfect in straight Henry Ford black. It's panels are as straight as the day it rolled off the line.

That stance we mentioned is down to the hot rod hauler being mounted on a TCI chassis, which uses a 46-inch dropped tube to get that front end "in the weeds."

For a truck that was originally intended to house a flathead 4-banger under the hood, it's a miracle that a ZZ4 crate engine should now find its home in a truck's engine compartment – especially without any modifications to the truck's sheet metal or firewall. A 700R4 transmission lives under the truck's floorboards and, in turn, spins a Ford 8-inch rear axle under the repro Brookville repro steel bed. Brookville also supplied a brand new tailgate and a set of fenders. So, while at least some of the cab was assembled from new old stock panels, going this route saves a lot of time in body prep, especially if you want to shoot it in black.

MAKE:	Ford
BODY STYLE:	Closed-cab Pickup
YEAR:	1929
ENGINE:	Chevy ZZ4 V8
BUILD STYLE:	Street Rod
OWNER:	Gary McCormack

▶ The simple design of Budnik's Famosa wheels compliment the so-straight black paint on this simple '29 pickup.

'40 Chevy Coupe

Few would dispute the fact that the "arrest me" red is what grabs your attention and demands that you spend time checking out this cool '40 Coupe. Nevertheless, it's the stance of the Chevy which really makes it something special. Get the stance wrong on a car like this, and folks probably won't dwell long enough to appreciate the long hours in the garage that it took to get the job done. Get it right, though, and you'll be beating them off with a stick! The low-level look of this '40 is made possible by the use of a Heidt's Mustang II crossmember, aftermarket A-arms and a set of 2-inch dropped spindles. The back is brought down to earth with a TCI 4-link, a homemade cross member and a Ford 8-inch axle.

A "Chevy in a Chevy" formula means that the Coupe runs a 350/350 engine trans combo. The engine receives an Edelbrock 650 Carb and polished Performer intake, to equal the shine provided by the Billet Specialties valve covers and air cleaner. Sanderson block hugger headers complete the engine's exhaust duties through a home-built system. All the stock trim has been retained on the fat 5-window. Yet, the contemporary look is very much there, with the v-butted windshield and the choice of billet wheels. Budnik Pentical are the rims of choice, with 17s and 18s gracing the fender wells both front and rear, respectively.

MAKE:	Chevrolet
BODY STYLE:	2-door Coupe
YEAR:	1940
ENGINE:	Chevy 350 V8
BUILD STYLE:	Street Rod
OWNER:	Wayne Streams

▲ Take your shades off for a moment and you'll see that this Chevy is actually two-toned in red and orange – just to add some subtle extra interest to the fat '40.

Acknowledgements and Picture Credits

Kev Elliott

Pages   14-15, 18-19, 20-21, 22-23, 24-25, 26-27, 30-31, 32-33, 34-35, 38-39, 42-43, 44-45, 46-47, 48-49, 50-51, 52-53, 54-55, 56-57, 58-59, 60-61, 62-63, 64-65, 66-67, 68-69, 70-71, 72-73, 74-75, 76-77, 78-79, 80-81, 82-83, 84-85, 88-89, 90-91, 92-93, 94-95, 134-135, 244-245, 248-249, 252-253, 560-561, 568-569.

Keith Harman

Pages   96-97, 98-99, 100-101, 102-103, 104-105, 108-109, 110-111, 112-113, 114-115, 116-117, 118-119, 120-121, 122-123, 124-125, 126-127, 128-129, 130-131, 132-133. 160-161, 162-163, 164-165, 166-167, 168-169, 418-419, 650-651, 674-675, 676-677,

Mike Key

Pages   86-87, 170-171, 174-175, 176-177, 180-181, 182-183, 184-185, 186-187, 188-189, 190-191, 192-193, 194-195, 196-197, 198-199, 200-201, 202-203, 204-205, 206-207, 208-209, 210-211, 212-213, 242-243, 346-347, 628-629, 630-631, 632-633, 634-635, 636-637, 638-639, 640-641, 642-643, 644-645, 646-647, 648-649, 652-653, 654-655, 656-657, 658-659, 660-661, 662-663, 664-665, 666-667, 668-669, 670-671, 672-673, 678-679, 680-681, 682-683, 684-685, 686-687, 688-689, 690-691, 692-693, 694-695, 696-697, 698-699, 700-701, 702-703, 704-705, 706-707, 708-709, 710-711, 712-713, 714-715, 716-717, 720-721, 722-723, 724-725, 726-727, 728-729, 730-731, 732-733, 734-735, 736-737, 738-739, 740-741, 742-743, 744-745, 746-747, 748-749, 750-751,

Mike Mueller

Pages 136-137, 138-139, 140-141, 142-143, 144-145, 146-147, 148-149, 150-151, 152-153, 154-155, 156-157, 158-159,

Mike Read

604-605 (by kind permission of Tony Thacker, So-Cal Speed Shop).

Chuck Vranas

Page 2, Contents Page, all Introduction pages, 16-17, 28-29, 36-37, 40-41, 106-107, 172-173, 176-177, 178-179, 214-215, 216-217, 218-219, 220-221, 222-223, 224-225, 226-227, 228-229, 230-231, 232-233, 234-235, 236-237, 238-239, 240-241, 246-247, 250-251, 254-255, 256-257, 258-259, 260-261, 262-263, 264-265, 266-267, 269-270, 270-271, 272-273, 274-275, 276-277, 278-279, 280-281, 282-283, 284-285, 286-287, 288-289, 290-291, 292-293, 294-295, 296-297, 298-299, 300-301, 302-303, 304-305, 306-307, 308-309, 310-311, 312-313, 314-315, 316-317, 318-319, 320-321, 322-323, 324-325, 326-327, 328-329, 330-331, 332-333, 334-335, 336-337, 338-339, 340-341, 342-343, 344-345, 348-349, 350-351, 352-353, 354-355, 356-357, 358-359, 360-361, 362-363, 364-365, 366-367, 368-369, 370-371, 372-373, 374-375, 376-377, 378-379, 380-381, 382-383, 384-385, 386-387, 388-389, 390-391, 392-393, 394-395, 396-397, 398-399, 400-401, 402-403, 404-405, 406-407, 408-409, 410-411, 412-413, 414-415, 416-417, 420-421, 422-423, 424-425, 426-427, 428-429, 430-431, 432-433, 434-435, 436-437, 438-439, 440-441, 442-443, 444-445, 446-447, 448-449, 450-451, 452-453, 454-455, 456-457, 458-459, 460-461, 462-463, 464-465, 466-467, 468-469, 470-471, 472-473, 474-475, 476-477, 478-479, 480-481, 482-483, 484-485, 486-487, 488-489, 490-491, 492-493, 494-495, 496-497, 498-499, 500-501, 502-503, 504-505, 506-507, 508-509, 510-511, 514-515, 516-517, 518-519, 520-521, 522-523, 524-525, 526-527, 528-529, 530-531, 532-533, 534-535, 536-537, 538-539, 540-541, 542-543, 544-545, 546-547, 548-549, 550-551, 552-553, 554-555, 556-557, 558-559, 560-561, 562-563, 564-565, 566-567, 570-571, 572-573, 574-575, 576-575, 576-579, 580-581, 582-583, 584-585, 586-587, 588-589, 590-591, 592-593, 594-595, 596-597, 598-599, 600-601, 602-603, 606-607, 608-609, 610-611, 612-613, 614-615, 616-617, 618-619, 620-621, 622-623, 624-625, 626-627,

Personal Acknowledgements

Keith Harman and Chuck Vranas would like to personally thank all those who have helped in the extensive research and preparation of this book, including all the owners and builders of the cars included (too many to list!) plus everyone who has influenced them personally over the years resulting in the enthusiasm required to carry out the daunting task. Special thanks also to Kev Elliott, Mike Key, and Mike Mueller for the additional images and input, thanks guys!

Chuck would like to thank the following people for their overwhelming support and inspiration over the years:

Kim Vranas, Jim & Ardie Vranas, Marge Corcoran, Eric Geisert, Brian Brennan, Ken Gross, Kev Elliott, Rob Fortier, Jim Rizzo, Richie Willett, Jim Lowrey, Dave Simard, Paul Gamache, Norm Grabowski, Andy Brizio, Roy Brizio, Art Himsl, Darryl & Terri Hollenbeck, Tom Fritz, Ray Tourigny, Russ Heslin, Pete Flaven, Jim Gove, Tony Dowers, Mickey Lauria, Mike & Margaret Ann O'Connor, Bob Moscoffian, Bob O'Connor, Jack Hennan, Lenny Biondi, Dick Morse, Tom & Marianne Clancy, Dave Paras, Schloz, Ron & Laura San Giovanni, Don Rooney, Larry Hook, Tony Muscatella, Bill, Marianne, Jeanette, & William Melahouris, and Mario & Julie Barros.